Directing scenes and senses

Manchester University Press

theatre
theory · practice
· performance ·

series editors
MARIA M. DELGADO
MAGGIE B. GALE
PETER LICHTENFELS

advisory board
MICHAEL BILLINGTON
SANDRA HEBRON
MARK RAVENHILL
JANELLE REINELT
PETER SELLARS
JOANNE TOMKPINS

This series will offer a space for those people who practise theatre to have a dialogue with those who think and write about it.

The series has a flexible format that refocuses the analysis and documentation of performance. It provides, presents and represents material which is written by those who make or create performance history, and offers access to theatre documents, different methodologies and approaches to the art of making theatre.

The books in the series are aimed at students, scholars, practitioners and theatre-visiting readers. They encourage reassessments of periods, companies and figures in twentieth-century and twenty-first-century theatre history, and provoke and take up discussions of cultural strategies and legacies that recognise the heterogeneity of performance studies.

The series editors, with the advisory board, aim to publish innovative, challenging and exploratory texts from practitioners, theorists and critics.

also available

The Paris jigsaw: Internationalism and the city's stages
DAVID BRADBY AND MARIA M. DELGADO (EDS)

Theatre in crisis? Performance manifestos for a new century
MARIA M. DELGADO AND CARIDAD SVICH (EDS)

World stages, local audiences: Essays on performance, place, and politics
PETER DICKINSON

Performing presence: Between the live and the simulated
GABRIELLA GIANNACHI AND NICK KAYE

Performance in a time of terror: Critical mimesis and the age of uncertainty
JENNY HUGHES

South African performance and the archive of memory
YVETTE HUTCHISON

Jean Genet and the politics of theatre: Spaces of revolution
CARL LAVERY

Not magic but work: An ethnographic account of a rehearsal process
GAY MCAULEY

'Love me or kill me': Sarah Kane and the theatre of extremes
GRAHAM SAUNDERS

Trans-global readings: Crossing theatrical boundaries
CARIDAD SVICH

Negotiating cultures: Eugenio Barba and the intercultural debate
IAN WATSON (ED.)

Directing scenes and senses
The thinking of *Regie*

PETER M. BOENISCH

Manchester University Press

Copyright © Peter M. Boenisch 2015

The right of Peter M. Boenisch to be identified as the author of this work has been asserted by him in accordance with the Copyright, Designs and Patents Act 1988.

Published by Manchester University Press
Altrincham Street, Manchester M1 7JA
www.manchesteruniversitypress.co.uk

British Library Cataloguing-in-Publication Data
A catalogue record for this book is available from the British Library

Library of Congress Cataloging-in-Publication Data applied for

ISBN 978 1 5261 2301 5 paperback

This edition first published 2017

The publisher has no responsibility for the persistence or accuracy of URLs for any external or third-party internet websites referred to in this book, and does not guarantee that any content on such websites is, or will remain, accurate or appropriate.

Typeset by Out of House Publishing
Printed by Lightning Source

In memory of
Jürgen Gosch (1943–2009)
Sven Lehmann (1965–2013)
David Bradby (1942–2011)
three playful thinkers in and on theatre

CONTENTS

List of illustrations	viii
Acknowledgements	x
Introduction. The dissensus of *Regie*: rethinking 'directors' theatre'	1
PART I *MISE EN SCÈNE* TO *MISE EN SENS*: TOWARDS AN AESTHETIC POLITICS OF *REGIE*	13
1 *Regie* beyond representation: directing the 'sensible'	15
2 The restless spirit of *Regie*: Hegel, theatrality and the magic of speculative thinking	33
3 Theatre as dialectic institution: Friedrich Schiller and the liberty of play	54
4 The essence of the text and its actualisation: Leopold Jessner, the playwright's radical servant	73
PART II THE THEATRAL APPEARING OF IDEAS: THE THINKING OF CONTEMPORARY *REGIE*	95
5 The tremor of speculative negation: on *Regie*, truth and ex-position	97
6 Seeing what is coming: on *Regie*, playing and appearing	118
7 The intermedial parallax: on *Regie*, media and spectating	142
8 Theatre in the age of semiocapitalism: on *Regie*, realism and political critique	164
Conclusion. The future of *Regie*?	189
Bibliography	194
Index	204

ILLUSTRATIONS

Cover: tg STAN's *Summerfolk* (2010). Photo: tg STAN/Tim Wouters

1	The 'magic triangle' of theatrality after Helmar Schramm	40
2	The central principles of Hegel's speculative thinking	44
3	Leopold Jessner's *Wilhelm Tell* (1919), original model box (set design: Emil Pirchan). Courtesy of Theaterwissenschaftliche Sammlung der Universität Köln, Schloss Wahn	84
4	Jessner's *Richard III* (1920), design sketch by Emil Pirchan. Courtesy of Theaterwissenschaftliche Sammlung der Universität Köln, Schloss Wahn	86
5	Jürgen Gosch's *Macbeth* (Schauspielhaus Düsseldorf, 2005; set design: Johannes Schütz). Photo: Sonja Rothweiler	100
6	Gosch's *Uncle Vanya* (Deutsches Theater Berlin, 2008; set design: Johannes Schütz). Photo: Iko Freese/drama-berlin.de	102
7	Michael Thalheimer's *Rats* (Deutsches Theater Berlin, 2007; set design: Olaf Altmann). Photo: Barbara Braun/drama-berlin.de	111
8	Thalheimer's *Orestie* (Deutsches Theater Berlin, 2006; set design: Olaf Altmann). Photo: Iko Freese/drama-berlin.de	112
9	tg STAN's *JDX – A Public Enemy* (1993/2014). Photo: Tim Wouters	121
10	tg STAN's *JDX – A Public Enemy* (1993/2014). Photo: Tim Wouters	125
11	tg STAN's *Nora* (2012). Photo: Magda Bizarro	126
12	Andreas Kriegenburg's *The Trial*, after Franz Kafka (Kammerspiele Munich, 2008). Photo: Arno Declair	130
13	Kriegenburg's *Heart of Darkness*, after Joseph Conrad (Deutsches Theater Berlin, 2009; set design: Johanna Pfau). Photo: Arno Declair	133

List of illustrations ix

14	Ivo van Hove's *Scenes from a Marriage*, after Ingmar Bergman's TV series (Toneelgroep Amsterdam, 2005; set design: Jan Versweyveld). Photo: Jan Versweyveld	143
15	Guy Cassiers's theatre adaptation of Marcel Proust's *Recherche du temps perdu* (Ro Theater, Rotterdam, 2002–5; set design: Marc Warning/Kantoor voor bewegend Bild). Photo: Ro Theater/Pan Sok	145
16	Ivo van Hove's 'Roman tragedies', incorporating Shakespeare's *Coriolanus*, *Julius Caesar* and *Antony and Cleopatra* (Toneelgroep Amsterdam, 2007; set design: Jan Versweyveld). Photo: Jan Versweyveld	148
17	The 'theatral square' illustrating the relational network of theatre performance	151
18	Guy Cassiers's adaptation of J. Bernlef's *Out of Mind* (Ro Theater, Rotterdam, 2006; design: Marc Warning). Photo: Ro Theater/ Sjouke Dijkstra	156
19	Frank Castorf's *The Duel*, after Anton Chekhov's 1891 novella (Volksbühne Berlin, 2013; set design: Aleksandar Denić). Photo: Thomas Aurin	167
20, 21	Frank Castorf's *The Idiot*, after Dostoevsky (Volksbühne Berlin, 2002; set design: Bert Neumann). Photos: Thomas Aurin	170
22	Thomas Ostermeier's *An Enemy of the People* (Schaubühne Berlin, 2012; set design: Jan Pappelbaum, with a chalk artwork by Katharina Ziemke). Photo: Arno Declair	178
23	Ostermeier's *The Marriage of Maria Braun*, adapted from Fassbinder's movie (Kammerspiele Munich, 2007; set design: Nina Wetzel). Photo: Arno Declair	182
24	The 'theatral square', applied to the relations of direction, *mise en scène* and *Regie*	190
25	Ostermeier's *An Enemy of the People* (Schaubühne Berlin, 2012; set design: Jan Pappelbaum). Photo: Arno Declair	193

ACKNOWLEDGEMENTS

It would not have been possible to work on this study between 2004 and 2014 without a lot of support. I am grateful to the Arts and Humanities Research Council, whose Small Grant for the Performing Arts scheme helped to launch my research, and to the University of Kent, which supported the work and completion of this project with two periods of research leave. I am indebted to Christopher Balme, Patrice Pavis and Hans-Thies Lehmann for their constant friendship and mentorship through several decades of 'growing up' in theatre research. Patrice has also, with his characteristic generosity, provided ample comments on a draft version of this book. Ever since I set foot in UK academia, Maria Delgado, Paul Allain and the late David Bradby have been the most generous and inspirational advisers and supporters of my work. Maria has now also, along with Maggie Gale and Peter Lichtenfels, included this study in their series 'Theatre: Theory – Practice – Performance', which is an honour and a privilege for my first book-length monograph conceived, written and published in English. I am grateful to all three series editors for their encouragement, support and feedback, and the same goes for Matthew Frost at Manchester University Press. Further thanks go to many colleagues who have in various ways commented on and supported my research over the years, in particular Erika Fischer-Lichte, Janelle Reinelt, Marvin Carlson, David Savran, Günther Heeg, Peter Marx and the peer reviewers who have patiently worked through early versions of the manuscript. Christel Stalpaert, Johan Callens, Katja Schneider, Katharina Keim and Clare Finburgh have been very special friends and colleagues on many joint adventures. The Working Group 'Directing & Dramaturgy', which I once inherited as co-convenor with Jacqui Bolton and David Barnett from our predecessors and mentors Maria Delgado, David Bradby and Brian

Singleton, has been instrumental in developing the thinking presented in this book. Jennifer Parker-Starbuck, Louise Owen and Theron Schmidt have permitted me to 'pre-launch' some of its arguments when they invited me to London Theatre Seminar. Finally, I would have become entangled in a far greater Babylonian dissensus without the help of Helen Gush, who made sure that my idea of English now actually corresponds to the rules of the language, except where I insisted on ignoring her scrupulous advice and her persistent admonitions about sentences spanning several paragraphs while lacking any detectable sense. The European Theatre Research Network at the University of Kent has enabled me to employ Helen, and also to obtain copyright permissions to reprint the photographs. I would like to thank in addition all the photographers and companies in question for granting permission to reprint these images in the present book. I dedicate this book to Johanna for her patience and support of theatrical madness.

Peter M. Boenisch
London and Berlin, August 2014

Introduction. The dissensus of *Regie*: rethinking 'directors' theatre'

One can hardly imagine a more contested area in the field of theatre arts than what is often (and most of the time disparagingly) called 'directors' theatre': the production of plays, in particular from the canonical dramatic repertoire, staged by an ensemble of resident theatre artists, usually at the public state and city theatres of Continental Europe. Ever since the new artistic practice of *Regie* emerged over the course of the nineteenth century, directors and their *mises en scène* found themselves in the spotlight, but also in the firing line of audience members and critics. Even today, 'directors' theatre' is frequently, and not only in the anglophone world, experienced as something outright outlandish, if not outrageous. In the memorable words of a New York theatre critic (reviewing Flemish director Jan Lauwers's New York performance of his celebrated *Isabella's Room*), it marks the fatal 'sins of Eurotrash theater', which the reviewer helpfully went on to classify as 'wilful obscurity, over-the-top stagecraft, auteur-ish egocentrism' (McCarter 2004, 19). *Regietheater* is – as another New York critic asserted after seeing German director Thomas Ostermeier's *Nora* – 'dumb', 'idiotic' and a sort of theatre 'that has to wallow in self-indulgence to prove to itself that it's alive' (Feingold 2004, 71). Needless to say, it is the very same directors, pathologically rejected by some, who find themselves (no less pathologically) embraced and idolised by others as *Wunderkinder* and prophets of a theatre of the future.

Ever since moving into UK academia from Germany more than a decade ago, I have been fascinated and puzzled by this perfect example of what French philosopher Jacques Rancière, one of several intellectual inspirations of the thinking behind the present study, terms *mésentente*, or dissensus. He introduces the term to describe a peculiar form of misunderstanding, which is not the conflict between one who says white and another who says black. It is the conflict between one who says white and another who also says white but does not understand the same thing by it or does not understand that the other is saying the same thing in the name of whiteness. (Rancière 1999, x)

The terms directing, *mise en scène* and *Regie* similarly divide us within a field where we appear, at first sight, to talk about the same thing. Upon closer inspection, though, an irreconcilable cultural divide opens up, not least between the insular English theatre culture and its geographically not too distant Continental equivalents. They seem to emerge from distant territories, from foreign planets even, with artists, critics and audiences alike conversing in mutually unintelligible tongues. Notions such as *mise en scène*, but also terms such as 'straight' theatre and 'devising', 'dramaturgy', 'performance' and 'postdramatic', to name but a few, resist easy translation and often add to the *mésentente* instead of confirming any truly shared understanding of theatre and its practices. In many conversations, whether in the classroom or at conferences, or just sitting in the theatre stalls on the rather rare occasion of a visit from a Continental theatre ensemble, it is a safe bet that within ten minutes at most, the discussion is transformed into a heated exchange about 'directors' theatre' *against* 'playwrights' theatre', 'text-based drama' *against* 'devised performance', being 'true to the text' *against* the (to my mind usually rather mild) excesses of the director on stage in front us, or, most fundamentally, of Continental *against* English theatre practice. I have been intrigued to find equivalent antagonisms between the Anglo-American pragmatic tradition of realist, analytic thought and Continental, French- and German-style philosophy. A most fascinating parallel world of rejections and allegiances thus opens up between what François Cusset aptly described as the influential export brand of 'French Theory' (Cusset 2008), and its counterpart on stage, Continental *Regietheater*. In often surprising ways, this parallel interlinks the present vogue and the concurrent hatred of figures such as Jacques Rancière or Thomas Ostermeier.

At this point, one cannot help here but be reminded of Hegel's interpretation, regularly quoted by Slavoj Žižek, of the geographic triad of Germany, France and England as expressing three fundamentally different existential attitudes: German reflexive thoroughness, French revolutionary hastiness and English pragmatic utilitarian moderation. Žižek, my other principal intellectual ally throughout the present study, notoriously connected this reading to respective differences in toilet design, demonstrating that even (indeed especially) the most mundane objects and most vulgar activities reveal such fundamental ideological truths (see Žižek 2006a, 16f.). Yet, do we not find these same attitudes, and the same traces of ideology, right at the epicentre of making and presenting theatre, too? Do they not underpin the cultural history of theatre directing, *Regie* and *mise en scène*? Are these three terms really mere 'translations' that talk about the same idea, the same theatrical practice, or even express some general principle of theatre? Where notions of *Regie* and *mise en scène* emerged in German and French theatre as early as the 1770s, the term 'director' entered English theatre language comparatively late, in the 1950s, mirroring the use of this word in cinema (Bradby and Williams 1988, 4). Before this, the theatre director was referred to as 'producer', placing the industrial organisation of theatrical entertainment and the pragmatics of cultural production and circulation over and above any sense of 'art'. From an English perspective, the idea of 'directing texts' can only be understood as pragmatism of efficient blocking and the smooth organisation of the text's proper enunciation and representation, measured by its conformity to the pre-written script. For this reason, in an English context, 'directing a play' is understood as 'a significantly different activity' from 'making a performance', as Christopher Baugh has suggested, the latter pointing to 'new practices, new technologies and a new stagecraft' (Baugh 2005, 17).

From a Continental theatre perspective, however, it has become utterly unimaginable that one would not break free from the authority of the text, not rethink the play afresh with every new reading and not 'make a performance' of the text with each new production. Directing here means 'choosing a direction, an orientation, an interpretation', while still 'taking as a starting point the text's givens as unalterable, to the letter', as Patrice Pavis explains (Pavis 2013, 294). He draws our attention to the difference marked by English writers where they use the verb 'to stage' as opposed to 'direct', where they refer to such a Continental approach as 'laying out [and] putting on stage' a dramatic text (35); yet this different use has certainly not become systematic or continuous. More recently, the term 'theatre direction', rather than 'directing', has become more and more prominent in an English context (see Shepherd 2012). It now appears on playbills and programme notes, most notably perhaps at London's Young Vic theatre, where (South African) artistic director David Lan, since taking office in 2000, has made very significant efforts with his 'Young Vic Directors' Programme' to productively challenge the way that emerging (English) directors think about their art. 'Direction' in this context marks an artistic and aesthetic approach different from the mere pragmatic execution of stage business.

Staying with names, terms and etymologies, in contrast to the Anglo-Saxon entrepreneurial producer, the *Regisseur* of German theatre directs us to the ties to state bureaucracy and to the German system of public financing, where art and culture are (still) provided for the citizens as a form of 'cultural health service'. It seems noteworthy that *Regie* – notwithstanding the bourgeois ideal of *Bildung*, of intellectual education and erudition – echoes the words 'regieren' and 'Regierung', of 'ruling' and 'government' in the German language. In French, meanwhile, the term *régie* has little connection to the creative art of theatre, but instead originated in the vocabulary of state administration and its budgeting system. Today, the 'régisseur de plateau' is the stage manager, whereas the actual French term for the theatre director, the *metteur en scène*, is semantically situated directly within the realm of art, reinforcing the ideal of artistic autonomy and freedom.[1]

The present book is an attempt to make some sense of this dissensus. We have today learned to consider the director no longer

> as a homogenous individual but rather as a construct that itself articulates wider debates around the intersections between theatre, nation, state and the broader structures through which geographical, political and cultural spaces intersect or collide. Directing is shown to be both a function and a profession, a brand and a process, an encounter and a market force. (Delgado and Rebellato 2010, 21)

The achievements of Bradby and Williams in their pioneering and infinitely valuable study on 'Directors Theatre' (Bradby and Williams 1988), and of Pavis's singularly systematic explorations of what he terms *mise en scène* (Pavis 1982, 1992, 2010, 2013), have helped us to arrive, in the English theatre discourse as well, at a consensus that 'the craft of directing is never simply a question of "interpreting" but rather about shaping, representing, positioning and creating' (Delgado and Rebellato 2010, 18). But if we start probing further, a lot of questions still remain unanswered, perhaps not even asked. For more than a decade now, theatre research has offered prolific, sustained and profound investigations into the art, techniques and problems of the actor, of acting and performing. We still lack a similarly in-depth interrogation, let alone understanding, of theatre direction. We are certainly well supplied with a range of survey studies and historiographical accounts that offer many facts and data on directors, *Regie* and *mise en scène*. Plentiful 'how to' manuals on the craft of the theatre director fill our bookshelves further, yet they often seem to perceive directing as little more than professional labour in an 'aesthetic service industry', whose core aim is the successful delivery of marketable, pleasurable experience products to its audience-customer-consumers.

This book does not set out to offer a(nother) 'new' history of theatre directors and direction, nor will it attempt to provide an exhaustive survey of the contemporary field of Continental European 'directors' theatre', nor offer a manual for what to do in the rehearsal room. For the encyclopedic overview of the field of directing in the English language, I refer readers to Innes and Shevtsova (2013); for a panorama of contemporary European *Regie* to Delgado and Rebellato (2010). Pavis's systematic exploration of present-day *mise en scène* (Pavis 2013), read alongside Shepherd's innovative 'practical theorisation' of 'direction' in a UK context (Shepherd 2012), provides further indispensable and inspiring ground for many of the questions raised and further developed in this study. Additionally, there are most useful editions of interviews, primary material and other writings on theatre directing offered by Delgado and Heritage (1996), Giannachi and Luckhurst (1998) and Schneider and Cody (2002). Within Anglo-American theatre (and performance) studies, the long-held, almost exclusively Anglo-centric perspective has subsequently been redressed through particular attention to Continental European theatre directing by Kelleher and Ridout (2006), Carlson (2009), Lavender and Harvie (2010) and Shevtsova and Innes (2009), as well as Finburgh and Lavery (2011). Furthermore, the English translation of German theatre scholarship by Lehmann (2006) and Fischer-Lichte (2008) has familiarised a wider international readership with crucial conceptual paradigms of postdramatic theatre and of a performative theatre aesthetics.

Since there is no need to repeat what colleagues have already achieved in the aforementioned marvellous work on the subject, I have taken the liberty of dedicating the present volume, at its most fundamental level, to a conceptual exploration of *the thinking of* Regie: of how to think about theatre direction, and how *Regietheater* thinks itself. My approach here is committed to the speculative tradition of Hegelian dialectic thinking, and to avoid disappointment, I should clarify some further methodological deliberations at the outset. To think through directing in a way that is able to account not least for these all-too-underexplored, (perhaps not so) subtle differences between English and Continental European concepts, conventions and expectations, it seemed necessary to attempt an outline of an alternative framework of categories. Above all, I wanted to resist the persistent slipping back to a handful of worn-out clichés and reductive stereotypes, which hardly do more than keep unhelpful controversies alive. The focus here therefore shifts from an exploration of what it is that 'the director does', or what they should do, to what *directing* does, and what directing can do, tapping into and realising the potential of *what theatre does and may do*. This has become a pertinent matter within our global configuration, where art and culture are no longer, in Marxist terms, mere aspects of the ideological superstructure, but have themselves become the very sites of alienation, conflict and exploitation. Today, certainly in the West, intellectual labour and the creative power of employees, rather than physical strength and manual work, are what the capitalist system exploits and appropriates. This crucial context not only of contemporary theatre making, but of human existence today, which Bifo Berardi and Jodi Dean have designated with their influential terms 'semiocapitalism' and 'communicative capitalism' respectively (Berardi 2009; Dean 2009), provides an important horizon for my own critical thinking about *Regie*, to which I shall repeatedly refer. Moreover, my own exploration of the dissensus of directors' theatre is inspired by an attempt to think through the *politicity* of twenty-first-century theatre performance, which is how Jacques Rancière describes a political potential that springs not so much from the content, as from the very formal and structural fabric of an art form. My most fundamental wager is that theatre directing should, above all, quite literally be taken to mean 'giving a direction' – or a purpose – to the text that is being staged, and to theatre at large, as a medium, a cultural form and aesthetico-political force within society, on every single night the curtain goes up.

Therefore, instead of further following the traditional academic focus on the interpretation of playtexts and on performance analysis, this study attempts to once more 'render strange' the problem of theatre direction. To trace theatre's politicity, I will start by delineating some crucial, basic parameters of the *formal* operation of *Regie* and its constitutive *structural* dynamics and problematics. The speculative methodology of theatre theory adopted here follows an explicitly Hegelian approach of speculative thinking. It is aligned with the emerging field within our discpline of 'performance philosophy' (see Cull 2012, 2013, and http://performancephilosophy.ning.com) Above all, I start by asserting that '*directing thinks*' and that it thinks in its own way. And by thus thinking, theatre *plays* – with theatre texts, the theatre stage and with us as theatre spectators. Confronted with that Rancièrian *mésentente* – which we may very liberally render as a 'messy understanding' – about *Regie*, I wonder whether precisely a genuinely emancipatory 'messing up' is not the briefest possible description of what the contested *Regietheater* does, of how it thinks and plays? Do not all the debates and misunderstandings precisely affirm the crucial shift its dissensus suggests, by challenging and going beyond established paradigms of meaning and standard patterns of the common 'partition of the sensible', as Rancière terms it (see Chapter 1 for a more detailed discussion of his concept)? By tackling the playful thinking, and thinking playfulness, of *Regie* with a no less playful, speculative and subjective methodology, which itself 'messes up' some widespread assumptions about theatre directing, I hope to initiate a thinking that resonates with current problems, challenges and the sheer 'mess' that confronts us, in the liminal field between contemporary Continental *Regie* and fresh approaches in English theatre direction, and most certainly everywhere beyond.

It has been a deliberate decision to present for this purpose an expressly partial study, which reflects selected episodes from (mainly German) theatre history in Part I, and then proceeds to isolate what I consider the core parameters of *Regie* by discussing, in Part II, a somewhat contingent choice of recent theatre work created in the first one and a half decades of the twenty-first century in European languages other than English, and within institutional contexts significantly different from the Anglo-American theatre market. While confining my study to theatre work I have followed and myself seen over the past decade of working on this book between 2004 and 2014, I leave out, quite notably given my proposed scope of 'Continental European theatre', work from the French, Italian and Spanish, and not least the Eastern European theatre world, which I have seen, but with which I cannot claim the same linguistic familiarity as with work emanating from my 'home turf' in the German- and Dutch-speaking world, in which I have worked, watched and researched since the rather accidental development of my enthusiasm for theatre at some point in the 1980s. Moreover, I also decided against including, as a foil, much work I have also watched from the anglophone theatre context, and not to present it side by side with the examples discussed here. This would have suggested a homogeneity and coherence that betrays the very dissensus from which this project started. In fact, throughout this study I insist on the strangeness, the 'foreign body', the partiality, particularity and the partisanship of *Regie* by applying this very term – *Regie* – instead of a universalising 'theatre directing' or a generic 'mise en scène', in order to dissociate us from assumptions, expectations and conventions, and instead encourage us to acknowledge the cultural and aesthetic differences and specificities in direction. My partial view from outside and as an outsider will, I hope, offer an opportunity to take a step back and reflect. I hope that this will be true for European readers as well, as they will be only too familiar with the *Regie* work under discussion in this study; perhaps I am able to offer for them a more sideways look that fosters fresh thinking, too, just as my own 'givens' were challenged after I moved into a rather different aesthetico-political framework in theatre and in higher education.

Against authority: the deadlock of 'directors' theatre'

The principal aim, then, in what follows is not to attempt an impossible comprehensive account of 'directors' theatre' and its most representative artists, but to arrive, via rather particular and subjective manifestations of *Regie*, at a sharper insight into theatre direction and its potential, its aesthetic possibilities and its political implications. *Regie* is here shown to be far more than the arrangement of signs and meanings that 'produce' the play on stage (as in a common but all too reductive understanding of *mise en scène*), far more than a functional craft of translating and adapting. Rather, it is a fundamentally relational practice of renegotiating and relating texts and theatre, scenes and senses, performances and audiences, directing/producing and spectating theatre, which sits *in the very form and structure of theatre as a cultural technique and as a cultural institution within the 'aesthetic regime of art'*. This is the name Rancière proposes for the cultural paradigm whose advent was signalled by the arrival of Romantic poetry, idealist philosophy and the new realism of the novel. They all marked a significant cultural shift at the backend of the momentous historical rupture of the 1789 French Revolution, lasting into the present (see Rancière 2013).

This study is thus, not least, an urgent call to finally abandon the blinding and intellectually stifling perspective that defines directing, and theatre-making at large, solely in terms of the one 'proper' and ultimate authority that brings to life and controls all aspects of the production. We should note here the more than trivial slippage between *Regietheater* (literally, 'direct*ing* theatre') and its English rendition as 'directors' theatre'. The latter places the individual artist rather than a theatral practice and process in the centre, thereby disclosing a rather different ideological mindset. Writing a history of *the* director as a celebration of original inventions of 'great men' (and mostly they still are, admittedly even throughout the present study), immediately pushes issues of authorship and authority to the fore. Conceiving of directing as the individual creative product delivered by the director as author-*auteur* inevitably stages a clash and competition between writer and director. It positions the director of 'directors' theatre' *opposite* and in opposition to the text, suggesting an insurmountable antagonistic tension between director and playwright, reiterating implications of command and obligation, of hierarchy, superiority, respect, of truthfulness and fidelity, and of master and servant. From this perspective, only two positions can be taken: either, directors are seen as dictators suppressing and crushing playwrights' 'democratic' voice, or conversely, they become ultimate liberators, the freedom fighters who deconstruct the despotic hierarchy and 'authority' of the Text, the pioneers who break into new territories against all odds (critical and other), somewhat like 'creative cowboys' who act (or rather: direct) against the rest of the ('commercial', 'conservative', 'old', 'outdated' ...) theatre world.

This remains an outright debilitating position, even more so since it assumes what appears to be a politically radical gesture of liberation: One of the positions must always appear as 'underprivileged', in need of this advocacy, engagement and liberation – whether it be the 'suppressed' text in *Regietheater*, or the director who is 'disabled' by playwrights' theatre. In fact, this very notion of a 'playwrights' theatre' only makes sense if it is based on the assumption of 'authorial competition', rather than collaborative co-creation. And where would 'performers' theatre', let alone a theatre of and for its audience, find its place within this power struggle? We can hardly get further away from the understanding of direction, and *Regie*, as the recognition (and indeed, celebration) of an essentially collective, social and political practice. The discursive paradigm of (individual) authorship – hence, the director's claim for authorship and superior authority – serves, first and foremost, the most regressive political purpose. It cleanses any emancipatory impulse contained in the expressly political *Regie* of theatre-makers from Schiller to Jessner, Brecht and the post-war *Regietheater* pioneers of the 1960s and 1970s, down to the contemporary generation of late twentieth- and twenty-first-century theatre-makers, who are as diverse and even contradictory as tg STAN and Frank Castorf, Thomas Ostermeier and Guy Cassiers (to name but a few of those who will make an appearance over the course of this book). We should not forget that describing the director as 'auteur' was once an emancipatory and somewhat radical proposition itself. For David Bradby and David Williams, who have been particularly instrumental in establishing the term in anglophone theatre discourse, it seemed obvious to link *Regietheater* to the simultaneously emergent directorial *auteur* of French *nouvelle vague* cinema. These radical interventions in theatre and cinema became equally influential at approximately the same time during the 1960s and 70s, sharing the spirit of the time (we should not forget here the radical philosophy that emerged from this same spirit, at the same moment in time, precisely the generation of Louis Althusser's student Jacques Rancière and Lacan's student Slavoj Žižek). Just as the director-*auteurs* in European cinema were seeking to counter the industrialised machinery of mass entertainment, symbolised in particular by Hollywood, theatre directors began to challenge the status of theatre as cultural capital of a middle-class elite. A young generation, who in the 1960s sought liberation in many different ways, thus reclaimed the canonical classics that had been the backbone of the institutionalised theatre system since the eighteenth century. The aesthetic and, even more significantly, the political values that underpinned the work of theatre directors such as Peter Brook, Joan Littlewood, Ariane Mnouchkine and Peter Stein could not be further from any attempt to solidify the hegemonic position of the individual director-artist, of the creative maker or of the producer who delivers his goods, or the inventive genius who commands and authorises performance practices and processes of directing and direction.

Were we to further perpetuate the ideology of a power binary between playwright and director, and equally between text and production, as representing distinct, competing forces, we would become complicit in the safe containment of any challenge posed by *Regie*, in its past and present incarnations. We would neutralise its explosive, dynamic potential as a dialectic 'style of thinking' (Helmar Schramm's notion is introduced in Chapter 2) to propose an alternative 'partition of the sensible', in Rancière's term. *Regie*'s political impetus would be reduced to rivalry within the walls of theatre. To remain truthful, as theatre critics and theatre-makers, to the vision of directors and playwrights who imagine theatre as a vital critical force engaged with contemporary society, we must first of all stop pondering whether playwright or director should have superior authority. We should reject any simplistic formula that constructs such hierarchically weighted oppositions in the first place, and escape the ideological trap of authority and authorship, of intentions and interpretations, and of the reductive, mechanistic idea of a 'translation' from page to stage, and finally call an end to the persisting caricature of *Regie* as the purely subjective, 'private' whim of an idiosyncratic director.

This does not mean rejecting dramatic narratives, realistic stories and recognisable characters. Neither, however, does it mean reducing the dramaturgic toolkit to these mechanisms of dramatic representations alone, and certainly even less so using these categories as indicators for assessing the artistic quality of *Regie*. If we define theatre solely as a semiotic machine of representation and meaning, transported from the written page via the stage to the audience, who have to decode this message (the author's 'meaning' and 'intention') in the 'right' way, we miss out as much as if we fantasise about theatre performance as a pure pre-semantic phenomenal experience. Far from exhausting itself in generating subjective interpretation, *Regie* triggers and instigates a genuinely theatral (and hence: utterly impersonal) negotiation of 'styles of thinking'. Therefore, it must, first and foremost, be understood as a process and a function – as a formal operation where the playtext remains ('objectively') the same, yet our perception and understanding is ultimately changed through the play-performance afforded by *Regie*.

Thinking *Regie*: an outline of this book

With its somewhat eclectic choice of fragments, moments and pertinent stories, this book offers a symptomal diagnosis, rather than a full history of *Regie* between 1771 and 2015. Part I outlines the social, ideological, political, cultural and aesthetic contexts of *Regie*, and some of its core intellectual and conceptual roots, and does so by largely circumventing standard reference points such as Antoine, Stanislavsky or Brecht. Chapter 1 begins by problematising the assumption of a 'watershed' moment in the birth of *Regie* around 1880. The emergence of *Regie* as a new and necessary form of cultural mediation is pinpointed long before the modernist rupture of around 1900, situating *Regie* within the Rancièrian 'aesthetic regime of art' and its specific 'partition of the sensible'; these philosophical ideas and concepts are further introduced and explained in this chapter. Applying them to *Regie* allows us to link its development to a whole tradition of European directors from the early nineteenth century onwards, from Heinrich Laube and Franz von Dingelstedt right through to Max Reinhardt in the early twentieth century. Their *Inszenierung* of, above all, canonical, historical classics is described as a genuinely aesthetic operation, establishing relations of the sensible and orchestrating what Rancière usefully describes as the 'silent speech' of things.

This early form of *Regie* already reveals its self-reflexive mediating movement, emphasising the ultimate present captured in the performance moment, as a response to what was more and more perceived as distance and unavailability of the past. This very problem of 'thinking representation', as the philosopher Alain Badiou describes it, again reminds us of the shared background of Continental *Regie* and the simultaneously emerging Continental philosophy of Kant, Hegel and the German idealist tradition of thought. Chapter 2 then specifically links *Regie* to Hegel's influential thought, maintaining that *Regie* expresses a cultural dynamic of making sense and making sensible, which is essentially energised by the force of dialectic thinking outlined by Hegel. Against static orders of duality, and mutual exclusivity (for instance, of notions such as 'subject' and 'object'), he posited a relational dynamic process of constant 'sublation' (*Aufhebung*), triggered by confronting existing ideas and assumed certainties with their inherent contradictions, their 'negation' that for him always already sits within them, rather than being added from the outside – an important line of thinking for my exploration of *Regie*. Furthermore, Hegel, like many of his contemporaries, emphasised the sensory dimension of thinking, refusing to dissociate sensory feeling and rational thinking. Accordingly, I will directly connect the dialectic thinking of *Regie* with what German theatrescholar Helmar Schramm has evocatively termed the 'magic triangle' of theatrality: a force field constituted by the three relating forces of movement (*kinesis*), meaning (*semiosis*) and perception (*aisthesis*). Chapter 2 introduces the key concepts of Schramm and of Rudolf Münz, the most influential scholars representing the German approach of 'theatrality studies', in order to further situate *Regie* within what Münz calls the 'cultural fabric of theatrality'. From a binary transition or translation, which Patrice Pavis quaintly described as the 'text-performance couple' (Pavis 2008), we arrive both via Hegel's triadic model of dialectic sublation and via the tripartite relational field of theatral dynamics at a triangular model of *Regie* that locates the practice as mediation between text, its production and its theatral performance, where it is perceived by the public. Thus interweaving directing and spectating, *Regie* is also historically situated. That is the very reason why there can be no general principle of 'directing', no universal method of organising dramatic texts for their performance *as such*, no normative prescription what it should be and do: far from being straightforward translations, even the very use of distinct terms such as *Regie*, directing or *mise en scène* already implies culturally and historically specific 'partitions of the sensible'.

On the basis of these dual relational forces of dialectics and theatrality, *Regie* thus necessitates relational encounters – with and between people, media and the texts of traditions and legacies. These encounters take place in the autonomous (but public) aesthetic space of theatre, an idea which Chapter 3 develops through a discussion of Friedrich Schiller. Circumventing the (pseudo-)Schillerian evocation of 'theatre as moral institution' and of the utopic idealism often associated with his idea of aesthetic autonomy, I will instead foreground Schiller's notions of liberty and play. His peculiar 'practice as research' experiment of reintroducing the chorus in his late tragedy *The Bride of Messina*, and its accompanying essay, will then reveal how already at Schiller's time, shortly after the turn of the nineteenth century, the space was carved out, and a structural necessity articulated, which *Regie* would then fill in the further course of the century. Schiller remained one of the central reference points for the politically engaged Leopold Jessner, an important mentor to both Brecht and Piscator, to whom Chapter 4 turns. His directorial innovations of the 1920s represent a major divide between Continental European and Anglo-American developments of theatre directing, which had not yet been evident in the work of Max Reinhardt a few years earlier. Jessner's practice allows me to pin down central concerns relating to the 'dissensus' around *Regie* and to discuss why a director may offer radical alterations to a printed playtext, yet will at the same time insist on his function as the 'playwright's radical servant', as Jessner expressed it. The dialectic thrust of *Regie* becomes clear here; it has never been, in Hans-Thies Lehmann's words, 'motivated simply by contempt for the text but also by the attempt of *rescue*' (Lehmann 2006, 52) – above all, a rescue from the threat of the reification of theatre and cultural legacy as a cultural commodity, which safely absorbs and contains the radical energies that had driven the playwrights to write their drama in the first place. The discussion of Schiller and Jessner does not intend to suggest a causal historical lineage. Instead, their respective positions, separated by over a hundred years, symptomatically capture central trajectories of thinking the conceptual space of *Regie*, both mobilising the speculative dynamics of theatral thinking.

Part II of the book then moves on to contemporary work. The four discussions that make up this section are, however, less concerned with analysing specific directors' intentions, their 'signature styles' or their interpretation of specific dramatic works. Instead of offering performance analyses, I explore the relational systems in which they are placed and from which they emerge, in order to arrive at a fuller understanding of some principal aesthetico-political operations that characterise contemporary *Regie* as a process and function of theatral mediation and dialectic sublation. The chapters will of course also offer discussions of some of the most prominent and innovative artists contributing to contemporary *Regie* in German- and Dutch-speaking theatre. I will introduce the *Regie* of Jürgen Gosch and Michael Thalheimer (Chapter 5), tg STAN and Andreas Kriegenburg (Chapter 6), Ivo van Hove and Guy Cassiers (Chapter 7) and of Frank Castorf and Thomas Ostermeier (Chapter 8), and delineate some of their central working methods, creative strategies and aesthetic principles. Again, however, the intention here is not to celebrate their individual 'artist-authority', their intentions and interpretations, or their 'creative vision'. The work of tg STAN, an Antwerp-based collective, illustrates my main point: they have been staging plays by Ibsen and Chekhov, as well as many contemporary playwrights, for some twenty-five years without any director ever directing their productions. Throughout this section, the detour via the personal and the individual, and via *Regie* work from a distant context and in different languages, will serve my central objective, which is to interrogate and explore some of the central (in Hegelian) 'concrete universal' principles, problems and coordinates of *Regie* and of contemporary theatre-making at large. The specific issues explored further include the contested notion of 'the truth of the text' (Chapter 5), the dialectic sublation of the play-text in play-performance (Chapter 6) and the mediation which the double-edged act of *thea* affords, with its emphasis on both performing (showing) and spectating (gazing), marked by the Žižekian notion of the 'parallax perspective' (Chapter 7). All these issues somewhat culminate in the discussion of the overarching political potential inherent in *Regie* and in the very formal structure of theatre, which may offer a playfully excessive resistance to the dominant logic of economy, efficiency, sustainability and austerity which defines present-day global neoliberal semiocapitalism (Chapter 8). Throughout this study, I draw exclusively on the practices, productions and experiences with which I am most familiar and which have left the biggest impression on me as a theatre spectator. Similarly, readers are invited to complement and to challenge the outlined ideas, phenomena, problems and potentials of *Regie* with their own examples, perhaps even their own artistic practices and experiments.

Notes

1 I thank Patrice Pavis for many useful discussions about terminology and nuances in the various languages in which both of us speak and write about theatre. He pointed out the affinity of *Regie* and the 'giving order' of *regieren*, and the way in which neoliberal politics and economics 'régir notre existence', control and direct our existence, in today's world.

PART I
Mise en scène to mise en sens
Towards an aesthetic politics of Regie

1

Regie beyond representation: directing the 'sensible'

Writing in the 1920s, Adolf Winds, an early historiographer of the art of *Regie*, was puzzled by the absence of discussions of directing from the most influential theatre writings of the eighteenth century, such as Diderot's essays on theatre or, most importantly, Lessing's seminal *Hamburgische Dramaturgie* (Winds 1925, 60). Still, the German theatre scholar set out to offer his readers a history of *Regie* that began with classical Greek theatre, at the very cradle of European theatre history. After all, Aristotle did mention *opsis*, the scenic presentation, in his *Poetics*. Yet, Winds's account, which follows the development of *Regie* throughout antiquity, medieval pageants, the baroque theatre of the courts and the Jesuits, right into the early twentieth century, does not sit quite right with today's reader. His narrative understands theatre directing in the broadest sense: as practice of arranging and managing the business of the stage. These are certainly efforts involved by necessity when- and wherever someone puts something on stage. Winds's broad brush strokes, however, make today's reader even more aware of the caesura that effectively separates *Regie*, personified by the emergent figure of the allegedly authorial and authoritarian theatre director, from other, earlier forms of 'staging theatre'. There is a moment prior to which the idea of 'directing' a play could simply not be thought. Winds himself was aware of this qualitative leap. He describes the progression from an external *Regie*, which focuses on the 'expressive design of the scenic environment' (9), towards 'interior *Regie*, implemented in the modern way', which aimed at 'saturating the word with spirit' (39).[1] Accounts of the history of theatre directing, by Winds and others, suggest that, at some point, the emergence of a specialised profession and of a specific process that follows its own logic and categories had become a necessity, whereas before, no such need had emerged, not within the collectively organised modes of theatre creation in English Elizabethan playhouses, let alone at the Dionysian festivals of old Athens. If *Regie* were a catch-all phrase which signified *any* artistic method for arranging stage practice, if its idea were exhausted by *any* organisation of theatrical means, there would have been no need to invent it.

Most histories of theatre directing mark this inaugural moment of *mise en scène* proper with the new naturalist theatre aesthetics of André Antoine's Théâtre Libre, founded in Paris in 1887, and its subsequent widespread followers, from Otto Brahm in Berlin to Konstantin Stanislavsky in Moscow.[2] Their naturalism (and likewise its obverse twin, symbolism) was in varying ways pitched against the predominant stage conventions of the time. It exploited, either in the name of truthfulness or of a 'true art of the theatre', the newly available technologies such as electric lighting, while also reflecting the new urban, cosmopolitan cultural situation, and the new conventions and expectations of 'bourgeois perception' that were triggered by the new medium of photography and, very soon, the moving images of film (see also Lowe 1982; Crary 2001). The accounts that follow this standard narrative about the emergence of directing are usually prefaced with nods to the internationally touring German Meininger troupe of the 1870s as influential pioneers, while not forgetting Richard Wagner's *Gesamtkunstwerk* idea either, including his Bayreuth innovation of the darkened auditorium. From this perspective, the advent of *Regie* heralds the modernist 'retheatricalisation' of theatre, as Georg Fuchs phrased it in his 1909 manifesto for the Munich *Künstlertheater* (Fuchs [1909] 1959). Or, following the influential take on modernism proposed by art critic Clement Greenberg, it could be seen as realising ultimate 'medial specificity' in the field of theatre (see Greenberg [1961] 1992 and Carroll 1996). Patrice Pavis also supports the association of *mise en scène* with an 'epistemological break around 1880', after which the notion 'took on its modern meaning, still signifying the passage from the text to the stage … but increasingly doing so while enjoying the status of an autonomous art' (Pavis 2013, 4):

> We should reserve the term mise en scène and especially that of director (metteur en scène) for stage practices from the 1880s onwards, since the era of directors did not start before Zola and Antoine's radical critique of theatre or before the counterpoint provided by symbolism (at least in the context of France). (Pavis 2013, 3)

Or did it? While I am certainly mindful of Pavis's explicit qualification *entre parenthèses* and also of the fact that my principal endeavour in this study is not a historiographic, but an aesthetic account of the idea of *Regie* and its cultural history, I propose to shift the usual perspective. What if what has become the default starting point, associated with the ground-breaking rupture of Pavis's 'epistemological break around 1880', was, in fact, the answer to aesthetic issues and problems that had already preoccupied several generations of artists throughout the nineteenth century, and far beyond the realms of theatre? What if *Regie* was far more than theatre's reaction to new media technologies, and to new modes of economic production as well as new approaches to the understanding of human behaviour from Darwinism to psychology and sociology? What if, instead, it was part and parcel of the same style of thinking that had propelled these significant developments in the first place – including Continental philosophy and above all Hegel's paradigm-shifting speculative approach? And what could such a wider perspective on the history of the idea of *Regie* offer to our understanding of contemporary practices, and to comprehending the true potential of theatre direction today, as theatre and all arts across the Western hemisphere face the onslaught of their neoliberal marketisation and effective absorption, alongside other forms of human creativity and so-called 'immaterial labour', by communicative capitalism (Dean 2009)?

My wager here is, then, that current understandings of *mise en scène*, of the 'rise of the director' and of *Regietheater* throughout the nineteenth and twentieth centuries can be productively connected to a wider cultural shift. *Regie* emerged out of the very 'time of birth and of transition to a new era', which Hegel alluded to in the Preface to his *Phenomenology of Spirit*. He describes it as a new era in which 'the Spirit broke with the previous order of existence and of imagination', which, arriving with the sudden force of a 'flash, in a single stroke erected the outline of the new world' (Hegel 1986a, 18, 19). I will here employ Jacques Rancière's term for this emergent socio-cultural configuration already referred to in the Introduction, above: the 'aesthetic regime of art' (see Rancière 2013). Emphasising the transition from the previous 'representative regime' to this emerging 'aesthetic regime' of art in the nineteenth century, Rancière challenges narratives that foreground the modernist break around 1900. For him, the latter was no more than the fine tuning of the new aesthetic *dispositif*.[3] I suggest that the advent of the director and, even more so, of *Regie* as a principally new technique of artistic mediation are also quintessential manifestations of this paradigm we can call the aesthetic regime.

Rancière connects this fundamental socio-cultural change to fundamental modifications within what he terms the 'partition of the sensible'.[4] Not unlike the 'Ideological State Apparatus' of Rancière's teacher Louis Althusser, and similar to his contemporary Michel Foucault's notion of the disciplining function of 'discourse', the 'partition of the sensible' marks a socio-cultural horizon that defines the modes, conventions and limits of what is sayable, thinkable, visible and perceivable within a given society and culture. More clearly than Althusser, Foucault and others, Rancière outlines a perspective where apprehension itself, our perception and cognition, our very senses and experiences (all, of course, fundamental aspects of theatre) are seen as *always already* political, even before the traditional sites of ideology – discourse, the symbolic order, the networks of medial representation – come into play. A 'partition' of the sensible is the prerequisite for meaningfully accessing and participating, or, in another key Rancièrian term, for 'par(t)-taking' in culture, politics and society. It establishes, in the literal sense, 'the common' of a community: its norms and systems of allocating (and reallocating) places and identities through the 'apportioning and reapportioning of spaces and times, of the visible and the invisible, and of noise and speech' (Rancière 2009a, 24).

Rancière uses the term 'sensible', which in French signifies much more than the English word suggests, where sensible, essentially, means rational and making sense. Rancière extends the spectrum of meaning of 'sensible' to what *makes* sense and what *is* sense, what is perceived by our senses. This ambiguity inherent in the word 'sense' had already fascinated Hegel:

> 'Sense' ... is this wonderful word, which itself is used with two contrary meanings. On the one hand it refers to the organs of immediate apprehension, on the other hand however we call sense the meaning, the thought, the universal of a matter. And thus the sense refers on the one hand to the immediate exteriority of existence, on the other hand to its very interior essence. A sensible reflection [sic! *Hegel did have a sense of humour ... PMB*] of course will not separate the two sides, but in any one direction it will also contain the opposite one, grasping in the sensuous immediate perceiving both the essence and the notion. (Hegel 1955, 160)

This is exactly what Rancière does. His perspective therefore productively speaks to this project of thinking *Regie* as a practice that directs scenes and senses. It also resonates well with the wider situation within our discipline at present, where we have finally begun to overcome the antagonistic confrontation that stifled theatre discourses during the 1990s and early 2000s, when the analysis of meaning (the semiotic 'sense' of interpretation) was irreconcilably pitted against attention to the experience (the Hegelian 'sensuous appearing' and the phenomenological sensuous experience).[5]

The development of *Regie* and *mise en scène*

Mise en scène was undoubtedly a 'brand new notion' (Pavis 2013, 6) revealing the assumed 'epistemological break'. Yet, once we move beyond the walls of theatre and its dominant historiography, this rupture shifts from 1887 towards 1789. Indeed, not even the Meininger were the first to think of *Regie*. Some of the earliest signs of life even predate the French Revolution: The first documented *Regisseur* in German theatre was Herr Stephanie der Ältere, who was appointed under this title at the Vienna Burgtheater in 1771. He succeeded a Herr von Brahm (of all people!) when the latter took up an appointment as secretary to the Austrian embassy in Sweden.[6] The new post of Stephanie's predecessor reminds us that his job within the administrative machinery of the Habsburg Empire had no artistic remit. In line with the original meaning of *régie* within the administrative structures of (French-speaking) court bureaucracy which had spread across Europe over the course of the eighteenth century, he was the theatre's administrative accountant, a 'controller' in today's business terminology. Yet, at the same time, Louis-Sébastien Mercier very much outlined the job description of the future theatre *Regisseur* in his influential essay *Du théâtre*, written in 1773 and translated by Goethe into German in 1776. Mercier pondered the hierarchy between playwright and actor, and concluded: 'One should therefore find a mediating power [*une puissance intermédiaire*] (even if this term should make us laugh) which privileges neither the concerns of the poet nor those of the actor' (Mercier 1773, 363f.). That same year, in Germany, actor-manager Conrad Ekhof (1720–78) launched his rather short-lived Academy for Actors. His ideal was the 'orchestration of the performance' [*Konzertierung des Spiels*], for which purpose he began to define his own task as 'the supervision of the actors in rehearsal, so that everyone knows their part and performs it well, and in new pieces takes their position well and not against the sense of the piece' (Ekhof, in Frenzel 1984, 257). In a similar spirit to Ekhof's 'supervision' (*Aufsicht*), the Theaterprotokolle, documenting the management of the Mannheim National Theatre between 1781 and 1789, reveal attempts to achieve the unity of the stage representation as well as early manifestations of Winds's 'innere Regie'. The *régisseurs* at Mannheim were the two elected representatives of the actors who served as technical-artistic directors to the company and represented the actors on the management board alongside *Intendant* Dalberg (1750–1806), himself a state minister, and principal actor August Wilhelm Iffland (1759–1812), who had previously worked with Ekhof at Gotha.

Similar to French actor and director Jean-Nicolas d'Hannetaire (1718–80), who in his *Observations sur l'art du comédien* of 1776 called for a 'maître', a master to guide the actors on stage, Goethe eventually drew up his famous 'Instructions for Actors' in 1803, in his role as Director-*Intendant* of the Weimar Court Theatre. For Winds, he was 'the first *Regisseur* in our sense of the term' (Winds 1925, 65). At their Weimar theatre, both Goethe and Schiller took the classical plays they produced in a vigorously updated, contemporary direction. Not least, they made Shakespeare – the most central cultural icon for their generation in its trajectory from the radical *Sturm und Drang* of the 1770s into the classical period of the early nineteenth century – fit for the Weimar stage. In his well-known reflections 'Shakespeare and no End', Goethe argued against the 'time-worn and unreasonable remark that in performing a Shakespearian play not a iota must be omitted' (Goethe [1813] 1900, 20). Although he also supported Schlegel's and Tieck's attempt to introduce the original Shakespeare into the German language, he still – with his director's hat on, as it were – supported actor-manager Friedrich Ludwig Schröder's amendments, including a new, happy ending for *King Lear*. Elsewhere, a Weimar playbill announced *Romeo und Julia* 'von Goethe' (by Goethe). Likewise, Schiller's remarkable adaptation of *Macbeth* (1800) aligned the play with contemporary sentiments. There was certainly another qualitative leap to be made from their Weimar stage aesthetics towards the 'modern' theatre *Regie* of the Meininger, Wagner and Antoine. Nevertheless, by the end of the 1820s, the *Regisseur* was already explicitly noted on theatre programmes. Berlin playbills from the 1824/25 season, and from Vienna dated 1829, are some of the oldest documents evidencing this momentous development (Bergman 1966, 70).

The role of the *Regisseur* had thus rapidly developed from a purely supervisory function of policing order and attendance at rehearsals and financial spending, to an artistic function, giving direction to the interpretation of the characters and the actors' stage performance – thereby, as some will argue, 'policing' the playtext and its production, too. Playwright and theatre director Heinrich Laube (1806–84) was particularly instrumental in this development. He was one of the first to reject conventions of rhetoric and oratorical declamation, which still notoriously dominated Goethe's Weimar stage. During his eighteen-year tenure as *Intendant* at the Vienna Burgtheater from 1849 to 1867, and his later work at the Stadttheater Leipzig and at the Vienna Stadttheater, Laube encouraged his actors to speak 'naturally'. He introduced the conversational tones of everyday language to the stage, and also paid careful attention to the dramaturgic meaning of the speech for the character. His innovative and influential style was characterised by what Paul Lindau, a well-known theatre critic and playwright of the time, described as

> the persistent infinite care and diligence, the persistent deep intellectual engagement, the persistent admirable talent to lead the actors to the deepest grasp and comprehension, while offering them simple, intelligible and effective means to transform their correct insight into an accurate presentation [*das richtig Verstandene zu richtiger Anschauung zu bringen*]. (Lindau, quoted in Hagemann 1904, 68)

Laube devised for and with his actors a nuanced play with gestures and stage props in order to channel the audience's attention and to thereby create an effortless focalisation of important moments in the play. At the same time, his stage remained rather bare, only containing sketchy sets, which make his work more reminiscent of the later Leopold Jessner (see Chapter 4) than of the sumptuous *mise en scène* à la Meininger. In this respect, his successor at the Vienna Burgtheater, Franz von Dingelstedt (1814–81), who had previously come to fame with his work as artistic director and *Regisseur* at Stuttgart and in particular at Weimar and Munich, was renowned for his atmospheric stage environments, which aspired to present integrated, coherent works of stage art. Dingelstedt was involved in the premiere of Richard Wagner's *Lohengrin* at Weimar in 1850, for which he provided a prologue, despite feeling little sympathy for Wagnerian aesthetics (see Roenneke 1912).

Personifying the approaches of 'inner' and 'external' *Regie*, Laube and Dingelstedt implemented new ideas of stage aesthetics which were soon described by another term borrowed from the French language. Around 1820, the concept of *mise en scène* was first used in the present-day sense.[7] Originally, it designated the composition of a painting (see Veinstein 1955) or referred to the adaptation of a literary text, such as a novel, for the stage (Dort 1971, 51).[8] It would not be long before the Francophile cultured class in the German-speaking countries adopted the term, translating it literally as 'in die Scene setzen'. As a result, the concept of *Inszenierung* emerged; difficult to translate, it is situated somewhere between a production, the idea or concept that drives it, and its realisation in each performance. More and more of the leading *Intendanten* of the time subscribed to this emerging aesthetics; apart from the key figures Laube and Dingelstedt, the most notable were Karl Immermann (1796–1840), whose (albeit short-lived) efforts in staging 'original Shakespeare' at Düsseldorf during the 1830s contributed to the reputation of his theatre as *Musterbühne* (exemplary theatre), and Eduard Devrient (1801–77), who worked at Dresden while Wagner was *Kapellmeister* (music director) in the city, and later at Karlsruhe, spreading Wagnerian ideas on the dramatic stage (Winds 1925, 74–86). Around this same time, we begin to find entries on *Regie* in contemporary dictionaries and encyclopaedias,[9] and critical writing addresses the new function in German theatre, too. In 1837, a now much-quoted essay by August Lewald in a German theatre magazine, the *Allgemeine Theater-Revue*, explicitly designated the *Inszenierung* as 'the business of the *Regisseur*' (Lewald 1837). In 1841, Franz von Akáts published another frequently referenced source. His early textbook on the new profession of the 'Scenir-Direktor', as he proposed to call it, evidently without lasting effect, was entitled *Kunst der Scenik in ästhetischer und ökonomischer Hinsicht*: 'Scenic art in aesthetic and economic regards'. While for him, as he makes clear from the outset, the practice of *mise en scène* did not imply an 'original creation [*eigene Schöpfung*]' (Akáts 1841, iv), he also reminds us of the fact that what we today, from a Continental perspective, understand as a primarily, if not solely artistic practice emerged to no negligible extent from an economic context – not at all unlike the English theatre producer, who, even in present-day direction, remains caught between 'artistry and organisation', where the latter may even be 'the crucial and defining activity of direction' (Shepherd 2012, 16).

The disciplining of actors as well as audiences, financial control and a newly unified style of representation in 'accurate' costumes and set pieces – these aspects became central for a new theatre aesthetics that was thus as much driven by the emerging 'aesthetic regime' as by new capitalist 'modes of (industrial) production' and the corresponding new modes of 'managing' and distributing labour in the name of profitable efficiency. It would soon turn works of art, too, into something that could be produced mechanically, even on an industrial scale, as the rise of new theatre impresarios and commercial entrepreneurs demonstrated. This trend was eventually epitomised in the new Boulevard theatres in Paris, whose model was copied across Europe. This aesthetic as well as economic trajectory of *Regie* throughout the nineteenth century continued earlier explorations of 'directed' performances that had been undertaken by actor-managers from the late eighteenth century onwards. These included Friedrich Schröder and Ernst August Klingemann in Germany and John Philip Kemble and Charles Kean in England, who mostly staged texts from the emerging Western theatre canon, particularly Shakespeare (see Williams 1990).

Regie as aesthetic mediation

The standard perspective that primarily associates directing with the modernist avant-garde discourse of theatricalisation tends to overlook the fact that *Regie* (apart from its direct economic aspect of 'producing' theatre according to new parameters of industrial manufacturing) reveals, above all, a characteristic relational and reflexive structure of mediation, or *Vermittlung* in Hegel's original term. This mediation goes beyond a process of adaptation between two media, 'from page to stage'. It does not seek to create an autonomous *mise en scène* that eventually supersedes the playtext; in fact, it challenges the assumption of a binary between text and performance (see Pavis 2008). It provides the text, the production and our experience of spectating with *sense* – and a 'sense' is, of course, also always some kind of 'direction'. It is this changing process of mediation which characterises the emergence of *Regie*, and which signals most directly its association with the aesthetic regime of art.

So, what does this mediation of *Regie* actually entail? As a medium, theatre establishes relations: via its production and performance, it relates the written playtext with the present moment, in which an audience sees and senses the playtext, mediated through the production or *Inszenierung*. The understanding of theatre as medium applied here does not, like many discussions, focus almost exclusively on theatre's appropriation of new media technology on stage. Rather, it looks at the underlying relations that are established for presenting, performing, and spectating, that is the processes and structures of mediation itself, which take the form of a 'partitioning of the sensible'. Today, we see that the 24/7 availability of mobile devices which connect us to the world also impacts on the way we perceive the world, and thus also theatre (see Crary 2014). In the nineteenth century, *Regie* arrived on a scene where the boundary between stage and auditorium had become very clearly demarcated. This was reflected in the disappearance of on-stage seating and the newly darkened auditorium opposite the lit stage. Yet, this demarcation did not negate the audience, but rather revealed a new relational structure: the audience is now conceived as its obverse part, affirmed in its dialectic relation with the *Inszenierung* on stage. The audience's 'aesthetic act' complements the *mise en scène* not as secondary activity of reception (or consumption), but as an integral component (see Boenisch 2006). As Alain Badiou suggested, the spectators should therefore be considered as the 'point of the real by which a spectacle comes into being' (Badiou 2008, 189).

Directing, performing and spectating (yet another 'magic' theatrical triangle) are thus structurally complementing activities that mutually presuppose each other without a clear hierarchy or privilege awarded to one or the other. As a process of mediation, *Regie* organises the scenes and senses that interconnect processes of directing (and performing) with acts of spectating. From this medial perspective, *Regie* directs the text, first and foremost, towards and for an audience. It thereby facilitates and allows for a vital public dialogue, as it requires a direct encounter and affective engagement: our encounter, as spectators, with the text whose scenes we see staged on stage, which speaks, above all, to our senses. On this basis, the true 'meaning' of a theatre production is no longer located in the interpretation (or, even more banal: the 'staging') of the playtext, and even less so in the intangible intention of the director. Instead, it emerges from the quintessentially public encounter facilitated through *Regie* and its reflexive relations: an encounter with cultural traditions and registers of cultural memory, but ultimately also an encounter with ourselves as spectators, in a most 'sensible' manner.

This brings us back to Rancière. His central notion of the 'partition of the sensible' pointed us to the essentially aesthetic organisation of senses, sensibilities and sensory perceptions which regulates what 'really makes sense', what (and who) can be 'naturally' perceived visually, acoustically, physically and verbally, and thereby become a 'sensible' thing or being. Giving direction to scenes and senses, *Regie* as an aesthetic practice reveals itself as an essentially political operation as it directly intervenes in the structuring and partitioning of the sensible. One of the most useful (and also most controversial) propositions of Rancière's thinking is his understanding of the site of politics, which for him goes far beyond the 'political order' of the state and the exercise of power, which Rancière instead describes with the term 'police'. The basic dimension of politics is for him necessarily an aesthetic one. As he reminds us, establishing any order of the sensible will inevitably be based on exclusion, on 'counting out' what (and who) has *no* part in the common, and must therefore remain unperceivable, invisible, unspeakable, untouchable, unheard of, unthinkable as nothing, nobody or mere rabble.[10] The partition of the sensible thus distributes, in another of Rancière's proverbial phrases, what (and who) counts as a voice, and what is merely considered a noise: any 'common good' can only exist by not being common to everyone. A political act happens when those who are thus 'counted out' and denied a voice, a vote and a body, begin to demand to be counted as part of society, hence to 'par(t)-take'.[11] This demand manifests itself as political dissensus, a concept we encountered in the Introduction. The truly political act insists that there is another way of seeing white, to again evoke Rancière's example quoted previously. It thereby proposes a different partitioning of the sensible (see Rancière 1998, x; Rancière 2009a, 24f.) This crucial notion of dissensus thus designates far more than 'a conflict of interests, opinions or values: it is a division inserted in "common sense": a dispute over what is given and about the frame within which we see something as given' (Rancière 2010, 69). From a Rancièrian perspective, the basic form of politics is therefore a dissensual *mise en scène* – or we can describe it even more appropriately as a dissensual *mise en sens*: political action creates a frame that claims the legitimacy of an alternative perspective and of a different perception.

Following this thought in our context, the charge against *Regie* of missing, failing, even distorting the playtext is not an indicator of its flaw and shortcomings. Instead, it marks the potential of *Regie* to stage dissensus, emerging from within the very process of mediation as it frames and potentially reframes our sensory perception. This inherent capability of dissensus marks the difference between 'mere directing' and *Regie*. It became possible only through the full-scale reorganisation of the relationship between, as Rancière terms it, the 'sayable' and the 'visible' (as well as the un-sayable and in-visible), which was marked by the advent of the aesthetic regime of art. The prior representational regime (also translated as 'representative' regime into English) relied on direct, that is unmediated identity. Art was simply a different way of doing, and not a matter of 'framing'. It was not yet perceived as a distinct, autonomous realm with its own artistic and aesthetic laws. The early modern logic of emblems and allegory, in particular, discloses in its symbolic readings a different layer of the world that, however, essentially 'is one'. The topos of *theatrum mundi* relied on this fundamental unity. Furthermore, the allocated place within the representational order governed both daily life and the representational politics of monarchy (and the church), as well as art and theatre, reflecting that same shared, encompassing worldview, 'whereby a human nature that legislates on art was tied to a social nature that determined place in society and the "sense" appropriate to that place' (Rancière 2009a, 14). The purpose of art was to represent the perfection of this 'natural order', based on norms and rules, and on technical artisanal mastery. It was governed by *mimesis* – the crucial link that connected the principles governing artistic forms and subjects and the experience of art on the one hand, and 'real' life as such, for instance, in the assumed correspondence of microcosm and macrocosm on the other.

The mimetic principle also shaped the relation between a playtext and its staging under the representational regime, to the degree that this very distinction was entirely anachronistic. There was not yet any aesthetic space for the *individual* mediation afforded by *Regie*, and even less for authorial originality. Still, the playtext could still be altered for performance, but on the basis of the common rules and principles of mimesis. They enforced an ideal, 'appropriate' order of representation, which, for the stage, was encapsulated in the French tragic conventions of *vraisemblance* and *bien séance*. Rancière repeatedly reminds us of Corneille's reworking of Sophocles' *Oedipus* (see Rancière 2007, ch. 5, and 2009c, chs. 1 and 2). Corneille amended the cruelty of the gouged-out eyes and the oracle's surplus of information that pre-empted the plot and thereby thwarted dramatic tension. Further, he introduced a love relationship by adding Oedipus' sister, Dirce, to the plot and allocating Theseus as her suitor. Such interventions into the playtext for performance are by no means a result of the later emergence of *Regie*. Yet, under the representational regime, they were prompted by a representational consensus, not by aesthetic dissensus. Corneille's alterations thus highlight the very different role of theatre within the cultural configuration of the representative regime:

> The preferred site of representation is the theatre, a space of exhibition entirely given over to presence, but held by this very presence to a double restraint: the restraint of the visible under the sayable and of meanings and affects under the power of action – an action whose reality is identical to its unreality. (Rancière 2007, 116)

This 'division of the sensible' performed by the representational regime of art thus installed a characteristic 'absoluteness of drama', to use Szondi's term, which underwrote the laws of the stage under the representational regime, yet which makes it, from our own present-day perspective, appear entirely artificial and unreal (see Szondi [1956] 1987).

Whereas this absolute framework of the representational regime did not function according to any rationale of the actually existing everyday world, with the advent of the new aesthetic order, the focus of art shifted from rule-bound logic to mundane reality – from the transcendental order to the thing itself. Romantic poetry, the realist novel and not least the emerging visual technologies of photography (and much later film and television) admitted *any* subject matter or object into *any* form of art. The problem that prompted Corneille's changes was no longer there. Similarly, *any* new technology (say, photography, a urinal or today's quick snapshot with the mobile) was able to 'become' and to produce art. The aesthetic regime thus introduced to the stage – most notably in the elaborate sets of the Meininger – what Rancière described as the 'silent speech' of things (see Rancière 2007, ch.1). He relishes pointing towards the banality of objects that surfaced in the nineteenth-century novel: Stendhal's water pump, Balzac's lopsided beams in the *Maison du Chat-qui-pelote* and Charles Bovary's hat in Flaubert's novel. Not only in literature, but even more so on stage, the pure 'prosaic objectivity', as Hegel phrased it (Hegel 1955, 558), especially of 'low', banal and ordinary objects, which would in the old regime not even have found entry into the 'high art' of representation, made a purely aesthetic experience available. Their affective perception in a theatre performance eclipsed any (mimetic) representation and fictional narration.

As Zola would confirm, naturalist sets 'took on in the theatre the importance that description took on in the novel' (from 'Naturalism on the Stage', quoted in Pavis

2013, 6). In his discussion of Dutch and Flemish genre painting, Hegel also replaces the classical ideal of 'eternal beauty' (of the eternal divine order, etc.) with the new, thoroughly aesthetic understanding of beauty as 'sensuous appearing of the Idea'. Therefore, at the heart of art in the aesthetic regime, there are contingent, prosaic objects, and their – in Hegel's term – 'appearing as such':

> The artist does not intend to give us through his work an idea of the object he presents us with. We have already the fullest idea of grapes, flowers, stags, trees, sandy beaches, of the sea, the sun, the sky, the décor and ornaments of the instruments of daily life: of these, there are enough in nature itself. Yet, what is meant to attract us is not the content and its reality, but the pure appearing which is without interest in regards to the object [*sondern das in Rücksicht auf den Gegenstand ganz interesselose Scheinen*]. What is isolated in Beauty is appearance as such, and art is now understood as mastery in representing all secrets of this self-absorbed appearing of external appearances. (Hegel 1955, 562)

What Rancière calls the 'obstinate silence' of these objects and their appearing likewise applies to the realism that characterised nineteenth-century *Regie*, once more confirming its status as medium affording a special aesthetic mediation. Rancière connects the fascination with 'self-absorbed appearing' to the dynamics proposed in Roland Barthes's (much later) study of photography, *Camera Lucida*. Here, his attention shifted from the primarily semiologic outlook of his earlier *Mythologies*, and he moved on from what he describes as the close 'studium' of signs to the 'punctum': the 'silent moment' that touches the spectator (Barthes 1980). Barthes here offers another instance of the two senses of the 'sense' of an artwork. The very *punctum* of the 'silent speech' of objects and traces, their 'appearing as such', rather than realist authenticity and the spectacular 'studium' of a scene energised *Regie*, not least in its early fascination with history, and likewise in its later naturalist aesthetics, eventually fostering the prominent directorial revolutions of Antoine, Brahm, Stanislavsky and Reinhardt.

The scope and purpose of *Regie* is rather accurately captured by this notion of the (aesthetic) 'punctum', rather than associating it with the 'studium' of semiotic representation. Within the aesthetic paradigm, a theatre production, like any other artwork created under this new regime, now drew its entire *raison d'être*

> from its belonging to a specific sensorium. The property of being art refers back not to a distinction between the modes of doing, but to a distinction between modes of being. This is what 'aesthetic' means: in the aesthetic regime of art, the property of being art is no longer given by the criteria of technical perfection but is ascribed to a specific form of sensory apprehension. (Rancière 2009a, 29)

Creating, but also spectating, art was no longer a matter of acquired skills and given conventions, but was a matter of *sense*. We begin to see more clearly why *Regie* had to emerge. Under the new order of the sensible, the artist himself became a medium, considered as gifted with unique sensibility, that German *Empfindsamkeit*, with which the artist complemented the pure rationalism of Enlightenment. They were therefore able to disclose a form of being behind the mundane surface of functional reality, and to point towards a deeper truth: the aesthetic truth. The 'moment of art', as it were, now became associated with this somewhat enigmatic, intimate and direct encounter between (intuitive, genial, original) artistic creation and a new spectatorial sensitivity, a specifically aesthetic 'sensory apprehension' that was equally intuitive and individual. In a paradigmatically dialectic way, art was at once identified and (re)defined *as aesthetic* – as a specific and different kind of experience, as an essentially autonomous partition of the sensible: 'For art to exist, what is required is a specific gaze and form of thought to identify it' (Rancière 2009a, 6). The process of mediation is not just the means (the 'doing'), but the very site of aesthetic art.

The aesthetic regime thus understands art, in a radically new way, as a site for sensory experiences which go beyond the existing, everyday order of discourses, bodies and images. Art becomes the site to suggest, through its aesthetic *mise en sens* of a sensory dissensus, alternative 'partitions of the sensible'. Art in the aesthetic regime is thus based on a paradox: On the one hand, the artworks, subjects and objects themselves became ever less distinguishable from the everyday world and its experience, as we see in the pinnacle of aesthetic theatre art, in naturalism. On the other hand, art was no longer subordinated to the demand of *mimesis* of an all-encompassing 'natural order' and instead withdrew into its own, autonomous realm. We see this paradox in the move from Kant to Hegel: the former still subjected art to nature; for the latter, the new law governing art was beauty or *Kunstschönheit* (see Szondi 1974b). Beauty negated the 'everyday' or 'natural' partition of the sensible, and therefore was able to sublate the contradictions of reality. Art thus became one of the various autonomous domains that began defining the make-up of our Western cultural fabric after 1800, a period described by historian Reinhard Koselleck as *Sattelzeit* ('saddle period'), a term with which he also referred to a threshold between two paradigms (see Koselleck [1959] 1988). Economy and politics were other fields now perceived as distinct spheres, and no longer 'as one' as under the representational regime. Hegel's philosophical 'system', meanwhile, sought to undercut this new separation, albeit from a distinctly 'aesthetic' perspective: for him aesthetic mediation was the one mechanism to still maintain a link between the separate, fragmented, even contradictory realms of society. Such a dialectic resolution of the gap between art and nature, or reality, the mediation between the autonomous aesthetic order of the sensible and the pragmatic functional world, between the universal and the particular, the abstract and the concrete and not least between artistic creation and the experience of art, was the role newly ascribed to philosophy; a mediating role that had simply not been necessary within the representative regime. This includes the emerging discourse of aesthetic theory, in its manifestations as philosophy of art, hermeneutics, art criticism and philology. These mediating discourses refracted art from their asserted autonomous domain back into the socio-cultural 'partition of the sensible'.

Regie, then, is nothing but another manifestation of these same discourses, practices and techniques of aesthetic mediation. Its emergence marks the moment where theatre (*qua mise en scène/mise en sens*) becomes an essential part of these new 'ways of sensible being' (Rancière 2009a, 11). Through the 'arrangement of the decoration' and the 'arrangement of the animation' ['Anordnung der Ausschmückung' and 'Anordnung des Lebendigen'], the two principal functions of *Regie* identified by Akáts, the theatral dynamics of performing and of scenography become important triggers of a unique aesthetic experience. *Regie* orchestrated this experience by striving for a coherent *Inszenierung*, or in Akáts's term, for a 'Gesammtwirkung' [*sic*], an experiential 'overall effect'. The same purpose guided Dingelstedt's *Regie* and later pivoted with the Meininger. During their Berlin seasons from 1874 onwards, and later when touring internationally, their much lauded productions of canonical classics eventually gave the new *Regie* its widespread, popular exposure. Their work was of course well backed by a PR machinery that worked on full spin to create the enthusiastic public reaction for Duke George II of Saxe-Meiningen's theatre enterprise that has lasted to the present day (see de Hart 1981; Koller 1984; Osborne 1988). Under the leadership of director Ludwig Chronegk, their work integrated the attention to the text and its 'natural' and accurate delivery we found in Laube's epochal 'internal' *Regie* with Dingelstedt's and Devrient's sense for atmospheric scenic environments, while adding the sense of an ensemble of actors. The major innovations of earlier *Regie*, which critics such as Akáts and Lewald had articulated, now became the default standard for stage production: actors were expected to be familiar with the entire play, its story, its 'sense' and ideas. Actors were also no longer assigned stock characters, which they specialised in, but were cast according to who fitted best with the fictional character. The shift in terminology from 'part' or 'role' to 'character' was concomitant. Further, the use of stock scenery recycled according to the type of setting required, was abandoned. Somewhat notoriously, the Meininger furnished their stage with scenery and costumes from Duke George's own possessions. For *Julius Caesar*, they accurately recast an antique Roman statue that the Duke had seen *in situ* as (unlike Shakespeare) he specifically travelled to Rome. For Schiller's *Maria Stuart*, he even went to Fotheringhay, where Schiller set his purely imagined encounter between Mary and Elizabeth I. In addition, the Meininger consulted the original playscripts when developing their acting versions, and no longer relied on contemporary adaptations.

The thoroughly aesthetic task of *Regie* was thus defined as facilitating an individualised representation – a notion that would have been an outright contradiction under the representational regime. This goal could simply not be achieved through stock sets, 'ham' acting and traditional stage rhetoric. The acting, the scenography, the props and costumes and other aspects of the *Inszenierung* were to resonate with the unique 'sense' of the play by means of sensual illusion and a scenic atmosphere. These attempts reached their peak in the early twentieth century with the influential historicist and atmospheric productions by another internationally successful German director, Max Reinhardt (1873–1943; see Carter 1914; P. Marx 2006a; Styan 1982). Famously, Reinhardt experimented in rehearsal to find the most appropriate way to direct each play; the opposite end of the rule-based conception of art in the representational regime. This is why *Regie* can be understood as expressing the aesthetic 'art-ness' of theatre. Its process of bringing together and organising a wealth of disparate and heterogeneous materials – text, space, bodies, voices and sounds, costume, light, not the least the spectating public – turned *Regie* into the ultimate 'art of the theatre'. As Alain Badiou suggests, such an 'assemblage of components directly produces ideas' (Badiou 2005b, 72). *Regie* thus marks the moment that had 'transformed the thinking of representation into an art in its own right' (Badiou 2007, 40). At the same time, Reinhardt's work points us to a further key aspect of *Regie* that aligns it with the aesthetic regime: it was informed by a sensibility for *difference* which was to be expressed through the autonomous realm of art, and it is this same sensibility that also underpins the historicism and the realism of nineteenth-century *Regie*.

Early *Regie* and historical realism

The celebrated historical realism of the Meininger, in productions such as *Julius Caesar*, Schiller's *Wallenstein* or Kleist's *Hermannsschlacht*, continued a new and notable engagement with history that had been a vital motor driving the new practice of *Regie* for some time. In the mid-eighteenth century, the question of how to represent the historical sites and contexts of a play already featured prominently in the context of the *Nationaltheater* movement. Later, Schlegel and Tieck attempted to introduce the 'original' Shakespeare into the German language with their influential translations, accompanied on stage by Immermann's and Dingelstedt's scenic efforts. Throughout the nineteenth century, the new art of *mise en scène* remained obsessed with history and historical settings, characters and circumstances. Great effort was put into assembling 'historical' scenographic décor. It is worth exploring this aspect more thoroughly, since it is all too easy to make the mistake of projecting the aesthetic concerns of the twenty-first century onto this fascinating prominence of historical realism in nineteenth-century *Regie*. Although the *Inszenierung* aimed at making present and sensible, through the mediation of the performance, the 'truth' of the past, this 'truth' was not perceived as 'correct' representation of historical settings, costumes and behaviour. The desire for 'sublime authenticity' (reflected elsewhere in emerging technologies, from the diorama to photography) was not simply a medial strategy employed to overcome or even efface a gap and a notable distance. On the contrary, the obsession with accuracy, with copying 'originality', emphasised and highlighted a feeling of rupture, loss and disconnection between past and present. It indicated actual historical separation. Following the categories of Hegel's philosophy of history, we can see this trend of historicism in early *Regie*, *pace* the Duke of Meiningen's obsession with 'real' props, going further than imitation (*Nachahmung*). Instead, it engendered a reflective, aesthetic transformation (*Nachbildung*) of the past. History and its artefacts, which made their 'real' sensory appearance on the theatre scene, refer us to distant, and simultaneously very distinct, moments in the past.

Karl Marx illustrated the fundamental problem of the distance between past and present, discussing Homer in a much-quoted passage from his *Grundrisse* manuscripts:

> From another side: is Achilles possible with powder and lead? Or the *Iliad* with the printing press, not to mention the printing machine? Do not the song and the saga and the muse necessarily come to an end with the printer's bar, hence do not the necessary conditions of epic poetry vanish?

> But the difficulty lies not in understanding that the Greek arts and epic are bound up with certain forms of social development. The difficulty is that they still afford us artistic pleasure and that in a certain respect they count as a norm and as an unattainable model. (K. Marx 1857)

We can research and recreate the context from which a past play emerged, but this does not offer any insight into its idea. Yet, it is precisely as a result of this aesthetic dimension that we remain fascinated and attracted to this past artwork. *Regie*'s focus on the past – whether of Greek classics or Shakespeare's plays – is therefore bound to an attempt to mediate and establish a relation, to a negotiation with this paradox of the 'artistic pleasure' and the 'unattainable model' of the past. Rather than reflecting the search for a sense *of* the past, attempts to capture the past through visual and performing art reflect the quest for a sense *for* the past. Rather than simply bringing the past into the present, its aesthetic re-presentation asserted the very impossibility of direct access to the past, without the aid of aesthetic mediation, of which Slavoj Žižek reminds us in his Hegel readings:

> The main feature of historical thought proper is not 'mobilism' (the motif of the fluidification or historical relativization of all forms of life), but the full endorsement of a certain *impossibility*: after a true historical break, one simply cannot return to the past, or go on as if nothing happened – even if one does, the same practice will have acquired a radically changed meaning. (Žižek 2012, 193)

Precisely for this reason, the disjunction requires mediation, as it can no longer be solved by a representational order governed by the principle of correspondence. The sense of time *as progress*, which underlies this new attitude to history in the nineteenth century, had been entirely foreign to the static representative order.

The momentous rupture of the 1789 Revolution, in particular, had fostered an acute awareness of the dimension of time, which became a further defining aspect of the aesthetic re-partitioning of the sensible.[12] Whether in Romantic poetry, in popular culture and certainly in Hegel's philosophy, time now acquired 'direction' and was experienced as progression of specific and unique moments. Most importantly, the past became a reference point from which to define one's own, necessarily distinct standpoint: it induced a distance from which to reflect on the present. From this perspective, the historicism of nineteenth-century *Regie* was neither entirely (nor inherently) a conservative looking back. Not unlike the *Nationaltheater* movement of the eighteenth century, it articulated potentially emancipatory dynamics which positioned themselves against the stasis of the representative order, in art and politics as much as in other cultural spheres. Hegel's understanding of art is, consequentially, strictly historical. His assertion of a periodisation of art *history* was in its time no less puzzling than Foucault's claim that sexuality should have a history has been in the late twentieth century. Hegel departs from classical Greek perfection. The ideal figure of classical Greece (not so much its historic reality, though – only Heidegger would once more be irritated by the odd harmony of democracy and slavery) served as a model for the ideal unison of sensuality and reason. This distinct 'mise en sens' offered an aesthetic alternative to the contradictions experienced in the present.[13] Typically, this newly felt historicity was experienced as a 'negative progress', which distanced us ever further from an idealised (and thoroughly imagined) past infused with all the positive values perceived as lacking in the present. From Schiller's reinstatement of the Greek chorus around 1800 (see Chapter 3) to the enthusiasm for historical remnants such as Elgin's Marbles or Schliemann's Trojan excavations (all to be displayed in the aesthetic autonomy of a Berlin or British Museum), to the productions of Greek tragedy and of Shakespeare's classics – the past was understood as a testimony of a different set of individual and collective relations, thus as a different 'partition of the sensible'.[14]

The historicism of nineteenth-century *Regie* thus positioned the spectators in a dialectic relationship to the represented historical time, emphasising an elemental difference. It asserted the key function of art within the aesthetic regime, which is to provide a 'special' experience different from the everyday, rather than disclosing the will to restore or vicariously relive the past on stage. Instead of the previously asserted immutable 'timelessness' of classical works by authors such as Sophocles or Shakespeare, their radically different 'sense' became the key to and the (to a degree almost contingent) trigger for a specifically aesthetic experience. Perceived as truer than the lacking, 'negative' reality of the present, it ultimately asserted the possibility of a different partition of the sensible. In its first incarnation as historical realism, *Regie* thus perforated and dynamised the perception of classical plays from the past. The very existence of ever-new *mises en scène* of the ever same classics confirms that the visible is no longer subordinated to the sayable, and that the 'double constraints' of the representative regime have been lifted. The interest shifted to the assertion of difference itself, which *Regie* actualised in the *Inszenierung* through aesthetic means.[15]

At the end of the nineteenth century, theatre may no longer have been the 'preferred site of representation' that Rancière described in the context of the representational regime in Baroque court theatres and on early modern popular stages (Rancière 2007, 116, as quoted above). No longer affirming an immutable order of being, the scenic dynamic triggered by the mediation of *Regie* sought to capture the unique idea of each play in new ways, and to make it sensibly available as an aesthetic experience to its audience. The new practice of *Regie* carved out a new space for a speculative 'aesthetic' mediation, which exploited the gap that had opened up between the dramatic text and its presentation on stage and in performance: a gap which revealed a dissensus, pointing to a different partition of the sensible. Previously 'a space of exhibition entirely given over to presence' (Rancière 2007, 116), this presence now became more and more punctured with its absent other – of silent objects, of other times, of different places, races and classes. Establishing relations with these sites of difference, theatre made them available for our sensuous experience in the present, without obliterating the difference and the distance, of which we were also persistently reminded through the new formal spatial separation between stage and audience. This is what directly links *Regie* to the Hegelian mode of dialectic, 'speculative thinking', against the representational logic of predication, correspondence and causality. *Regie* is the very name given to this new dialectic process that makes sense, gives sense and makes sensible by playing with the forces of Schramm's 'magic triangle of theatrality', briefly alluded to in the Introduction, above. The next chapter will now look more closely at this dialectic and theatral way of thinking engendered by *Regie*.

Notes

1 Throughout, translations from German sources are my own, unless stated otherwise. In her introductory essay to their edited volume of source material on directing, Helen Krich Chinoy draws on Winds's account (Cole and Chinoy 1963, 1–78), also adopting his distinction of *innere* and *äussere Regie*, albeit in exactly the opposite way, arguing for a development where 'modern theatre tends more and more toward an *äussere Regie*, a unity imposed by historically accurate sets and costumes, by realistic imitation, and ultimately by the external hand of the director' (13f.) In this case, we should side with Winds, not least since 'interior direction' is also a term used by Antoine (Antoine 1903). (I am grateful to Patrice Pavis for sharing a copy of the original document with me.)
2 Historical accounts of the emergence of directing, the director and *mise en scène* are manifold. See among many others Blanchart 1948; Bradby and Williams 1988; Braun 1982; Brauneck 1988; Cole and Chinoy 1963; Fouquière 1884; Innes and Shevtsova 2013; Kennedy 2009; Pavis 2013; Roselt 2009; Roubine 1980; Shepherd 2012; Veinstein 1955.
3 We should take care not to reduce this opposition to a simple stand-off between figurative imitation, realism and three-dimensional illusion, on the one hand (an all-too-simplistic shorthand for the representative regime of art), and new forms of modernist 'abstract art' that expose their materiality and insist on their autonomy, on the other. The latter is nothing but a caricature of the aesthetic regime, reducing it to an attitude where 'anything goes', also with regard to the staging of a text. Rancière keeps insisting that the aesthetic regime never simply abandoned mimesis and imitation in favour of principles such as abstraction and medial purity. He interprets the later anti-bourgeois rupture of turn-of-the-century modernism around 1900 as principally rooted in the same aesthetic partition of the sensible. Modernism was an attempt to cut out the transcendent bridge of aesthetic mediation, instead creating immanent art that either purported to be 'pure art' (*l'art pour l'art*) or assumed a direct identity with life. What both of these opposed principles nevertheless share is the central topology of the aesthetic regime that sees in art the site for a 'truer' sensory experience.
4 Rancière's concept of *le partage du sensible* is frequently rendered in English as 'division of the sensible'. I prefer the more literal 'partition', that is closer to the meaning of the French word 'partage' which is sharing, not dividing. It also maintains the echo of 'having a (or no) part' in the aesthetico-political stakes, which is the central aspect within Rancière's emancipatory political philosophy. For a concise outline of the principal tenets of his argument, see the first section, 'Politics of Aesthetics', in Rancière 2009a.
5 This shift was probably best mirrored by the progression in the work of German theatre scholar Erika Fischer-Lichte: from her pioneering *Semiotics of Theatre*, published in the early 1980s, she arrived via a sustained engagement with phenomenology throughout the 1990s at her 'aesthetics of performativity' (Fischer-Lichte 2008). What she describes as the 'emergence' of meaning is stimulated by an 'exchange of energies'. Rather than the old model of transmitting 'semiotic meaning' from sender to receiver, a dynamic 'autopoietic feedback loop' connects the stage with the auditorium, and the performers with the spectators.

6   As stated by Winds 1925, 10, who refers to a 'Schmids Chronologie des deutschen Theaters' as his source.
7   In French, this transition was marked by the move, in theatrical terminology, from the bureaucratic-managerial terms of *régie* and the *régisseur* to the new terms of *mise en scène* and the *metteur en scène*. Jean Vilar, founder of the Avignon festival and director of the Théâtre National Populaire, programmatically referred to himself as *régisseur* (Roubine 1980, 20).
8   For French theatre history, Roxane Martin has in two seminal studies traced the use of the term in the field of theatre as far back as post-Revolutionary contexts: see her *La féerie romantique sur les scènes parisiennes 1791–1864* (2007), and *L'émergence de la notion de mise en scène dans le paysage théâtral français 1789–1914* (2014). I am grateful to Patrice Pavis for pointing me to Martin's important research.
9   The leading German encyclopaedia, *Brockhaus*, includes a short article on *Regie* in its 1836 edition, explaining it as 'the organisation of the matters of the stage, in as much as they refer to the performance of plays' (vol. 9, 139).
10 Rancière traces such gestures of exclusions all the way back to Plato's 'counting out' of artisans and poets from his utopian *Republic* (see Rancière 2009a, 26).
11 Rancière's approach, not unlike Chantal Mouffe's emphasis on agonism, challenges models of the public sphere that emphasise rational consensus, most prominently in the works of Jürgen Habermas (see Mouffe 2005; Rancière 2010; Reinelt 2011).
12 Where the equally paradigm-shifting discovery of America in 1492 had given urgent emphasis to the dimension of space (see Sloterdijk 2013), the Revolution of 1789 prompted the reflection (one may critically argue: the overestimation) of the dimension of time. In philosophy, this is manifest in a line of thought from Hegel via Heidegger to postmodernism.
13 Hegel introduces the triad of symbolic, classical and Romantic art. There is an echo in Rancière's distinction of the 'ethical', the 'representative' and the 'aesthetic' regime of art (see Rancière 2004, 2009a).
14 Rancière frequently uses Schiller's discussion of the *Juno Ludovisi* statue to articulate the distance to the past experienced in the aesthetic regime.
15 It is interesting to note the link between this craving for historical authenticity and the craze for 'exotic' foreign art or cultural displays, including the displays of actual 'savages' (some dead, some living) in the 'anthropological' museums of major Western European cities. Both phenomena were fed by the same contradictory spectatorial desire, and both were the product of an orchestrating *Regie*. These very contradictions pushed the awareness, fostered by historicism, of individual situations and circumstances, for time in general and *our time* in particular, to its limits. This is why Naturalism became a necessary next step within the trajectory of the aesthetic regime: workers, women, slaves, foreigners and other repressed aspects of the grotesque and often immoral social reality, which Brahm emphasised exemplarily in his manifesto for the Freie Bühne, gained a place in the works of Ibsen, Jarry, Hauptmann, Gorki, Schnitzler and Wedekind. At the same time, no analysis of naturalist aesthetics should forget the crucial role of the fundamental distance, and the mediated relation.

2

The restless spirit of *Regie*: Hegel, theatrality and the magic of speculative thinking

There is an intriguing suggestiveness in the etymology of the German term *Schauspiel* that gets lost in translation, whether it is rendered as 'drama' or by using any other term to invoke the genre of theatre dedicated to the staging of playtexts. A composite noun, it contains the words 'Schau' and 'Spiel'. The former is the direct equivalent to the Greek *thea*, which signifies both the act of 'showing' and the act of 'gazing' at this ostentatious display. This double-edged 'Schau' is at the heart of any performance where actors put themselves on display – *sich zur Schau stellen*, as one says in German – while the audience (the *Zu-schau-er*) watch. We also encounter 'Schau' when we reflect on the world, as *thea* importantly reminds us of the close link between *thea*-tre and *theo*-ry, which existed from the outset in Western European culture (see Wilson Nightingale 2004). In philosophy, *thea/Schau* also surfaces in *Anschauung*, a notion quintessential to the German idealist philosophy of Schelling, Fichte and Hegel. It, too, is a concept much richer than the literal rendering 'in-sight' suggests, as the word also points us to the sensory process of perception (the 'on-sight'). These etymological ruminations provide useful ammunition against current mind-numbing debates that place 'theory' and 'practice' in opposition to one another, completely misunderstanding the Greek notions of *theoreia* and *praxis*, and suggesting that one would be able to create performances, or to otherwise 'practise' one's art, without thinking; or that the intellect stood in the way of creativity and active doing.

But let us return to 'Schauspiel': the second term that complements the polyvalent idea of *Schau* is, of course, the 'Spiel' of playing, players and playhouses – the very term that remained common parlance for theatres and actors long into the nineteenth century. Considering drama and its performance as *Schauspiel*, as a game or play of sight and showing, enables us to further develop our understanding of *Regie*, and our grasp of its mediation, introduced in the previous chapter. Theatre, from this perspective, designates first and foremost an art that plays with thoughts and thinking, performed in public, observed and responded to by those who watch, witness and engage – it is the *public play of thea*. This chapter reflects on the relevance of *theatre* in both these senses, as theatral *Schau* and as public *Spiel* in order to further think through the aesthetic 'revolution of *Regie*'.

To start with, we will explore the idea of 'theatr(ic)ality' in greater detail. For Roland Barthes, it famously signified 'theater-minus-text … a density of signs and sensations built up on stage starting from the written argument' (Barthes [1954] 1972, 26). In his text, Barthes considered Baudelaire, a key informant of the Rancièrian aesthetic regime, to arrive at a definition of theatricality as 'that ecumenical perception of sensuous artifice – gesture, tone, distance, substance, light – which submerges the text beneath the profusion of its external language' (26). Here, he hinted at what Rancière later captured in his formula of the 'silent speech' of things, which remains unattainable without aesthetic mediation. Yet, as Barthes's listed elements suggest, his approach conceived of theatricality as yet another term for *Inszenierung* and *mise en scène*, starting from the text and eventually 'submerging' it. To fully grasp the potential of the Janus-faced notion of *thea*, and to exploit its dynamic ambiguity for our conceptual modelling of *Regie* as an intervention in the aesthetic sensible, this chapter takes a different route and considers this 'public play of *thea*' through the lens of what has become established in German theatre scholarship as *Theatralitätsforschung* (theatrality studies). Some core ideas of this approach – the notion of 'theatrality' as a cultural relation and as a 'style of thinking' – are then linked to Hegelian 'speculative thinking', and I will outline some core Hegelian ideas which productively resonate with *Regie*. I will, however, not engage that much with Hegel's writing on theatre, or on art in general, found most notably in his lectures on aesthetics. Instead, I concentrate on some of the central principles that inform his mode of thinking, in order to offer a 'Hegelian understanding of post-Hegelian art' (Pippin 2014, 53). I am indebted here to Robert Pippin's discussion of Manet's revolution in painting, which he analyses through a Hegelian lens. The chapter works through a more detailed outline of Hegelian thinking, mainly to mark a distance from 'the caricature [Hegel] has been for so many years' (Jameson 2010, 17): the reduced portrait of Hegel as an advocate of a closed system that, by means of a teleological dialectic synthesis, resolves all contradictions in an 'end of history' harmony. Other than Pippin, my return to *Regie* via Hegel has been inspired by the recent revaluations of his thought by Herbert Marcuse, Gillian Rose, Fredric Jameson, Catherine Malabou and Slavoj Žižek. Above all, Hegel's insistence on the inseparability of understanding from *Anschauung*, his emphasis on sensible experience as anything but disinterested (Pippin described this radicalisation of Kantian ethics as 'Hegel's practical philosophy', see Pippin 2008) and his idea of speculative thinking, all offer crucial prompts for thinking through the actual potential of *Regie* as something other than the representation of an independently existing text and its ideal(ised) truth. Instead, *Regie* will reveal itself as genuinely 'theatral thinking'. Let us therefore turn to this somewhat idiosyncratic notion of 'theatrality' first.

Theatrality: the theories of Rudolf Münz and Helmar Schramm

The 'German school' of *Theatralitätsforschung* ('research into theatrality') is internationally far less well known than the simultaneously emerging discipline of US performance studies. It was established during the 1970s, in what was then the German Democratic Republic, by its founding pioneer Rudolf Münz, alongside Joachim Fiebach and their principal students and assistants, Helmar Schramm and Andreas Kotte. The concurrent German and North American revisions of our discipline both extended the notion of theatre beyond the narrow definition that solidified in the nineteenth century. They aligned the field with a wider anthropological perspective: in the USA, Richard Schechner engaged in an interdisciplinary dialogue with Victor Turner, while Eastern European theatrality studies were able to draw on a legacy ranging back to Nicolai Evreinov in the early twentieth century. The latter's somewhat eccentric theorisations of a Nietzschean human 'will to play' in his books *The Theatre as Such* and *The Theatre for One-Self* (published in 1912 and 1915) not only prompted the modern philosophical discourse on 'theatricality' but also offered, as an aside, a fascinating early instance of 'performative writing' (see Golub 1984; Jestrovic 2002; Lukanitschewa 2013). More solidly academic in scope, East German *Theatralitätsforschung* built, above all, on robust historiographical investigations far beyond the realms of scripted drama, while also taking up prompts from Brechtian theatre-theoretical thinking (his 'Street Scene' offered a central contribution to the debate), and reconsidering the legacy of the European modernist avant-garde, from Futurism to Bauhaus (Fiebach 2002) and Artaud, who remained a persistent reference point for Helmar Schramm's writing. Rudolf Münz's methodological manifesto of theatrality as historiographic research tool (Münz 1998) and Schramm's systematic archaeology of the term 'theatre' as a metaphor, a rhetoric medium, and as art (Schramm 1990) demonstrate the depth and breadth of this research, which soon popularised the term within German and wider Continental European theatre research. By 1998, Andreas Kotte could not but note that the idea of 'theatrality' had become 'a free-floating element of discourse' (Kotte 1998, 188), at least within this geographical research context. Meaning everything for everybody, the notion had turned into what Lacanian cultural critique terms 'empty signifier'.[1]

The distinct coinage of the term theatrality, as opposed to the more common 'theatricality', signalled, on the one hand, an explicit stance against the canonised institutional matrix of bourgeois theatre, which Münz in his writing referred to as the 'theatre of Monsieur Diderot'. It was an attempt to avoid the major theatre-historiographic pitfall of projecting contemporary ideas and concepts (mainly those of the post-eighteenth-century Western European theatre institution) onto the past, thereby making other, alternative and less popular forms of theatre conform to this 'master narrative', or erasing them from official theatre-historic memory altogether. On the other hand, the explicit choice of this term sought to defend the cultural practice of theatre against those who dismissed it as conservative and outdated, and who accused it of 'theatrical' fake appearance, deceitful 'acting' and the staging of falsities and fiction. In everyday speech, the term 'theatrical' is used to express the opposite of 'truth' and 'reality'. This continues the long history of theatrophobia, the fear of dissemblance, fictional illusion and simulation right through history (see Barish 1981). More recently, these attitudes have gained fresh currency in the context of postmodern and feminist critique, from the Debordian analysis of the 'spectacle' to Baudrillard's critique of 'simulation'. Further, the strategically termed 'performance art', as well as the new (inter-) discipline of (US) performance studies, declared performance to be 'the basic stuff of social life', as anthropologist Victor Turner once phrased it (Turner 1986, 81). At least in its early years, it pitched performance against theatre, text-based drama against devising, 'theatrical' representation against the 'presence' of performance (see Féral 1982). Too often, constructions of hierarchical dichotomies were merely displaced, cementing yet more binary models of thinking within our discipline.

In its engagement with previously marginalised theatre forms – whether popular Western performance traditions, such as the *giulliari*, harlequins and the German *commedia* tradition, which Münz extensively researched, or non-Western forms of performance such as Fiebach's pioneering work on African theatre – the East German branch of theatrality studies offered an understanding of theatral practices that sought to avoid their persistent (or at least implicit) comparison with standard forms and normative assumptions about 'theatre'. Münz rigorously modelled his definition of 'theatrality' on a thorough reflection on the notion of *thea*, the dual activity of 'gazing' and 'showing' expressed by the Greek verb *theorein*, alluded to at the outset of this chapter (Münz 1979, 1998). Departing from a literal understanding of *thea*-tre, his argument productively complements the emphasis, within performance studies, on 'performativity'. Münz maintained, above all, that *thea* is not merely a secondary adjunct to 'performance', its 'other side', as it were, but that it is always already included, 'counted in' in any ostentatious presentation of technique (i.e. performing). The approach of 'theatrality research' was stronger than performance studies in its assertion that theatre simply cannot take place without an audience. Here, the spectator was conceived of differently to the silent observer in the darkened auditorium introduced by the tradition of fourth-wall psychological realism in its predication on the drama of the bourgeois subject. Theatrality, as signalled in the very term *thea*, implied the spectators' unique and indispensable contribution, involvement and cooperation. This further confirms that we will not be able to think directing, either, without also considering spectating.

The tie between performance and perception, between representation and spectating, which is asserted by the notion of theatricality, can also be traced beyond the immediate discipline of theatre and performance studies.[2] Art critic Michael Fried found the ambiguous duality of *thea* famously confusing. In his notorious 1967 treatise on *Art and Objecthood*, he rejected any 'awareness' of the presence of the spectator in the artwork itself and instead favoured what he termed 'absorption' (Fried 1980).[3] During the 1950s and 1960s, the terminology of roles, scripts, settings and performances became particularly prominent within the social sciences and cultural anthropology. The works of Erving Goffman, Milton Singer and Clifford

Geertz, in particular, popularised an extended idea of 'theatricality' in society and culture, which exploited the actor/character paradigm of dramatic theatre. As the subtitle of her influential 1972 study announced, Elizabeth Burns compared the 'theatrical conventions in the theatre and in social life', underlining the centrality of the spectators' involvement and their vital cooperation in any theatrical event. Moreover, she did not characterise theatre in terms of its 'media specific' artistic properties – an approach that had dominated art research across the board at the time. Instead, she explicitly introduced theatricality as 'an audience term' and presented it not as a matter of artistic intention but as 'a mode of perception' (Burns 1972, 12f.).[4] More recently, Christopher Balme utilised, for his post-colonial study of Western representations of cultural performances from the Pacific and South Sea, the idea of a 'theatrical mode of perception' as a conceptual framework that applies both in institutionalised (Western European) contexts of theatre as well as in wider cultural performance events (Balme 2007). Above all, his argument countered the assumption that theatricality is inherent in certain actions or people. Instead, he drew on Goffmann to argue that a complex interplay of aesthetic conventions and other expectations generates a 'frame' of theatrical perception around phenomena: what is perceived as theatrical is what is framed in this way. Importantly for my argument, theatrality here was grounded in processes of mediation, rather than in specific media technologies.

This leads us straight to the second of Münz's vital propositions which moved beyond the theoretical assumptions of performance studies. By insisting on the indispensable complementary relation between performing and spectating, announced by the cultural process of *thea*, he considered theatrality as 'a relation, not behaviour' (Münz 1998, 70). Where performance was understood, within the horizon of performance studies along Schechner's and Barba's lines, as 'twice-behaved behaviour' or 'restored behaviour', we can consider these theoretical positions themselves as expressions of a specific 'partition of the sensible', which is deeply imbued in the Western, and especially US, ideology that privileges, above all, the individual. Where theatrality is, instead, conceived as a relation, the focus no longer remains on the individual as the originator of the performative act. Instead, a relation within the cultural fabric is foregrounded. Theatre only ever exists as such a particular relation within a specific socio-historic situation, and therefore also within a specific aesthetico-political framework or 'regime'. Consequentially, Münz persistently corrected any student of his who used the definitive article and spoke of 'the theatre' without further qualification. For Münz, *the* theatre as a definitive, trans-historical universal does not exist; there was only ever, for instance, 'the theatre of Monsieur Diderot', or, of course, the Continental *Regietheater* of the twenty-first century. Therefore, the term 'theatre' always implies a historically specific snapshot of a wider, dynamically changing sphere of human action and cultural activity. Münz described theatre as the articulation in a specific historic moment of the wider network of theatrality, which he termed *Theatralitätsgefüge*, a 'texture' or 'fabric' of theatrality (Münz 1998, 69f.). Münz outlined four intertwined components that make up this dynamic formation, which he also sets apart typographically in his writing in the way introduced below. He distinguished:

(1) first, **theatre** – the institutionalised theatre, theatre as art, with its codified modes of performing;
(2) then, by **"theatre"**, Münz referred to wider socio-cultural, non-artistic forms of theatrical (or, rather 'theatral') situations of performance and *thea*. Modelled on Brecht's 'Street Scene', these instances take place outside institutionalised frameworks: this is the field of 'cultural performance', from social 'role playing' to the Benjaminian aestheticising performance of political power, to religious processions and rituals, public executions and royal celebrations;[5]
(3) next, **'theatre'** designates forms of theatre (1) and "theatre" (2) that differ from, counter, subvert or undermine the respective hegemonic understanding of the initial two fields. From his solidly historiographic perspective, Münz used as examples the performances of medieval travelling troupes that created travesties of the conventions of the dominant religious mystery and morality plays, and the German *teatro dell'arte* and its interaction with traditions of humanist Renaissance theatre. More recent examples may include Performance Art, Live Art and 'Devised Performance'. All of these counterforms of 'theatre' (3) may therefore stimulate, in Rancièrian terms, a remapping of the partition of the sensible, reminding us of the fluidity of this relational texture that neoliberal capitalism, in particular, disavows. Over the course of time, many forms, productions and artists which started out in alternative performance, hence 'theatre' (3), have moved into institutionalised frameworks of theatre (1). Further, Münz included in this bracket the obverse of innovative experimentation: productions that were prompted by melancholic nostalgia for a past theatre that is *no longer* theatre (1). Notably, opera emerged from the attempt to recreate the lost form of Greek theatre;
(4) fourth, there is **'non-theatre'**: those practices of *thea* which are explicitly forbidden and prohibited, either by law or on moral grounds, by explicit or implicit censorship. This is theatre which must not take place, and which is expressly excluded from the boundaries of legitimate theatre (1). Even Shakespeare's Globe was built outside the city walls, and Naturalist productions initially could only be staged in non-public membership venues.

These strata of institutionalisation, codification, wider cultural performance and aestheticised representation of power, playful rituals, sites of counter-culture, subversion, cultural melancholy and displacement, and also legal and moral instances of prohibiting 'non-theatre' overlap, react and contradict each other. Thereby, they contribute to this socio-cultural texture of theatrality and to its specific concretisation at any given moment in history. This idea of a stratification can be productively extended to cover the whole of Rancière's notion of a cultural regime, structured by a specific partitioning of the sensible. These regimes, such as the aesthetic regime out of which *Regie* emerged, should not be understood as monolithic blocks, but similarly as cultural *Gefüge* made up of various strata.

Once we no longer define theatre in strictly literary and (in the narrow sense) aesthetic terms, it becomes obvious that, as a relational fabric, it is most essentially interwoven with society: even when it insists on its radical autonomy from society and everyday life, theatre is still a public cultural phenomenon, a 'public play of *thea*', fulfilling its 'mediating' function of establishing cultural relations. Where Münz examined the macro-relations that define theatrality within a socio-cultural regime, Helmar Schramm, his successor as director of the Leipzig Institute for Research in Theatrality and, after the end of the GDR, a professor at Berlin's Freie Universität, concentrated on the micro-dynamics that underpin it. For Schramm, theatrality discloses and defines, first and foremost, a *Denkstil*, a 'style of thinking', or a *dispositif* of thought. He suggested that, as a productive 'formalization of thought' (Schramm 1995a, 115), theatrality points us to the historically specific combination of what he called, inspired by Lyotard, the 'three decisive agents of cultural energy' (Schramm 1996, 44): *aisthesis* (perception), *kinesis* (motion) and *semiosis* (meaning), the relational micro-dynamics that mark out the 'magic triangle' of theatrality (Schramm 1995a, 115f.; 1995b, 158f.; 1996, 249ff.; see Figure 1). Again, we encounter an essentially relational model of interacting parameters. It productively resonates with the idea of the 'partition of the sensible', and offers an especially useful concretisation of the abstract idea of the 'sensible', giving them a more concrete shape as the three theatral categories of movement, meaning and perception. Once more, it is highlighted that the 'sense' of theatre is always more than the (semiotic) meaning, as it necessarily triangulates with kinetic and aisthetic 'energy'.

The energy triggered by this triangular force field always spills over the sanctioned borders of theatrality, creating sites of 'wild' thinking that transgress habitualised *dispositifs* of normality, and offer something akin to the Rancièrian dissensus. Mikhail Bakhtin associated such transgression famously with the liminal state of carnival, and its temporary reversal of the order of society. Accordingly, Schramm called his authoritative German-language study on theatrality *Karneval des Denkens*, 'Carnival of thinking' (Schramm 1996). His relational triangle was thus no attempt to create a geometric, scientific mapping; the triangle becomes 'magic' precisely because there is no stable centre, because the three forms of cultural energy reverberate, interact and mutually interfere.[6] Schramm asserted: 'No other traditional, cultural phenomenon contains the artificial, stylized interaction between perception, movement and language to the same extent as theatre' (Schramm 1995a, 115). Yet, his research took the notion of theatrality *qua* style of thinking far beyond the confines of stage performance proper. He scrutinised, for instance, the use of the term theatre in the philosophical writings of Erasmus of Rotterdam, Paracelsus, Montaigne, Bacon, Galileo, Descartes, Pascal, Hobbes, Locke and others. His follow-up large-scale research project *Theatrum Scientiarum* went on to investigate what he describes as the 'analogical, structural correlation between the history of theatre and the history of science' (115).

Complementing Rancière's interrogation of the move from the representational to the aesthetic regime, Schramm concentrated on the historic juncture of the seventeenth century, as the printed dissemination of writing, the geometric systematisation of space, the 'scientific' rationalisation of knowledge and the emerging capitalist industrial economy, with its imperatives of profitability and productivity, prompted a new 'style of thinking'. This shift introduced, above all, firm new boundaries between 'productive' work and 'un-productive' play, and similarly, a new hierarchy between

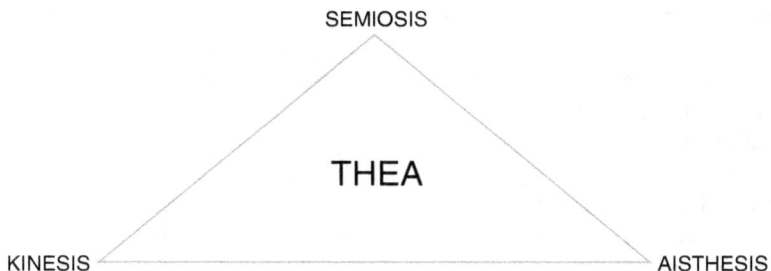

Figure 1 The 'magic triangle' of theatrality, as suggested by Helmar Schramm.

impressible physical and sensory 'feeling', on the one hand, and calculable, systematic intellectual knowledge, on the other. A veritable redistribution of the sensible took place in the name of (economic and intellectual) 'rationalisation'. The new *dispositif* dissolved the fluid spontaneity of the three fundamental parameters of theatrality, in clear favour of *semiosis*, and it fostered a bias towards the functional and efficient order of language. As a result, an irrational, non-calculable, anti-geometric, non-linear and simply non-productive underside of our enlightened, bourgeois civilisation emerged to provide alternative sites of different thinking. The growing body of texts on alchemy, which Schramm attended to in detail, attempted to maintain the dynamic, spontaneous vitality even in the newly privileged written form.[7] Similarly, the essentially kinetic performance form of *commedia* emphasised perpetual movement and the fluidity of conversion and (as in alchemy) essentially physical transformation. Alchemy as well as *commedia*, for Schramm,

> derive their vital impetus from the spontaneous physical interaction of perception, motion and language. With the gradual victory of the printing press, the ambivalent balance of forces between these three aspects of physical experience is destroyed. Language in the service of writing loosens itself from the physical context of its oral tradition and becomes the organizing violence in a hierarchical structure of representation. In the light of the public nature of the printed word, the two great arts of bodily transformation themselves undergo a decisive modification. (Schramm 1995b, 160)

Both fields now attempted their 'methodical stylization', measuring and conceptualising 'their thinkability and their worthiness of being thought' (158). The assertion of the 'remarkable mimetic correlation' between science and theatre (158), of theatre and philosophy and of *commedia* and alchemy, all under the umbrella of 'theatrality', becomes clearer. They share an underlying partition of the sensible, reflected in the theatral dynamics of perception, motion and language, all of which have become central organising principles to measure and conceptualise the world. Science *and* theatre are both fundamentally based on systematically organising and synchronising these basic cultural principles.

At this point we should add Hegel and the deliberately 'false thinking' (Marcuse 1955, 130) of the dialectic logic, to which we will return in greater depth below.[8]

Žižek wondered whether Hegel's system of thinking would have been at all capable of absorbing the rational mathematisation of modern (natural) sciences, with their reliance on measuring and empirical testing, which characterised the further course of the nineteenth century. He described Hegel's approach as 'the last great attempt to "sublate" empirical-formal science into speculative Reason' (Žižek 2012, 458). Similarly, in his seminal reading of the *Phenomenology of Spirit*, Jameson reminded us that through speculative thinking, Hegel

> wishes systematically to unmask and to denounce the attempt to think the thought of reality in terms of what we may call spatial thinking, the thinking of externalities and of quantities. For this kind of thinking – technically called *Verstand* or Understanding, following Kant's usage – is a thinking organized around the law of non-contradiction, a thinking for which only one pole of a given opposition or antithesis can be true at one time.
>
> ...
>
> [Hegel's] fundamental polemic target is *Verstand* or empiricism: ideologies of non-contradiction which produce the mirage of an affirmative action as well as the reifications of a substantialist worldview. (Jameson 2010, 47f., 50)

Alchemy (as opposed to chemistry) as well as 'other' theatre forms, such as *commedia dell'arte* (as opposed to the 'regulated' dramatic theatre), continued to insist on, in Schramm's terms, the 'spontaneous interaction of perception, motion, and language' (Schramm 1995b, 160). They thereby create a dissensus, pushing the limits of the now dominant logical order of language by 're-linking language to processes of perception and motion' (161), while equally reconnecting perception with motion and *semiosis*.[9] Their theatral 'carnival of thinking' persistently reconfigures the architectonics of the discursive borders of the 'sensible'.

The momentous shifts of the past may well assist us in considering our own position in the early twenty-first century, where, in Jodi Dean's term, the 'communicative capitalism' built on pervasive social media and digital technologies has once again significantly altered our 'kinetic style of movement' as well as reshaping the ways we perceive and attend to information (the *aisthetic* dimension) and how we produce meaning (the *semiotic* dimension). Schramm's theatre-philosophical operation, therefore, also performed one of *Regie*'s central purposes. He revisited and 'restaged' texts from another time for an audience of the present, and established through this mediation a short-circuit between different 'partitions of the sensible'. He further extended the invitation of theatrality research to open up our perspective beyond standardised modes of thinking in order to arrive at new and relevant conclusions for our own present-day concerns. Following Schramm's perspective, theatrality, at its very heart, discloses the 'stylisation' of relations between its three forces (*semiosis, kinesis, aisthesis*) across various socio-cultural fields. Theatre, then, as a cultural institution and as a medium of cultural (again, not solely technological) mediation, marks a space and situation of ostentatious presentation, transmission and specular perception of the organisation of these cultural forces. The negotiation of their relations is particularly intensified as a result of their framing through *thea*, that dual force of ostentatious performance and sensible perception. Through *thea*, theatre puts the (hegemonic) 'style of thinking' or, in Rancièrian terminology, the dominant 'partition of the sensible' in play.

Bringing together the perspectives of Schramm and Münz with our own field of *Regie* and the understanding of theatre as a relational situation leaves behind the emphasis on 'fiction', or 'role-playing', and hence helps us reduce the prominence of aspects of representation and narration in the proposed concept of *Regie*, too:

> A situation (performance, governed by *thea*) results from the interaction of bodies (corporeality/*kinesis*), and because it is structured in a specific way (*Inszenierung/semiosis*), it is recognised and perceived in its function (perception/*aisthesis*). If theatre is perceived as a situation, it cannot be analysed solely from one side, the representation (*Darstellung*), but must instead be explained as a specific relation between performer(s) and spectator(s). (Kotte 1998, 120; translation modified)

Conceiving of theatre as a theatral relation and situation imbued with the energies of *semiosis*, *kinesis* and *aisthesis* emphasises that theatre is always a (socio-political) 'reality': both performers and spectators 'really' act, they par(t)-take within the specific 'partitioning of the sensible'. Precisely in its multiple (relational) dimensions of the Münzian *Gefüge*, theatrality may, as a cultural force, both stabilise aesthetic, semiotic and kinetic configurations, or function as the reservoir for alternative styles of thinking, which remain marginalised or altogether excluded within the hegemonic institutionalisation of theatral thinking and theatre practices. *Regie* can then be grasped as the cultural force that sets in motion a complex and dynamic theatral process where *semiotic* signs, text and language bind themselves to the forces of *kinesis*, of moving and 'transporting' information, and *aisthesis* – its address of experiencing spectators.

Speculative thinking: a Hegelian perspective on *Regie*

Regie is inscribed in the specific historic situation and the 'theatral fabric' of Western European culture from the nineteenth century onwards – Rancière's aesthetic regime of arts. It thus shares its 'style of thinking' not least with German philosophy of the early nineteenth century, in its decisive developments between Kant and Hegel (for useful overviews, summaries and introductions, see Bowie 2003; Förster 2012; Henrich 2003). Specifically, *Regie* can be considered as a form of what Hegel calls 'speculative thinking', based on a dialectic mode of thought. Hegel's system of thinking, which he himself only occasionally referred to by the name of 'dialectic', should not be reduced to a closed system or a 'machine' of logical necessity. Rather, it offers a vital reinforcement of the potentiality of the 'carnival of thinking' inherent in theatrality, where it thinks, for instance, the unity of opposites, the identity of subject and substance, of thinking and its object. Against empiricism and formal logical reasoning, both of which, as Marcuse expressed it, dutifully pray 'the gospel of everyday thinking (including ordinary scientific thinking) and of everyday practice', Hegelian speculative thinking offers, in effect

> rules and forms of false thinking and action – false, that is, from the standpoint of common sense. The dialectical categories construct a topsy-turvy world, opening with the identity of being and nothing and closing with the notion as the true reality. Hegel plays up the absurd and paradoxical character of this world, but he who follows the dialectical process to the end discovers that the paradox is the receptacle of the hidden truth and that the absurdity ... contains the latent truth. (Marcuse 1955, 130f.)

Regie is the word for a new theatral thinking that dramatises this same speculative leap beyond the closed logic of representation, hence beyond the standard partitioning of the sensible: it moves from reality towards what Hegel calls 'actuality' (*Wirklichkeit*). His philosophy, *Regie* and alchemy all reach beyond the instrumental, economic, pragmatic logic of rational, intellectual Understanding, the 'common sense' of *Verstand*, that principal 'villain of the piece' in Hegel's theatral thinking (Jameson 2009, 82).

As a practice of speculative thinking, *Regie must* offer a re-presentation of the dramatic text which seems false at first sight – but which nevertheless gestures towards its 'latent', 'actual' truth, as we will explore further in Chapter 5. It discloses itself in what Hegel, in his famous, previously quoted expression, termed the 'sensuous appearing of the Idea' (Hegel 1955, 146). Such 'sensuous appearing', which we can imagine as an appearing directed by the three forces of theatrality, achieves according to Hegel far more than the mere representation of an objective, external idea that already existed *a priori*, similar to the shadows that dance on the infamous wall of the Platonic cave. At the very heart of his notion of intelligibility, or *Erkenntnis*, the 'sensuous appearing' emphasises the sensory dimension of *Anschauung*, often translated as 'intuition'. We should be attentive here to the reappearance of *Schau/thea* in the German word. The concept thus also evokes the dimension of *Vorstellung*, the re-presentation (*Vergegenwärtigung*) of an idea, precisely in its full semiotic, but equally its kinetic and aisthetic dimensions. Where Jameson translates 'representation' freely as 'pictorial thinking', I suggest linking *Vorstellung* with Schramm's 'theatral thinking': a thinking that gestures towards the Hegelian dimensions of Essence and the Notion, what he describes as 'Absolute', meaning full self-consciousness and recognition.[10] Importantly, this absolute consciousness is never purely rational and intellectual, but essentially sensory and affective: it is achieved, precisely, by 'theatral thinking'.

The functioning of *Regie* – of theatre direction as an art of dialectic, speculative thinking – is underpinned by central principles, which reflect fundamental structural (as it were, 'dramaturgic') aspects of Hegelian thinking: the basic 'dialectic triangle' of historicity, reflexivity and (concrete) universality, and furthermore the central speculative principles of mediation and negativity (see Figure 2). Let us briefly survey these principles; they will resurface time and again in our further discussion of the thinking of *Regie*.

First, Hegel's insistence on strict **historicity** extends the emphasis on the historical situatedness of the 'fabric of theatrality', which we encountered in Münz and

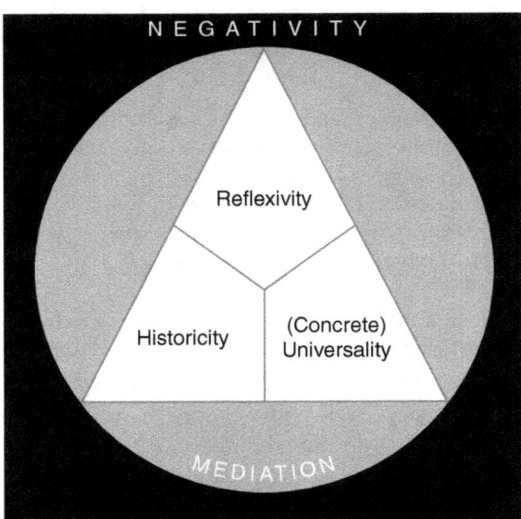

Figure 2 The central principles of Hegel's speculative thinking.

Schramm, who of course themselves argued within a solidly dialectic framework. As previously noted, in its first instantiations in the nineteenth century *Regie* introduced historicity into the *Inszenierung* of dramatic texts. By articulating a new conception of the present through the medium of the past (see Szondi 1974a), a new realism (expressed not least as the 'silent speech of things') marked the momentous break with the classicist order of representation, which (re)produced 'eternal art' and an eternal (socio-political) order. Similarly, Hegel turned philosophy from pondering eternal metaphysical truths (or Kantian 'purity') into a diagnosis of society in its own distinctly historic moment *qua* strict application of Reason (*Vernunft*). With him, philosophy became critical theory. Against empiricism and formal reasoning, his dialectic materialism (here I deliberately use Žižek's challenge to standard assertions of Hegel's 'idealism') draws its energy from a critique of the reality confronted by actuality. The latter Hegelian notion marks the true ('actual') potential of being, which Hegel associated with his term 'Notion'. Consequently, existence (and history) were no longer perceived as stable givens, but as constant movement towards actualising these notional possibilities. Hegel's philosophy thus opened up the 'really existing' (historic) reality towards this actual potentiality, and the same movement underpins the thinking of *Regie*. It turned theatre into an art form in its time and of its time (the historicism of early *Regie*), which in its dialectic turn at the very same time transcended its time by gesturing towards the actuality of a now distant and inaccessible past. The past (in Hegel, in particular, Greek antiquity) came to stand in for the actual potentiality not achieved in our present reality. Their distance thus becomes a means by which 'to reintroduce the openness of the future into the past, to grasp that-which-was in its process of becoming' (Žižek 2012, 464). Likewise, *Regie* rejects closure and the impressions of teleological progress as well as immanent necessity of the present hegemonic ordering of the sensible. Because of its dialectic core, *Regie* discloses aspects beyond representation (*Darstellung*) and points to a dimension of *Vorstellung*: to a speculative theatral thinking that always remains dialectically anchored in the ultimate contemporaneity of theatre, its *Zeitgenossenschaft*, as German director Leopold Jessner called it in the 1920s (see Chapter 4).

The second core Hegelian aspect of **reflexivity** must not be misunderstood as the (unmediated) 'isolated reflection' of Understanding that 'divides the world into numberless polarities', as Hegel rejected it in his earliest philosophical writings (see Marcuse 1955, 43ff., here 45). Rather, the movement of reflexion is connected with what Hegel describes, in the *Science of Logic*, as the 'Essence' of things. True being is reflected back in itself: 'Something is *in-itself*, in so far as it has returned to itself from its Being-for-Other' (Hegel 1986b, 129). Reflexivity is at the heart of Hegel's complex assertion of the 'Substance as Subject', his vital move beyond the antagonism of subject and object, a dichotomy which, far beyond a merely epistemological problem, 'denoted a concrete conflict in existence, and [time and again Hegel stressed] that its solution, the union of the opposites, was a matter of practice as well as of theory', as Marcuse asserted (Marcuse 1955, 25). Introducing a consequential term, Hegel described the historic form of this conflict as 'alienation' (*Entfremdung*). Reflexivity designates the dialectic force that works against the alienating reification of this and other relations. Within a dialectic dynamic, as it is characteristic for art in the aesthetic regime, the aesthetic experience is triggered by the strangeness of the art object or practice itself, by its immediate unavailability to standard modes of perception and experience, as they dominate the functional regime of everyday life. At this point, one may think of Schiller's discussion of the *Juno* statue, or of Hegel's reflections on the self-reflexivity of Dutch and Flemish genre painting in his *Aesthetics*. Yet, just as Hegel interpreted the latter as a work of art that is an 'archive of its own process' (Rancière 2009a, 9), in a crucial move, the force of reflexivity, as such 'archiving' of the very process of (theatral or other) mediation, fosters an awareness that even these strange objects (the Hegelian substance) are not 'alien' to the subject. As spectators, we are instead invited to reflexively find ourselves in the object, to return to ourselves through the object. Far more recently, Michel Foucault, in his late lectures, and after him Leo Bersani, prominently called for similar 'new relational modes' based on an 'extensibility of sameness' (Bersani 2010, 118): on the recognition of *the same* in the other. This creates a relation to oneself and to the other, which is not based on hierarchy, on implications of superiority/inferiority, identification and forceful appropriation, and thus an 'othering' that eventually exterminates difference, even in the name of diversity and tolerance.

Such (self-) reflexive moments constitute an important (structural) push beyond the (semiotic) content of theatre as symbolic practice. By forming a relation to this content, they reveal a collective practice of meaning that goes beyond individual interpretation. Here, the reflexive dynamics support the development of the (self-) consciousness of Spirit (*Geist*), another much misunderstood Hegelian concept. Often anthropomorphically distorted, as if referring to a single 'supreme being' (as in Kojève's famous allusion to the 'Sage' with explicit echoes of Napoleon and Stalin), Hegel's term should instead be read as designating 'collective life as such' (Jameson

2010, 75), not unlike the Marxian 'general intellect' or the notion of 'soul' in the work of Franco Berardi. From this perspective, referring to the Hegelian Spirit first and foremost expresses a stance against the privilege afforded to (alienated) individuality, even more so in the present-day 'style of thinking' described by Jodi Dean as 'communicative capitalism' (Dean 2009). When Hegel spoke of the consciousness of Spirit as the ultimate outcome of reflexivity, we should not take this as mere self-'awareness'. We should instead bear Lukács's understanding of 'consciousness' in mind, which emphasised its inherently practical aspect, its capacity to actually create, produce and change awareness in the reflective subject through its (reflexive) link within a 'community of interpreters' (the term is Rancière's; on this aspect, see Žižek 2012, 388, and Henrich 2010, 'Hegels Logik der Reflexion', 95–157).

Reflexivity further emphasises the structural necessity of **mediation** in its rejection of any privilege to immediacy and unmediated 'authenticity'. From this angle, *Regie* becomes a prime instance of what Schiller described as the 'doctrine of the middle term' (see Chapter 3).[11] Yet mediation not only 'sublates' what initially appeared as antagonistic opposition; as Hegel had already asserted in some early writings of the Tübingen period, it also suggests the mediation between the subject and its objective, material conditions. For Hegel, 'mediation is the proper function of the living self as an actual subject, and at the same time it *makes* the living self an actual subject' (Marcuse 1955, 38). The principle of mediation, therefore, becomes vital for any negotiation between the other central Hegelian constants: the abstract and the concrete, and the particular and the universal. They directly point us to the third principle of speculative thinking – to **concrete universality**. Corresponding to the dialectic aim of sublating the purely particular in the universality of the Notion,[12] the particular *Inszenierung* is the necessary stand-in for a playtext's 'concrete universality', which cannot be actualised directly, without mediation; this aspect will be more fully developed alongside the discussion of Leopold Jessner's work in Chapter 4. Understanding *Regie* as negotiation of abstract and concrete universality is a principal argument against the misinformed perception of the director as authoritarian *auteur* who allegedly (ab)uses the playwright's work according to his individual will. Instead of misrecognising the director in this way as transcendental figure, we can emphasise the fundamentally immanent character of the function of *Regie* – as historically situated, reflexive mediation, hence as process of 'concrete actualisation'.

Together, these tenets of the Hegelian dramaturgy of thinking assert its fundamental **negativity**, the core aspect of his thought which recently preoccupied Žižek, and which is probably the most complex and difficult to grasp. Hegel considered the conditions and relations of being and reality as necessarily negative, as they fall behind their actual ('notional') potential, determined by ultimate reason and liberty. Speculative thinking induces, above all, what Hegel himself described in his *Jenenser Logic* as 'restlessness', 'diese absolute Unruhe', stirred by the plaguing negativity of not being what, according to its actual potential, it truly is (see Marcuse 1955, 65f.) It thus enables 'the detection, where common sense presumed a continuous field of uninterrupted phenomena in an unproblematic real world, of strange rifts or multiple dimensions, in which different laws and dynamics obtain' (Jameson 2009, 23). This restlessness, this constant being on the move is perfectly exemplified in the heterogeneous plenitude of Hegel's own writing, in its persistent mobility of thinking (rather than a conventional 'representation of thought'), which rejects the laws of logic coherence and of linear dramaturgy. It thereby operates as 'de-reification', which is how Jameson summed up the overall purpose of Hegel's huge project.[13] Inherent in *Regie* is this same restless mobility of negativity that avoids the standstill of the status quo and which prevents, rather than facilitates, the commodification of the playtext. Far beyond the categories of 'interpretation' and 'representation', *Regie* indeed discloses the essential negativity of the playtext. It 'negates' the playtext, but not because it would ignore pre-existing authorial intention, or replace the original work of art with a different, secondary artwork, the director's production. Instead, the idea of negativity further destabilises the assumption that the playtext is, in Lacanian terms, 'Law' and authoritative 'Master Signifier'. It equally works against the (essentially Platonic) antagonism of the text as idea and of its performance as its 'materiality'.

Regie operates differently. As Hegel suggested in another famous formula from his *Phenomenology*, by deploying *Geist*, the marker of society as collective, of what Hegel terms ethical *Sittlichkeit*, one can split the one into two:

> Spirit is in its simple truth consciousness, and forces its moments apart. *Activity* splits it into the substance and its consciousness, and it likewise splits the substance and the consciousness. (Hegel 1986a, 327; original emphasis)

Regie induces such a split. Yet this is not an *external* split, inflicted on the otherwise harmoniously unified, 'complete' work of the playtext by the director. On the contrary, the split must be thought of as strictly immanent in the text. It asserts the contradictions and makes them tangible in the text's *mise en scène/mise en sens*, thereby staging a speculative unity that undermines the stability of any one of its constituent terms. What appears as secondary 'negation', as distorting or imposing its own interpretation onto the playtext, in fact *affirms* the text, in properly dialectic terms: it actualises the text by revealing the distortion as constitutive contradiction inherent *within* the text. *Regie* thereby asserts the text itself as a Hegelian work of art – as activity of the 'Spirit', 'forcing its moments apart'. Once more, we are pointed towards a theatral, speculative excess of 'false thinking' that generates a dissensus and ultimately leaps beyond the standard patterns and partitions of the sensible: this negativity mobilises change, and sets forth history, which Hegel conceived as a chain of mediated antagonisms and sublated contradictions. It likewise guarantees that there will be ever more productions of the same classics in Western European theatre.

Regie, the playtext and the 'non-identity of identity'

The above five core principles of speculative thinking will guide our explorations of *Regie*'s central conceptual aspects throughout this study. *Regie* actualises the play, in the German sense of *verwirklichen*: it brings it to 'real', actual life. Thinking of

Regie as speculative theatral thinking does not, however, imply or advocate a specific directorial approach or style, whether radical, deconstructionist, conservative, *werktreu* or other. First and foremost, the five key parameters outlined above determine the relationality which *Regie* negotiates

(a) between (play-)text and production;
(b) representation (of fictional worlds characters) and presentation ('the performative');
(c) the theatre production and its audience; and
(d) 'the world'/'the public' (as socio-cultural formation and political institution) and art/'the audience' (the realm of 'aesthetics').

The dialectic perspective challenges the primacy afforded to any of the two terms in the above list of relations. They are no longer conceived as independent terms, neither as 'cause' and 'effect', nor as terms providing the context or condition for the other. Instead, the negativity of dialectic thinking confronts us with the persistent tensions and contradictions between both terms, where no one term is fully complete or 'positive' when considered on its own. *Regie* sublates the dichotomic relations outlined above.

Because of its fundamental negativity, its dialectic nature challenges any beautiful idea of harmonious reconciliation of contradictions or oppositions. On the contrary. In his lectures on *Aesthetics*, Hegel confirmed the fundamental, outright monstrous and shocking (thus, 'sublime') multiplicity of art:

> [A]rt turns every one of its objects into a thousand-eyed Argus, so that the inner soul and spirit can be seen in every point. And not only the physical shape, the expression of the face, the gesture and posture, but likewise all actions and events, speeches and sounds, and the course of events through all conditions of appearance has turned art into an eye, in which the free soul reveals itself in its inner infinity. (Hegel 1955, 181)

For Robert Pippin, this passage is the pivotal expression of Hegel's understanding of art as philosophy (see Pippin 2014, 49f.). We can add this argument to our thinking of *Regie*: it does not turn the playtext into a thousand-eyed monstrosity by defacing it or imposing its own external power; dialectic thinking precisely rejects the assumption that a harmonious *Ur*-state existed prior to *Regie*'s intervention. This means: without its staging, the text, in itself a thousand-eyed Argus, is not yet actualised. It remains a neutral nothing. Only the assertion of its immanent split allows the positive authority of 'the Text' to appear – as, in fact, a secondary effect, not as some kind of 'original' essence. This retrospective appearance of the assumed cause, another vital moment of Hegelian dialectic thinking, further undoes the assumption of the text as transcendental authority which expresses authorial intention.

As works of art, the dramatic text and its production on stage are likewise monstrous expressions of the multiple ambiguity of the (strictly historic and collective) *Geist*, of 'time in its being', as Hegel elsewhere defines his prominent concept of Spirit. Therefore neither can be afforded hierarchic primacy. Playtext and theatre production both invite the spectators' encounter with the *Geist* of their time, as they make sense-able 'time in its being'. In their act of spectating, the spectators are no longer addressed here as ideal reference point, or as disinterested beholders. They themselves are being watched by the artwork's 'thousand eyes': the *Geist* of the artwork stares at us. As Žižek reminds us, this is the very reason why Lacan, in his *Seminaire XI*, described art as the 'attempt to cultivate, to tame, this traumatic dimension of the Other's gaze, to "put the gaze to rest"' (Žižek 2012, 388). Yet, as imaginary symbolisations of the Real ('time in its being'), as affective 'sensory appearing' of Spirit, *both* text and stage production *fail*. In his discussion of the movie *Billy Bathgate* and its source, Žižek makes a similar point, suggesting that not only does the film 'fail' the novel, but in an odd way, contrary to linear temporality, the (source-) novel also 'fails' the later film. For him, both are attempts to repeat the unrepeatable 'true novel' which only emerges from the gap created once the actually existing novel had been adapted for film. Žižek went on to connect this virtual reference point to the working of the Lacanian *objet petit a*, the psychoanalytic 'object cause of desire' that can never be captured but in its effects: 'This virtual point of reference, although "unreal", is in a way more real than reality: it is the *absolute* point of reference of the failed real attempts' (Žižek 2012, 617; original emphasis).

Similarly, a dialectic understanding of *Regie* suggests a shift in perspective in accordance with the same movement of a repetition that only retroactively posits its cause or origin. Both the playtext and its production in performance actualise the unrepeatable, entirely virtual 'true play' of Spirit, which signifies, according to Jameson's definition stated earlier, 'collective life as such':

> It is not that we should simply conceive the starting point (the novel) as an 'open work', full of possibilities which can later be deployed, actualized in other versions; or – even worse – that we should conceive the original work as a pre-text to be later incorporated in other con-texts and given a meaning totally different from the original one. What is missing here is the retroactive, backwards movement: the film inserts back into the novel the possibility of a different, much better novel. (Žižek 2012, 618)[14]

Adorno's discussion of theme and variation in the field of music offers another model to think this principle of 'identity as non-identity', which is at the heart of speculative *Regie*. It helps elucidating further the relation between the thousand-eyed text and its 'monstrous' staging as its inevitable alteration while asserting their (speculative) identity. His perspective clarifies the aspect of the dissolution, even inversion, of time, which we also come across in Žižek's discussion of *Billy Bathgate*:

> The thematic material is of such a nature that to attempt to secure it is tantamount to varying it. It really does not in any way exist 'in itself' but only in view of the possibility of the entirety. Fidelity to the demands of the theme signifies a constantly intervening alteration in all its given moments. *By such non-identity of identity music achieves a completely new relationship to the time within which a given work takes place. Music is no longer indifferent to time, since it no longer functions on the level of repetition in time, but rather on that of alteration.* However, music does not simply surrender to time, because in its constant

alteration it retains its thematic identity. The concept of the classic in music is defined by this paradoxical relationship to time. (Adorno 2004, 55f.; my emphasis)

This offers a new understanding of 'the classic' in theatre, too. As Fredric Jameson reminds us, Adorno's discussion is embedded in an essay on Schoenberg, where he suggested that the latter's transgression of limits was already foreshadowed *in the limit itself*, at which point Adorno turned to Beethoven, whose music he discussed in the section quoted above.[15] Jameson's conclusion about Schoenberg and Adorno may certainly be applied to *Regie*, and to the canon of classics it keeps staging: 'they can be rewritten in the present with a certain effective afterlife, even though they cannot but remain dead. It would be tempting to call this distance the dialectic' (Jameson 2010, 26).

Adorno's apt idea of the 'non-identity of identity' opens up a useful link to the Hegelian Absolute, which underpins his notion of the 'sensuous appearing of the Idea'. The latter is, of course, Hegel's famous definition of beauty, as he saw it exemplified in Greek antiquity: the 'shining forth of meaning in a sensuous medium, not the representation of an external meaning which is not at one with the medium of presentation' (Rose [1981] 2009, 132). Beauty makes the Absolute – the self-consciousness and recognition of collective Spirit – intelligible through the sensory and affective means of art; it cannot be measured 'relatively to' an antecedent, primary order, whether of an idea, an ideal or a playtext. *Regie* gestures towards 'Absolute Knowing' in its strict Hegelian sense, not as omniscience but precisely as assertion of the 'non-identity of identity', as 'constant alteration', in the face of the hegemonic order of the sensible: 'it is not *stasis* but *metamorphosis* that characterizes Absolute Knowledge. Consequently it forms and transforms individuals, fashioning their ways of waiting for and expecting the future' (Malabou 2005, 134). We will return to this aspect and the meaning of the Absolute in and for *Regie* in Chapter 6.

Theatre, therefore, 'knows'. As expression of the Real/Spirit, it presents us with a mode of thinking through our time and the time to come, which is the opposite of representing 'eternal truth' pre-written in the text. As kinetic and aisthetic dimensions add to a purely semiotic intelligibility, *Regie* affords a text's full 'sensuous appearing' by inducing *qua mise en scène/mise en sens* constant Hegelian 'restlessness'. The true 'magic' of theatrality does not reveal itself, thus, in theatre's ability to create fiction and a 'false' appearance, but precisely in its ability to trigger a 'false thinking' that gestures towards the Absolute, understood here as the expression of the self-consciousness of Spirit, of 'collective life as such' in all its thousand-eyed monstrosity: of 'time in its being'. Beyond the functional mode of 'sensing' the world that we call 'reality', theatral thinking (whether in alchemy, Hegelian philosophy or *Regie*) offers us a shift of perspective, a different outlook. In Schiller's productive term for this magic that is evoked and 'directed' by art, theatre and *Regie*, it offers us 'play' – an 'absolute' dimension which insists on its ultimate autonomy. It thereby remains irreducible to the orders of representation, of *Verstand* and to today's demands of global neoliberal semiocapitalism that seeks to commodify and market knowledge, thinking, art and play itself, turning them into goods with measurable profits (see Berardi 2009). The very 'play of thinking', the 'impure repetition' of *Regie* that always adds its surplus mark of 'theatral thinking', maintains a minimum of the Lacanian Real or Hegelian category of the Absolute Spirit: the spectral presence of this thousand-eyed monster with which Art looks at us. This look of the Other is the horizon of our self-consciousness as it returns us to ourselves through the other, and thereby ultimately grounds our agency as subjects in reality: the fact that we are – thinking.

Notes

1. Leading German theatre scholar Erika Fischer-Lichte began to integrate theoretical positions developed in the context of theatrality studies into her emerging framework of an 'aesthetics of performativity' (Fischer-Lichte 1995, 2008; Fischer-Lichte *et al.* 2005). Her recent, large-scale international research networking project is called 'Interweaving Performance Cultures', alluding to Münz's key idea of a cultural texture or fabric of theatrality.
2. In special issues on the topic, *Theatre Research International* (20(2), 1995) and *SubStance* (31(2/3), 2002) compile a range of essays that give a comprehensive overview of various research strands and approaches. See also Davis and Postlewait 2003 and Fischer-Lichte *et al.* 2005.
3. In her revaluation of Fried's argument, Rosalind Krauss points out how theatre in his argument actually becomes an 'empty term' to promote its opposite – 'the nontheatrical' (Krauss 1987, 62), which for Fried is exemplified in modernism and its model of 'absorption'.
4. While Burns pointed to important aspects that were at the time (and, to a degree, are still today) ignored in much theatre research where it exclusively focuses on artists and their works, her study also palpably exposes the limitations of this branch of theatricality research. Burns, as before her Goffman, thought almost exclusively within the paradigm of (essentially realist) 'the theatre of Monsieur Diderot' with its central parameters of role-playing and the reproduction of a script as implied norm. In her approach, she particularly emphasised the notion of 'authenticity', whereby she considered strategies of acting that aim to persuade an audience that I really am *Hamlet* and not an actor, hence to attempt not to engage the audience with, and even distract them from, the fact of them watching theatre. What becomes evident here is, once more, the implicit privilege afforded to 'theatrical' fiction as 'real' content and action of a play.
5. Of course, until the seventeenth century, the term *theatrum* was not confined to playhouses and the stage, but signified any place where some form of *thea* happened (Schramm 1990, 215). This could include theatres of war, anatomy theatres and certainly lecture theatres. This unity reflected the ideology of the representative regime, which did not yet conceive of art as a distinct, autonomous sphere, but simply as another mode of 'doing'. The English language has maintained this wider use of the term far more consistently than, for instance, German, where the term 'Theater' is no longer used beyond the field of stage performance.
6. Schramm himself links his model in an aside to Lacan's likewise 'empty' triangle of the symbolic, imaginary and the real (Schramm 1996, 260).
7. Schramm models his investigation of alchemy and theatre as a 'complex system of mutually reflected allegorical and metaphorical references' (Schramm 1995b, 160) on Walter Benjamin's influential investigation on the *Origins of German Tragic Drama* and its distinction of medieval allegory and the poetics of the seventeenth century. Additionally, he

repeatedly refers to Artaud's reflections on 'The Alchemical Theatre' in *The Theatre and its Double,* where the latter speaks of the 'deeper resemblance' and the 'mysterious identity of essence between the principle of the theater and that of alchemy' (Artaud 1958, 48; see also Demaitre 1972). We should not forget the philosophical dimension of alchemy, either, which, in its laboratory experiments, undertook 'a practical philosophizing which circled around the cosmological interaction of microcosm and macrocosm' (Schramm 1995b, 158), again realising the full dimensions of *thea* as theatre and theory, of scenes and senses.

8   Hegel himself used the term 'magical relationships' when referring to phenomena such as hypnosis (or, 'magnetic somnambulism' in the terminology of his time), which establish a link between the pre-reflexive 'sentient self' and external processes.

9   From a different theoretical perspective, Guido Hiss reads (departing from Schelling's aesthetic writings) some of the major reforms and innovations in drama and music theatre since the Romantic era as (utopian) attempts to achieve new aesthetic unity through a synthesis of various art forms. This can also be connected to the search for 'recalibrating' the economy between the three theatrical factors of perception, motion and language. *Regie,* for Hiss, results from the 'synthetic vision of a planned *Inszenierung',* which integrates the dramatic text into a richer synthetic aesthetic framework – a thought parallel to Barthes's idea quoted at the outset of this chapter (Hiss 2009, 130). Inevitably, for Hiss, too, the new notion of *mise en scène* fostered a 'creative tension between several levels of authorship', which he sees as energising the 'vitality' of modern theatre to the present (125).

10 With Jameson, I here maintain as a central concern of Hegelian thought not only the issue of intellectual *Erkenntnis* (self-consciousness), but also of social and cultural *Anerkennen* (recognition). Jameson develops the latter aspect lucidly in his reading of the famous Master/Slave (*Herr/Knecht*) section of Hegel's *Phenomenology* (Jameson 2010).

11 Schiller's aesthetic thought offers contours of dialectic thinking in the very sense later elaborated by Hegel. We also find (*pace* Engels) a similar insistence on mediation in Marx's *Theses on Feuerbach,* where he rejected any materialism which acknowledges the sensuousness of objects 'only in the form of the object, or of contemplation, but not as human sensuous activity, practice, and not subjectively', whereas idealism will embrace this more active side of reality – 'but only abstractly, since, of course, idealism does not know real, sensuous activity as such' (Karl Marx, 'Theses on Feuerbach' [1845], in Marx and Engels 1976, 6–8, p. 5). More recently, Žižek's reading of Hegelian materialism through Lacanian psychoanalysis took a similar stance.

12 'The universality of the dialectic notion is not the fixed and stable sum-total of abstract characters, but a concrete totality that itself evolves the particular differences of all the facts that belong to this totality. The notion not only contains all the facts of which reality is composed, but also the processes in which these facts develop and dissolve themselves. … The notion of capitalism is no less than the three volumes of *Capital,* just as Hegel's notion of notion comprises all three books of his Science of Logic' (Marcuse 1955, 158f.).

13 Most relevant in this context is Jameson's chapter on 'Spirit as Collectivity' with its perceptive re-reading of Hegel's *Antigone* discussion as ultimate invalidation of 'the myth of Hegel as a teleological thinker' (Jameson 2010, 75–95, p. 79).

14 Žižek of course does not miss the irony that this logic of repetition links the anti-Hegelian Deleuze with a central Hegelian principle, as it

relies on the properly dialectical relationship between temporal reality and the eternal Absolute. The eternal Absolute is the immobile point of reference around which temporal figurations circulate, their presupposition; however, precisely as such, it is posited by these temporal figurations, since it does not pre-exist them: it emerges in the gap between the first and the second one – in the case of *Billy Bathgate*, between the novel and its repetition in the film. (Žižek 2012, 618)

15 With Beethoven, we once more arrive in the time period concurrent with Hegel and the emergence of *Regie*, which paradigmatically focuses our attention beyond the standard assertion of a 'modernist rupture' around 1900, exemplified here by Schoenberg.

3

Theatre as dialectic institution: Friedrich Schiller and the liberty of play

We have started exploring how *Regie* reveals through scenes and senses a historically situated 'style of thinking', associated with the post-Kantian, post-1789 Western European 'aesthetic regime of art'. No longer serving the functional semiotic economy of representation, it uses the three theatral 'sensibles' of *kinesis, aisthesis* and *semiosis* to insist on a subjective, affective intelligibility and sensibility. Already in 1803, we find a detailed outline by none other than German poet, historian and dramatist Friedrich Schiller (1759–1805). Responding to Kant and, in many ways, prefiguring Hegel, Schiller was, above all, a man of the *thea* of theatre *and* theory (see Beiser 2005). His ample reflections on playwriting, tragedy, dramaturgy, and on wider questions of poetry – and certainly his own plays, poems and other writings – were an early and widely influential articulation of the fundamental changes concerning the place and function of art within the emerging aesthetic regime.[1] His relevance for our present reflections on *Regie* becomes immediately clear from his following description of the force of *Regie* that transgresses the surface level of written words, of characters and action, hence of representation:

> [It] leaves behind the narrow arena of the plot to engage with the past and the future, with distant times and people, with humanity in general, to calculate the big results of life and to give words to the teachings of wisdom. But [it] does so with the full power of imagination, with a bold poetic freedom which comes along at the high summit of human affairs like with the strides of Gods – and [it] does so with the full sensuous power of rhythm and the music accompanying [it] with sounds and movements.
>
> [It] thereby *purifies* the tragic poem separating reflection from action, affording it in turn, as a result of this same separation, with its own poetic power. (Schiller 1970, 111; original emphasis)[2]

This section is taken from the articulate essay with which Schiller accompanied, for its publication, the playtext of his *Die Braut von Messina* (*The Bride of Messina*). At its Weimar premiere, his 1803 play was considered an outright mess, a flop and a failure. It never came to equal prominence with the playwright's Weimar classics such as *Maria Stuart* of 1800 or *Wilhelm Tell*, which premiered the year after. *The Bride of Messina* was indeed an odd dramatic experiment: Schiller reintroduced the device of the Greek chorus within a contemporary tragedy. Yet, this awkward 'tragedy with chorus', as Schiller called it in the subtitle, may also be read as a complex and mature investigation, as a piece of 'practice as research', as we would say today, which sought to explore some of the most urgent concerns and problems of theatre art as it entered the aesthetic regime.

Of course, Schiller never *really* wrote an early manifesto of Continental *Regietheater*. He neither uses the term *mise en scène* nor does he speak of the *Regisseur*. I have slightly manipulated the above quotation from his essay entitled 'Über den Gebrauch des Chors in der Tragödie' ('On using the chorus in tragedy'), simply replacing Schiller's original references to 'the chorus', marked by my elisions of the 'it' in parenthesis. Yet, if we actually do read *Regie* each time he speaks about his 'chorus', his 1803 essay (in both the practical and theoretical sense of the French term) in fact becomes a rather detailed reflection 'On Using *Regie* in Theatre', too. The point of the following chapter is not, however, to present Schiller as director *avant la lettre*, or as the hitherto overlooked inventor of modern *Regie*. Yet, his theatre-theoretical thinking articulates the very gap in the theatral fabric that *Regie* would come to occupy in the further course of the nineteenth century. With the figure of the chorus, he attempted to give a body *on stage* to a new function at the heart of staging texts that soon was to be 'directed' *off stage* with the emergence of *Regie*. This becomes strikingly clear right from the first paragraph of his essay, where Schiller asserts that a playtext must be considered as necessarily 'non-all', to use slightly anachronistic Lacanian terminology:

> [T]he tragic poetic composition only becomes a complete whole by means of its theatrical representation: it is only the words which the poet provides; music and dance must be added to bring them to life. (Schiller 1970, 104)

In terms of theatrality, Schiller here asserts that the dramatic playtext (the *semiosis*) must necessarily be supplemented with kinetic and aisthetic 'life'. Similar to Hegel's later idea, discussed in the previous chapter, Schiller, too, maintains that only such a process of mediation will make the sensible Idea of the drama fully available. It is this mediating function which Schiller's chorus articulated and embodied in a concrete and literal way. Therefore, this chapter will not turn to Schiller's rich opus of dramatic and dramaturgic writings, but I will instead focus on his aesthetic theory in order to consider the central implications of his chorus model for our understanding of *Regie*. We will in the course of the chapter develop some further, crucial structural principles of *Regie*, taking our prompts from Schiller's description of the chorus:

- as intervention of a 'fremdartiger Körper' intruding the play, whereby Schiller here uses the very term of the 'foreign body' that would later become central for Walter Benjamin's aesthetic (Schiller 1970, 104);

- as the third term in a dialectic motion of mediation, not least between the ideal and the sensual, and between action and reflection;
- as a prime instance of theatral 'play' which strategically insists on its autonomy both from the laws of the playtexts just as much as from the realm of performance practice; and
- as a transcritical aesthetic device in the name of human liberty. (Karatani 2003)

In his idiosyncratic understanding of the chorus, Schiller thus outlines further vital building blocks for a concept of *Regie* as an aesthetic practice of mediation, whose purpose is something other than to reproduce or translate, and which is not concerned with issues of identity with an 'original'. Instead, following the Hegelian terminology introduced in the previous chapter, *Regie* is here, too, asserted as an 'absolute' principle: It follows (Žižek's reading of) Hegelian 'Absolute Freedom', which refers to the literal etymological meaning of *absolvere* as 'releasing' and 'letting go': 'the supreme moment of the subject's freedom is when it sets free its object, leaving it alone to freely deploy itself' (Žižek 2012, 402; see also Chapter 6 below).

Freedom – or, in the French coinage of Schiller's time, *liberty* – is indeed the fundamental premise of all of Schiller's ideas. His aesthetics at large, and his chorus experiment in particular, his theory and his practice, in all their many forms, were animated by his robust insistence on liberty as the most essential condition for humanity to exist. According to his well-known formula from the 'Kallias' letters, he thinks of aesthetic beauty as being one with 'freedom in (the) appearance' (Schiller [1793] 2003, 160).[3] He shares this core political as well as formal-philosophical value with much of German Idealism, from Herder, Fichte and Kant to Hegel and beyond (see Beiser 2005; Bowie 2003; Hammermeister 2002).[4] A key prerequisite of any position of 'true' liberty is a somewhat radical *autonomy*. While this has often been misunderstood as advocating a withdrawal from reality, it is much rather an insistence on a structural, relational position which finds its most astute articulation in another key notion of Schiller's thought: *play*. He developed this quintessentially humanistic concept at the centre of his 1795 *Letters on the Aesthetic Education of Man*, where he famously concluded: 'one only plays when one is, in the full sense of the word, a human being; and one is only fully a human being when one plays' (Schiller [1795] 2009, 64).[5] Liberty, autonomy and play: let us explore these important notions in turn, as they will prove to be most crucial elements within the thinking of *Regie*. They help us describe further the characteristic space which this theatral thinking has come to occupy within the Continental European cultural fabric until the present day.

Beyond the 'moral institution': theatre as play

Twice in his career, Friedrich Schiller was practically involved with theatre-making. Following the success of his *Die Räuber* (*The Robbers*), *Intendant* Heribert von Dalberg appointed the young Schiller for a season as resident theatre poet to the Mannheim

Nationaltheater in 1783, where his *Kabale und Liebe* (English title: *Luise Miller*) and *Don Karlos* premiered (see L. Sharpe 2005). Following a gap of almost a decade, Schiller then became famously associated with Goethe's influential Weimar court theatre; their pairing is widely considered as the pinnacle of the classical, idealist period of German literature. It was here at Weimar, in the years before his early death in 1805, where Schiller outlined some of his most radical propositions on the 'thinking of representation'. Exemplarily expressed by his chorus experiment, they reflect what Herbert Marcuse described as 'one of the most advanced positions of thought' of its time (Marcuse [1955] 1987, 188). Schiller's legacy is, meanwhile, certainly ambiguous. He remains a principal icon of the German *Bildungsbürger* establishment, in the field of theatre and elsewhere. In addition to his rich legacy as dramatist and poet, Schiller's 1784 lecture-essay on 'Theatre Considered as a Moral Institution' ('Die Schaubühne als moralische Anstalt betrachtet'), in particular, has become the prime manifesto to articulate the self-definition of the institutionalised German *Stadt-* and *Staatstheater* culture; to the present day, it remains compulsory reading in any introductory class on the country's theatre studies programmes.[6] The Mannheim Nationaltheater, where Schiller was employed at the time, reflected a crucial eighteenth-century cultural movement across the many autonomous German principalities, which remained not yet unified in a single state for almost a century to come. In the period leading up to the French Revolution in 1789, supporting 'national theatre' did not reveal outright conservative national*ist* cultural values (as popularised, most notably, by Herder), but rather advocated a hitherto non-existent theatre repertoire in the 'national' German language, as spoken by the emerging middle class, as opposed to French tragedy or Italian comedy championed by the aristocratic court theatres. For the lack of much else (and above all, an actual nation state), culture, literature and art at the time assumed (and still do so today) a pivotal role for the cultural self-fashioning of the emerging German bourgeoisie. *Bildung* (education/erudition) became as indispensable for advancement and distinction within middle-class German society as capital for their British (and later US) counterparts (see Hein and Schulz 1996; P. Marx 2006b). We should keep in mind the crucial contrast between the British Empire of capital and the Continental 'republic of letters' as two fundamentally different mechanisms of bourgeois emancipation from absolute monarchy and feudalism. Theatre was the medium of choice of the German middle classes – much more so than the novel which dominated elsewhere in Europe. Some fifteen years prior to Schiller's time in Mannheim, Lessing was part of a similar, failed, *enterprise* at Hamburg, immortalised in his *Hamburg Dramaturgy* (Bruford 1950; Fischer-Lichte 2002, ch. 3).

Within this context, the offer of a 'theatre as moral institution' as a means to grow 'splendid fruit' (Schiller 1970, 10), as Schiller phrased it in his over-enthusiastic rhetoric, was eagerly taken up. Following in the footsteps of Lessing, Diderot and Pope, Schiller (who was only twenty-five at the time) rehearsed staple Enlightenment arguments, commending a permanent theatre institution as a means to spread knowledge and familiarity with human (and notably new middle-class) virtues and vices:

> The *Schaubühne* is the shared channel through which the light of wisdom spreads from the thoughtful, better part of the nation downwards, from where it disperses in milder

beams throughout the entire state. From here, more correct notions, more refined principles and purer emotions will flow through all veins of the nation; the fog of Barbary, of dark superstition will lift, and the night will give way to the victorious light. (Schiller 1970, 10)

This Schiller certainly embodies the elitist values of a white European, male, middle-class Enlightenment culture, for which he has undergone some critical Eagletonian grilling (Eagleton 1988, 1990). Some subtler suggestions in his speech can easily be lost behind the apparent imperative to 'educate' and 'enlighten' top-down the less worthy members of audiences, nations and 'humanity' at large. On the surface, Schiller asserts that theatre is 'more than any other public institution of the State a school of practical wisdom, a signpost through civic life, an unerring key to the most secret access of the human soul' (Schiller 1970, 7). Yet, even in the very next sentence, he voices his own scepticism, admitting that theatre's educational 'influence is not infrequently nullified':

> Personally, I think that Moliere's Harpagon may not have reformed a single usurer, that the suicide of Beverley has only kept very few of his brothers from succumbing to the heinous addiction to gambling, or that the robber Karl Moor's tragic story has scarcely made the highways any less dangerous. (Schiller 1970, 8)[7]

In a similar vein, yet with far more venomous sarcasm, Schiller had already 'personally' lamented the incompetence of actors, playwrights and audiences that populated this allegedly exemplary 'school of wisdom' in his lesser-known article 'On the German Theatre of the Present Day', published two years earlier, in 1782. Here, he asked the rhetorical question: 'Are fewer girls seduced, because [Lessing's] Sara Sampson paid for her lapse with poison? Is a single husband less zealous, because the Moor of Venice acted so tragically rushed?' (Schiller [1782] 1818, 367f.).

While Schiller was thus sceptical about the efficacy of the stage as a pulpit to preach, instruct and educate, he nevertheless affirmed another effect of the *Schaubühne* which he considered far 'deeper and more lasting than morals and laws' (Schiller 1970, 5) – an effect more important to him than the enlightened yardstick of measuring art by its effect of 'improving' and educating the audience. This 'deeper and more lasting' effect is what he gestures towards with *play*, his central notion in his post-Revolution (and also post-Kantian) aesthetic outlook from the 1790s onwards. Schiller's understanding of 'play' by no means refers to harmless, 'childish' *divertissements* nor to playful romantic irony, as it would surface in European arts a few years later. To think of theatral play as providing some momentary relief from the hardship of reality or from the pressures of the political state of the ('superior') 'adult' world would precisely mean to reduce *theatre as play* to being barely more than the 'court jester' of society. Schiller's notion, however, goes far beyond the evocation of ludic qualities of performance, and the stage's aesthetic un- or anti-reality. His 'play' activates the full spectrum of meaning of the German term 'Spiel haben': to have the tolerance and flexibility in a technical sense – to 'play' in order not to get stuck. As agile and mobile mediator, 'play' thus makes opposites meet and establishes a link between what appeared as mutually exclusive. Precisely thereby, play will lead towards true, actual, formal liberty, the essential condition for truly human existence, as it is manifest in Schiller's all-important call for 'freedom of play': in a genuinely free society, Schiller sees no need for opposition, separation and antagonisms, or for a contest for primacy and superiority. His aesthetic play is thus a *formal* regulating function that insists on a necessary third perspective on any perceived binary opposition. Play as quintessentially human structural function not only facilitates a proto-Hegelian dialectic sublation of contradictions and opposites; above all, it corrects any wrongly tuned 'partition of the sensible': in particular one that conceives of the world in binary and exclusive terms alone.[8]

Such a playful meeting of opposites, far from idealist escapism, insists on a utopian dimension that Schiller locates right at the heart of aesthetic beauty in its true meaning. By the time Schiller fully articulated these ideas, he had influentially absorbed Kant's writings. Simultaneously his earlier enthusiasm for the French Revolution, for which he had been awarded the title of 'honorary citizen' of the French Republic – an enthusiasm which infused his early plays such as *Die Räuber* (1781), *Fiesco* (1783), *Kabale und Liebe* (1784) and eventually *Don Karlos* (1787), after which he would not write another drama before *Wallenstein* in 1800 – had turned into bitter disillusion during the Jacobin *terreur* and the subsequent Napoleonic wars. Schiller, in contrast to Goethe and Hegel, would not live to see and experience the debilitating conservative restoration after 1815, which provided a crucial background for the (later) writings of the latter two. From Schiller's point of view, then, even the Revolution had turned sour precisely 'because it still adhered to the model according to which an active intellectual faculty constrains passive sensible materiality' (Rancière 2009a, 32). In the tradition of Leibnizian Enlightenment, it had relied too exclusively on 'rationality' alone, while denigrating experiential parameters, even fearing sensory perception and sensual feeling as mere interference distracting from the 'primary' logic. The answer, for Schiller, could not be merely to turn the tables and emphatically embrace all things sensual, while mistrusting enlightened rationality. Above all, he critiqued this binary perception that underpinned, in particular, Kant's thought:

> Intuitive and speculative reason now withdrew in animosity to their separate fields and began to guard their frontiers with distrust and jealousy. Limiting our allegiance to a single sphere, one subjects to a master who regularly ends up suppressing all other abilities. While in one case the luxurious imagination ravages the carefully tended plantations of reason, in another case the spirit of abstraction quenches the fire that was meant to warm the heart and kindle the fantasy. (Schiller [1795] 2009, 24)

He persistently warns against any one-sided activity of isolated faculties, insisting instead on 'having it both ways'. While he never explicitly turned away from Kant, his thinking broke through the antinomies of the latter: the contrasts of form and matter, of ratio and feeling, of sensuality and morality, of pure and practical reason. Instead, Schiller outlined a new synthesis that became characteristic for German Idealism, not least for Hegel, whose 'speculative thinking' was precisely an attempt to incorporate intellectual logic into a sensuous existence, figured as 'Absolute Spirit'. Schiller already went the decisive step beyond Kant's own 'third term' of transcendental apperception, and judgment, in the problematic dualist equation between the rational (intellect, understanding) and the sensual (passions, impressions).

Schiller's principal proposition in the *Aesthetic Letters* is to start by outlining the two opposing forces of the *Stofftrieb* or *Sachtrieb* (sense drive, 'matter drive') on the one hand, and *Formtrieb* (form drive), on the other, which are his terms to describe the contrasting forces of sensory, physical experience, and of rational, intellectual categorisation and comprehension. His originality lies in not leaving it to the individual to balance out this opposition, but to posit a common facility of mediation in the name of beauty and humanity: the vital third instinct of 'play' (*Spieltrieb*):

> Reason demands, on transcendental grounds, that a partnership between the form drive and the sense drive should exist, namely a play drive, because only the union of reality with form, of contingency with necessity, of suffering with freedom makes the idea of humanity complete. (Schiller [1795] 2009, 61)

His aesthetic philosophy of art was, above all, an attempt to insist on the beauty of sensuality and sensory experience, while not giving up the importance of the enlightened mind's rational reflection, either. His *Letters*, in particular, mark the moment where he suggested that *Sinnlichkeit* is not to be seen as an obstacle to morality, but on the contrary, as the only possible pathway that will eventually afford ethical *Sittlichkeit*.[9] Instead of presenting, and thus privileging, the human mind and morality as conquering (animalist or, for that matter, childish instinctive) sensuality, Schiller locates true human freedom in the aesthetic field – where reason and senses meet. Should we not sense the future site of *Regie* in precisely such an act of playful mediation, in the liberating impulse of the human *Spieltrieb*, which avoids what Schiller perceives as harmful excesses of either 'cold intellect' or equally of an 'unreflected' sensuality? The stage, which Schiller had commended in his *Schaubühne* lecture for its unique powers of '*Anschauung* and living presence' of the most ultimate truths (Schiller 1970, 4), should prove an ideal site to realise actual freedom by realigning form and matter, subject and object, abstraction and fantasy, reflection and representation, the sensory and the sensual, the semiotic with the kinetic and aisthetic aspects of theatrality – and thereby to create aesthetic beauty and offer a site for 'freedom in (the) appearance'.

Yet, in order to realise fully the mediation offered by the 'play instinct', one has to insist on theatre as a fully autonomous aesthetic practice, on theatre as – in an anticipatory echo of Badiou's later assertion – a 'purely ideal space' (Schiller 1970, 108). Having doubted the efficacy of the *Schaubühne* as moral institution even while pragmatically canvassing for sponsorship in his 1784 lecture, by the 1790s Schiller insisted on theatre as a radically 'aesthetic institution'. This insistence on absolute (aesthetic) autonomy of art has often been interpreted as call for a retreat from mundane life and from everyday politics, similar to the clichéd notion of aesthetics as purely ornamental intellectualism that simply cannot be bothered with the pragmatics of worldly human affairs. As a professed Kantian, Schiller certainly owes something to the former's idea of 'disinterest' as prerequisite for aesthetic judgment. In his twenty-sixth Letter, Schiller distinguishes deceitful Platonian appearance (appearance as illusion) from aesthetic appearance (appearance as play); the world of appearance (*Welt des Scheins*) is aesthetic 'only in so far as it is truthful (expressly renouncing all claim to reality), and only in so far as it is self-reliant (bare from any support from reality)' (Schiller [1795] 2009, 112). A decade later, in the 1803 chorus essay, he conceives of the function of the chorus as a 'wall, which tragedy builds around itself to seal itself off in purity from the real world, to preserve its ideal ground, its poetic liberty' (Schiller 1970, 108). We should in particular note the crucial contrast here between a pure, ideal and poetic truth and the deceitful reality. Typically for Schiller's argument, the 'true' reality asserts itself in terms of the ideal, and not of everyday disillusions and sufferings: idealism and realism from his point of view are no longer contradictions but in fact become 'one and the same thing' (107). Art is, for Schiller, only truthfully real (in Hegel's terms: truly 'in-and-for-itself') when it is utterly ideal, that is insisting on its absolute autonomy. To grasp this position, we need to bear in mind that, by the mid-1790s, Schiller was – representative of an entire generation – thoroughly disillusioned. In the post-Revolutionary political trauma of the 1790s, he experienced reality as chaotic and as causing human suffering, of *Leiden*, which remains a central term throughout his aesthetic as well as dramaturgic reflections. In his fifth Letter, he gives a damning assessment of what may be described as 'dialectics of enlightenment' *avant la lettre*, describing what he perceives as 'the spirit of the time between wrong doing and savagery, between perversion and mere nature, between superstition and moral disbelief' (Schiller [1795] 2009, 22):

> Society set free, instead of advancing into organic life, collapses into the reign of the elemental. ... The enlightenment of the mind, on which the refined classes pride themselves not entirely without reason, reveals on the whole so little of an ennobling influence on the ethical disposition that through its maxims it instead confirms corruption. ... In the midst of the most refined community, egotism has built its system, and without developing a communal sense, we experience all the contagions and all calamities of society. We subject our free judgment to its despotic opinions, our feelings to its bizarre customs, and our will to its seductions ... and as if fleeing a burning city, every man solely seeks to save his own wretched property from the destruction. (Schiller [1795] 2009, 21)

Schiller even explicitly takes to task what he terms the new bourgeois 'leisured class', for presenting an 'even more repugnant spectacle of languor and a depravity of character' (21) than even the hated, corrupted aristocracy, which Schiller had exposed in many of his earlier works, such as *Kabale und Liebe* (1784). The cultured middle class, for him, now presented a spectacle 'all the more outrageous because culture itself is its source' (21). Disavowing the emancipatory impulses of the revolution of the 'third state', they fell for the lure of personal possessions offered by the emerging capitalist industrialisation.[10] Schiller critiqued not least the all-pervasive drive towards individualism that had, by the mid-1790s, relentlessly supplanted the spirit of equality, liberty and brotherhood of the 1789 Revolution.

The human suffering that is a key prerequisite for tragedy was hence for Schiller no longer caused by 'passions' as in French tragedy, or by an internal flaw of a character's mind: it was caused by the very tangible frustrations, the painful misery and the chaos of the external, material world around him. The response is the withdrawal of theatre (and art) from its former direct participation in politics that characterised the 'representative regime' of art, as described by Rancière. Art becomes instead the surrogate for a political revolution that failed in reality, as Schiller implies in his ninth Letter by way of reflecting on the decline of the Roman Empire:

> Humanity has lost its dignity, but art comes to its rescue and preserves it in stone that is full of meaning; truth lives on in the midst of deception, and the original will once again be restored from its copy. Just as noble art has survived noble nature, it also leads its way through its instructing and inspiring enthusiasm. Even before truth sends its victorious light into the depths of all hearts, the force of poetry captures its beams and lets the summits of humanity radiate already, even while humid night clouds the valleys. (Schiller [1795] 2009, 36)

Precisely from here, Schiller goes on to ask in the following sentence the decisive question that preoccupies him, and which remains pertinent for us today: 'But how will the artist avoid the corruption of his time which encloses him from all sides?' (36). This is where Schiller's call for autonomy comes in: art 'counts itself out' and emphatically rejects the hegemonic partition of the sensible. Instead, it asserts its vigorous dissensus. Already in 1784 Schiller had strictly set apart his *Schaubühne* from 'any other public institution of the State' (Schiller 1970, 7). He famously insisted: 'The jurisdiction of the stage begins where the realm of worldly laws expires' (4). Theatre is thereby affirmed as an *alternative* site that is to be kept strictly separate from any function within any political, legal or political context. We should note here the explicit but negative *relation with* the 'public institutions of the State' precisely by insisting on being different from these institutions and autonomous of any of their functions. Historian Reinhart Koselleck stresses that this insistence on aesthetic autonomy *against* reality reveals, in Schiller's aesthetic politics, the very opposite of *ignoring* reality:

> The moral tribunal became political criticism not only by subjecting politics to its stern judgment, but vice versa as well, by separating itself as a tribunal from the political sphere. This removal already presaged criticism of the State. The stage, by consolidating itself as an independent jurisdiction and positing itself against secular laws, exercised its criticism of the State more incisively and strongly than through the individual verdicts it proclaimed. The dualism of politics and morality in Schiller's assertion thus serves apolitical criticism, yet simultaneously it forms the basis of that criticism. Political criticism is based on this division and is at the same time responsible for it. (Koselleck [1959] 1988, 102)[11]

The turn away from and against the everyday business of state (and in today's world, certainly, party) politics could therefore not be further from the stereotypical interpretation as retreat into blissful ignorance of an ivory tower of art. The 'liberation from reality' facilitated by art, in Herbert Marcuse's words, 'is not transcendental, "inner," or merely intellectual freedom … but freedom *in* the reality' (Marcuse [1955] 1987, 188; original emphasis). The insistence on apolitical autonomy reveals itself as the ultimate political act. Asserting the superiority of what, in his rhetorical gesture, he calls 'moral' law over the 'worldly' law and over politics, Schiller ascertains the place for art to stage a tribunal over 'real' everyday politics in the very name of 'true' morality.

Here, Schiller offers a rather more elaborate perspective on the title he chose for the printed version of his famous lecture. Rather than asserting *established* bourgeois values, ideologies and 'morals', theatre as a true moral institution must assert an alternative partition of the sensible, offering what we may describe with Kojin Karatani as an essentially *transcritical* perspective. His term describes the shift towards a decentred subject position which Slavoj Žižek emphasises in the later Hegel: a transcendental position that facilitates an immanent critical stance.[12] We should proceed to link Schiller's insistence on the autonomy of the aesthetic with the imperative of mediation in Hegelian dialectics. Schiller positions art between (or, perhaps, beyond) law and politics, as another, as a third field, which is characteristic for his proto-dialectics of 'aesthetic play'. Theatre becomes a forum for an indirect, transcritical engagement. The very autonomy of aesthetic play and experience expresses the potential for a redivision of the hegemonic sensible in its fullest sense: a shift of the aestheticopolitical order that is essentially 'sensibly' experienced. From this perspective, *Regie* becomes an instrument of both aesthetico-political intervention and mediation in the name of (aesthetic) beauty, and precisely for this reason of Schillerian (political) liberty that is the idea of play, even against *the* play itself: against the text as a cultural commodity, against canonised and reified words.

A 'cross-eyed experience': the poetic interruption by the chorus

Let us return to Schiller's chorus experiment around his *Bride of Messina* to take these considerations further. Both intervention and mediation are central characteristics which Schiller attributes to the device of the chorus. Throughout his essay, he reminds us of his central value, insisting on the quality of true freedom as 'the liberty of mind in the lively play of all of its powers' (Schiller 1970, 105). Any such 'truth', however, would never emerge from the unmediated (textual) surface, nor as the first spontaneous impression, but requires mediation. Schiller, like Hegel after him, favours beauty in art (*das Kunstschöne*) precisely as effect of mediation against the unmediated, intuitive and spontaneous beauty of nature, which featured prominently in the Kantian notion of the sublime. Structurally, the chorus is thus afforded a similar position to the Hegelian reflective spirit, and Schiller certainly associates the chorus with reflection, as opposed to the dramatic action. While truth, for Schiller, remains the prime aim of his idealist conception of art, realism stands in its way. He vociferously rejects any 'naturalism' (as he interestingly terms it, somewhat *avant la lettre*) in his principal statement of intent for introducing the chorus, hinted at above:

> [T]o declare openly and honestly war against naturalism in art, [the chorus] should serve us as a living wall which tragedy builds around itself to seal itself off in purity from the real world, in order to preserve its ideal ground, its poetic liberty. (Schiller 1970, 108)

Within the chorus essay, this notion of the realm of 'poetic' truth takes the place of Schiller's earlier emphasis on the 'aesthetic'. It is set against the logic of verisimilitude, which he perceives as inevitably banal in its unmediated duplication of everyday reality: this can only leave us 'painfully thrown back into the mean and narrow reality by the very art which ought to liberate us' (106). Where realism insists on 'the common notion of the natural', it achieves for Schiller 'nothing but the outright suspension and annihilation of any poetry and art' (107). Even at its artistically best and aesthetically most pleasing, realistic illusion, on stage and elsewhere, 'would only ever be a poor impostor's con' (108). As simulation of reality that seeks to deny its own existence and impact, realist theatre for Schiller is thus inevitably what Rancière later terms 'stultifying': it wants to make us forget that we are seeing theatre, and hence also forget ourselves in that eponymous Romantic 'suspension of disbelief'. In the end, we would all but mistake the fiction for reality – a critique that resonates well with contemporary critical thought about our global media economy of semiocapitalism, expressed from positions of discourse analysis, deconstruction or a Lacanian critique of symbolic-imaginary misapprehension.

As long as it fails to actually implement a much more radical formal *relational freedom* that is entailed by the Schillerian notion of (aesthetic/poetic) play, theatre 'cannot have the beneficial effect of art, which is liberty' (106) – even where it attempts well intentioned (symbolic) representations of freedom or subversive alternative perspectives. Any 'true art', as he stresses once again, will 'not merely aim at a momentary play; its serious intention is not to excite us with a fleeting dream of liberty, but to genuinely *make* us free' (106; original emphasis). This assertion is crucial: even plays like Schiller's own *Don Karlos* or his *Wilhelm Tell* may inspire us momentarily because of their political impulses; yet actual freedom can only ever be achieved on the basis of a structural liberation, where – in the theatre – stage and audience relate in an 'emancipated' way, as Rancière would express it. The mere *appearance* of truth, however, does not yet constitute truth; the mere *representation of liberty* on stage is not in itself an act of liberation. For the same reason, Schiller also discards the antidote to realism which is fantasy, *das Phantastische*. In clear distinction to imagination (*Fantasie*), which occupies the highest status in his idealist aesthetics, fantasy, as the obverse of 'naturalism', permits everything. Nothing remains tied to even a semblance or pretence of reality. In effect, such fantastic art is no less stultifying as it, too, offers only an illusion of liberty, and not true liberty. Even more so, it relegates liberty to a realm of fantasy by portraying it as remote from actual reality and beyond its reach and limits, and therefore has a discouraging, disempowering effect.

Achieving liberty through play – this shall remain Schiller's yardstick for his own thinking and poetic practice. The chorus intervenes precisely by generating a poetic shortcut with the electrifying effect of play that truly liberates. As a foreign body outside and beyond the domain of narration and fiction, it irritates, halts and interrupts the effortless progress of *the* play through play. From Schiller's aesthetic point of view, it is indispensable as poetic intervention: a rupture, an interval, a border that opens up in the otherwise seamless imaginary fabric of the play – and as such it is ultimately real, as Alenka Zupančič has argued, connecting Schiller's discussion of the chorus with the operations of the Lacanian order of the Symbolic, the Imaginary and the Real (Zupančič 2006). As a cut through reality, and thereby always at least minimally different from reality, the Schillerian 'Ideal' that is realised by 'poetic art' is not a transcendental realm *beyond* reality, no utopian escapism. Similar to Schiller's positioning of the *Schaubühne* as moral institution beyond the reach of the state and politics, and simultaneously prefiguring the core Hegelian principle of negativity discussed in Chapter 2, it is *negatively related* to reality. This is why true art, which realises actual liberation through play, is according to Schiller 'at once ultimately ideal, and still in the most profound sense real': an art which 'can entirely leave behind the real, and still may and will be in precise accordance with nature' (Schiller 1970, 106). Fulfilling both demands simultaneously, which 'seem to annul each other in common opinion' (106), results in the characteristic 'awry perspective', which Žižek cherishes as a critical tool (see Žižek 1992). Similarly, according to Schiller, the *Anschauung* engendered by such a 'true' theatre art, or poetry and plastic art in his example, causes a 'cross-eyed experience': 'was die Ansicht poetischer und plastischer Werke so schielend macht' (Schiller 1970, 106). This points us to what Lacan describes as anamorphic structure: the 'parallax perspective' that Kant had already referred to, and which Žižek more recently elaborated (Žižek 2006b; see also Chapter 7 below).

As it effects – in a term closer to Schiller's own time – the poetic interruption of a Hölderlinian *caesura*, we should link the Schillerian 'poetic' with the notion of the 'silent speech' of things as it underpinned historicist *Regie* throughout the further course of the nineteenth century. Accordingly, this silent speech should not be grasped as evoking an unspeakable immanent 'truth' of the Thing-itself. Rather, the, in theatral terms, kinetic and aistheic excess points to the difference of the thing to itself: the point where the thing is no longer identical to itself but begins to relate to itself – not as an imaginary other, as exemplified in the well-known Lacanian concept of imaginary identification in the mirror stage, which is essentially a mis-recognition. Here, we recognise *the same* in the other, and thus begin to establish a 'real' relation to oneself, facilitated through that minimal, parallax difference, through the interruption and interval of the poetic. This points us towards an inherently ethical moment that underpins the aesthetic politics of Schillerian play. In a complex way, the poetic perspective is 'really' truthful – but not on the grounds of any replication of everyday reality, but because it captures and renders mimetically the intervention of the Lacanian Symbolic as it separates reality from the Real by splitting reality from within (see Žižek 1992). Expressed in the terms of Schramm's magic triangle, the Symbolic Order separates the semiotic from the kinetic and aistheic energies. Because Schiller's idealist poetic/aesthetic field insists on its radical autonomy, it, too, performs the 'alchemy' of impacting on the order of the sensible. It thereby articulates central concerns of how we constitute reality within a non-representational regime of thinking.

Schiller's own attempt to stage such an elaborate 'irruption of the real', as we may call it by borrowing a term from Hans-Thies Lehmann (Lehmann 2006, 99), is, paradoxically, his introduction of the most artificial device of the chorus. Its poetic function is to achieve actual liberty, and to truly fulfil the promise of 'emancipated spectating' (Rancière 2009b). Via the poetic mechanism of the chorus, theatre allows us as spectators to properly *own* the work, as it becomes 'the product of our creative mind':

> [I]t does so by awakening, exercising and perfecting within [us] a power that enables [us] to push back into an objective distance the sensual world, which normally weighs upon us only as raw material, bearing down on us as a blind force; to then transform it into a free work of our mind and to master the material through ideas. (Schiller 1970, 106)

Schiller once more emphasises the central liberating effect of autonomy within his aesthetic philosophy. Far exceeding the functional satisfaction of entertainment, it points to a refined pleasure of insight – *thea*, again: an *Einsicht* offered by aesthetic play, no longer as its separate, reflective after-effect, which may or may not arise. Offering the experience of a different, alternative partition of the sensible in aesthetic play, the intervention of the 'poetic' device has a fundamental, potentially life-changing impact. Therefore, the effect of 'true art', which is only possible as a result of insisting on its autonomy, does not stop when the curtain falls.

At the same time, this poetic dimension is also grounded in mediation. This becomes clear even from a historical perspective. Schiller's reanimation of the Greek chorus is in many ways reminiscent of his response, almost a decade earlier, to the fragmented Graeco-Roman *Juno Ludovisi* statue he articulated in his fifteenth Letter on Aesthetic Education, which serves as repeated reference point for Rancière's discussion of Schiller as key herald of the 'aesthetic regime'. In both instances, Schiller's interest was not motivated by a melancholic longing for a lost past ideal. Instead, it served him to point to the future through the past – against the debilitating present. Via the chorus, he hinted at a new way of thinking theatre: the chorus, he suggested, even 'offers a far more essential service to the modern dramatist than to the old poet' (Schiller 1970, 109), precisely by aiding today's playwright in transforming 'the common modern world' where, as Schiller writes, the palaces of kings are now closed, the people have become a 'raw mass', and where 'writing has displaced the animated living speech' (109). Once again, we encounter the, at the time, new, dynamic relationship to history, which gravitated, for many thinkers of German Idealism and beyond, to the classic Greek culture (see Szondi 1974a). Importantly, it reveals a *projective force* that is also relevant for the dynamics of emerging *Regie*. Crucially, the new *Geschichtsphilosophie* insisted on instilling an at least minimal distance, maintaining that no present appearance or manifestation can be fully understood purely from within its own moment of the present, but only ever in retrospect, from a later point in the historic development. The new historic dynamism thus forces a structurally necessary (temporal) gap, which in the case of theatre creates the new rift between the playtext and its performance. Schiller fills this gap with the chorus. It becomes his instrument (or 'moment') that will retroactively 'make sense' of the text; in Lacanian terms, it serves as *point de capiton*, or quilting point, which unifies and gives meaning to the entire symbolic field. And this is also what *Regie* does with its *Inszenierung* of the playtext.

Regie induces a poetic 'irruption of the Real', a *caesura* that pierces through the eternal and static present, which had characterised the earlier representational regime of art – and which still continues to reappear in debates about the unique immediacy, ephemerality and ultimate presence of 'performance'. Without this aesthetic intervention, there is no antecedent 'work' to be staged in the first place. The very 'authority' awarded to the material playtext as original work of art in its post-Romantic sense can be bestowed on it only by this transcritical projective retrospection. Yet, *Inszenierung* is not just the play in performance: as an essential function of theatre it also signifies the Schillerian notion of an autonomous third term that will transcend binaries through the motion of aesthetic play – including the binary between text and performance. The positions of play, chorus, aesthetics, *mise en scène* and *Regie* all revolve around such a third position that offers this transcritical space. It is located *vis-à-vis* both the (generalising) normative, rule-bound classicism of the representative regime and the essentially modernist (particularising) notion of individual artistic vision that would later haunt so-called 'directors' theatre'. With Schiller (and, equally, Hegel), we remain still in a space of thought *before* Romantic individuality, and more precisely, in an interim space, between the representational and the aesthetic, whose mediating autonomy *Regietheater* vociferously defends to the present day.

Where Schiller sublates the binary between text and its performance, between words and their framing through kinetic and aisthetic 'life', he emphasises the crucial aspect of theatre as facilitating an 'intermediate condition' as early as 1784: in the very first paragraph of his *Schaubühne* lecture, he introduced theatre's 'aesthetic sense' as a regulatory capacity to negotiate the harmony between rationality and sensuality (Schiller 1970, 3). In 1803, his chorus was then a practical attempt to install a 'playful' counterpoint to immediate action through reflection, and vice versa, mediating between the 'sense drives' and the 'form drives' we also encounter in theatre. If works of art were to address only the intellect, or to cater purely for the senses, he argues, they would forsake the true effect of poetic beauty. Schiller locates its emergence thus in what he terms the 'Indifferenzpunkt des Ideellen und Sinnlichen' – the 'point of indifference' where the ideal (the rational/*Form*) and the sensual (the material/*Stoff*) converge and become indistinguishably entwined (110). This prefigures Hegel's later evocation of beauty as 'the appearing of the idea in its sensuous form'. To illustrate this poetic 'point of indifference', Schiller draws on the image of the two pans of a scale which, even if they were not in perfect equilibrium, might still be kept in persistent oscillation so that no single side pulls the scale down entirely (111). This most apt image evokes the permanent motion as well as the fragility that are characteristic for the dialectic mode of thinking, as opposed to the static representative regime of art. The restless mobility of dialectic thinking (which we similarly encountered in Hegel's universe explored in the previous chapter) is, then, in Schiller's view the prime aim of the artist's skill: 'Und dieses leistet nun der Chor in der Tragödie' – 'This is what the chorus achieves in tragedy' (111).

Its mediating intervention guarantees *both* sensual pleasure *and* intelligent reflection, aiming for that approximate equilibrium in mobile flux: 'Just as the chorus brings *life* to the language, so it brings *repose* to the action' (112; original emphasis). Where the dramatic text embodies an idea, it awards sensuous power and, quite literally, gravity: it bestows on the idea an 'exhaustive presence', as Schiller terms it (111).

Thus, the chorus also serves as the mechanism that elevates the drama from the mere representation of a particular story to its universal dimension. It does so because the chorus represents on stage the public character of theatre as a cultural institution, or in Hegel's term the *Geist* as 'time in its being', or 'collective life as such' – and this is precisely what Schiller's term 'moral institution' means: it evokes theatre as necessarily *public* in scope, or, in Chantal Mouffe's terminology, as an *agonistic* practice. As Schiller explains, this was clear and natural in Greek theatre: 'The actions and fates of the heroes and kings are public in themselves' (109). However, in his present (and moreover in our own), an artistic instrument becomes necessary to somewhat artificially (or 'artistically') implement this constitutive public nature of theatre, and to remind us of it. This dimension must be carefully distinguished from any represented 'public' *within* the dramatic fiction, or from the idea of the chorus 'representing' the audience on stage. The *public* nature of the theatre experience rather refers us to yet another instance of transcritical aesthetic play which, in its effect, transcends any purely *binary* conception of the individual versus the collective; hence its association with the Hegelian notion of Spirit.

The chorus thereby completes the theatral dialectics: as Schiller had argued at the outset, the play, the drama and the words of the playwright are not complete when they are not performed; they require performance as the playtext's inbuilt negation. The chorus will sublate the hiatus between text and performance (and no less so between the idea and the real). It occupies the position of playful mediator, whose presence and interventions, according to Schiller, bring the invented world of the stage and its artificial fiction to life in a meaningful way, connecting it with both the grand horizon of humanity ('freedom/liberty') and with the immediate 'public sensible' ('play'). The chorus turns the fictional characters of the plot from 'real individuals' into representations of ideas and ideals, but it also endows merely abstract, immaterial reasoning with tangible, sensuous qualities. It thereby offers the spectators freedom to think, to contemplate and to thus take ownership of *the* play *in* play. Ultimately, the chorus achieves the all-important liberating poetic effect: it counterbalances feelings and affects with the calmness of reflection and distance, and prevents us as spectators from being entirely blown away by the 'storm of affects', thus losing our freedom:

> The mind of the spectator must maintain its liberty even amidst the fiercest passion; it should not fall prey to impressions, but instead detach itself, always clear and bright, from the emotions it suffers. ... The chorus, by keeping the parts apart and stepping between the passions with its calming reflection, hands us back our liberty. (Schiller 1970, 112)

The politicity of *Regie*

In the name of no less a goal than 'true' liberty and humanity, Schiller's device of the chorus thus 'explodes' the regime of representation. It is not so much a dramatic tool, as a structural mechanism of theatre which, quite literally in his play, embodies *play*. It injects the energies of *aisthesis* and *kinesis* into the semiotic dimension of the written drama, while at the same time remaining distant from the material excess of theatrical motion and perception. The Schillerian chorus in the *Bride of Messina* thus also marked the gradual transition from an aesthetic thinking about the art of drama towards the art of theatre, a transition that reflected the opening of the gap between the playtext and its *Inszenierung* which the art of *Regie* eventually came to occupy. Schiller began what Walter Benjamin later attested as the key achievement of Brecht's 'epic theatre': his experimental chorus rather forcibly re-inscribed *theatre* into the thinking of drama (Benjamin 2003; see also Lehmann 2013; Lukács [1914] 1965; Szondi [1956] 1987). Around the same time, August Wilhelm Schlegel set out to identify a distinct 'theatrical' domain, beginning his *Lectures on Dramatic Art and Literature*, delivered in spring 1808 in Vienna, with a 'discussion of the basic notions of the dramatic, theatrical, tragic, and comic'('Erörterungen der Grundbegriffe des Dramatischen, Theatralischen, Tragischen und Komischen') (Schlegel 1817, 29). Schiller himself meanwhile asserted that his peculiar reintroduction of the chorus anticipated a future theatre to come. To do full justice to his idea, 'one must hence transpose oneself from the actual state to a *possible* one' (Schiller 1970, 104), to which he added, 'one must do so wherever one intends to achieve something higher' (104). Making such an attempt to transcend the actual (that is, the material, artistic, socio-cultural, political, etc.) limitations of the present is, in fact, a key trait of his aesthetic mode of thinking as a specific, radicalised assertion of Kantian 'dis-interest'. It is here where Schiller's idea most of all reveals the contours of a Badiouian (re)thinking of representation, and with it a Rancièrian dissensual shifting of the partition of the sensible – and all this most vitally so by means of *theatre* and aesthetic *theory*.

With his striking – and strikingly impractical – vision that gestured towards 'a possible theatre', which would indeed soon emerge, Schiller affirmed theatrality. In a typically idealist mode of thought, and an equally typical chemical metaphor, Schiller himself referred to the 'higher organisation' that should be achieved by the all-important mediating poetic sublation of duality of text and performance in the absolute autonomy of *Regie*, or the 'true art' of theatre:

> In a higher organisation, the material or the elementary must no longer be visible; the chemical colour dissolves in the subtle carnation of living matter. But the material, too, has its glory, [*and this certainly holds true for the material of the playtext, PMB*] and as such, it can be integrated within a work of art. But then, it must through vitality and plenitude and harmony earn its place, and it must reinforce the forms which it surrounds, and not smother them with its weight. (Schiller 1970, 110)

Schiller's writings, as well as his practical attempts to tackle the actual problems he perceived, illustrate how the emerging preoccupation with the sensuously perceptible world, and how the negotiations of the Hegelian 'sensuous appearing' of ideas presented new challenges for art, which importantly added to simultaneous challenges by the invention of new technologies, and by new socio-cultural and economic contexts arising from the progressive urbanisation and industrialisation of Continental Europe. Long before the later modernist synthetic 'theatricalisation' with Wagner, Craig and Artaud, who sought different answers to the same basic problems, Schiller tentatively outlined the transcritical force that *Regie* would become: it marks a relational position that is no longer hierarchically weighted, that is not about 'understanding' and thereby 'commanding' (the text, the audience …), nor about consuming and thereby turning the other into a commodity, nor about appropriation, ownership and authority. Far more than a new 'craft' of staging a text, hence a solely *functional* 'practical' aspect of 'producing' representation, the space was here opened for *Regie* as a 'speculative' practice, in the Hegelian sense: a critical activity related to the force of *thea* in theatre and theory. Stepping in to actually fulfil the 'poetic function' which Schiller had sought to realise through the chorus, it positioned itself as an agent of mediation in the gap between text and performance, where it, importantly, redivided the representative unity of text and performance into three, not two.

At the moment when the gap between text and performance, just as much as the gap between the material world and our rational understanding, became a prime concern, it entered the scene as a resolutely autonomous third factor that set in motion a dialectic process: a process in which we are dealing with the continuous metamorphosis of the *same* substance-subject which keeps developing in complexity, persistently mediating and thereby sublating its contents and contradictions. It is, above all, this sense of persistent motion which cannot afford any static standstill that the new theatral practice of *Regie* shares with Hegelian aesthetic philosophy, introduced in the previous chapter. Schiller's name for this ceaseless transposition that never arrests a structure in a fixed hierarchy or a stable position is play. Underpinned by the humanitarian values of liberty and emancipation, it engenders an artistic ethos, more effectively than much manifestly 'political' art, then and now. Precisely its paradox of 'radical autonomy' – its rejection of any other motif outside play, beauty and liberty, whether the theatre director's intent to make money, the actor's desire for fame and recognition or the audience's expectation of an entertaining hour at the theatre, away from the mundane worries of the day (see Schiller 1970, 105) – is the site of theatre's intrinsic 'politicity', as Rancière terms it (Rancière 2009a, 26, and elsewhere): a political core in the formal structure and fabric of theatrality, ingrained in this 'style of thinking'. This dialectic aesthetico-political force confronts binaries, antagonisms, hierarchies, assumed symmetries – that is, the hegemonial partitions of the sensible. Set in motion on the theatre stage by *Regie*, it offers the non-standardised, non-unified, non-homogenised cross-eyed gaze of aesthetic play that makes our perception *schielend*, offering a different, parallax perspective on the same world we are in. This ethos of the liberty and politicity of theatral thinking, of the freedom of *scenes and senses*, certainly inspires *Regie* to the present day. While the political German *Regietheater* of the 1960s and 1970s, in particular, found a central reference point in Brecht, we shall now turn to Leopold Jessner, who mentored Brecht as well as inspiring, with his largely forgotten and abruptly terminated efforts, German post-war directors, from Jessner's former lead actor Fritz Kortner to Peter Stein, who started his career assisting Kortner.

Notes

1 Schiller's prominence in Rancière's considerations of the aesthetic regime (as in many other philosophical as well as artistic reflections, including Hegel) gives evidence of his central place within the cultural ideology of the emerging Continental European *Bildungsbürgertum*, the educated 'bourgeoisie of letters'. On the impact and wider reception of Schiller's aesthetic thought, especially in the twentieth century, see L. Sharpe 1995.
2 I will provide my own translations for citations from Schiller's essays throughout. In English, the 'chorus' preface is readily available (www.gutenberg.org/ebooks/6793, accessed 9 July 2013). Together with Schiller's other central writings on theatre, it is included in Schiller 1970, to which my quotations refer.
3 Schiller revisits these considerations in his twenty-third Letter on Aesthetic Education.
4 It is important to differentiate Schiller's notion of 'liberty' from bourgeois (economic and political) liberalism. We should not forget that Schiller in his time did not write for a (not yet established) bourgeois cultural elite of the eponymous *Bildungsbürgertum* (nor would Hegel after him). Prior to its own appropriation, reification and commercialisation, the art – and theatre – of the emerging aesthetic regime (solidified for Germany in Schiller's *Schaubühne* essay) was indeed energised by impulses that were to a certain extent radical. It was only when the Freedom of Trade Act was extended to the whole of the newly created German Reich in 1871 that a genuinely 'bourgeois' theatre established itself in Germany. Within a short time, many new, commercial theatres were founded and owned by the financially well-off middle classes, who introduced a new repertoire of classics from the canon of 'proper German education'. Among the most prominent was the Deutsches Theater at Berlin, founded in 1883 in what used to be a typical Parisian-style 'boulevard theatre' in the centre of the city.
5 Again, all translations are my own, drawing on a recent German paperback edition (Schiller [1795] 2009). An accessible translation of the Letters and of more of Schiller's key aesthetic writings can be found at www.gutenberg.org/files/6798/6798-h/6798-h.htm, accessed 9 July 2013.
6 'Schaubühne' is of course the literal German translation of the Greek *theatron*, 'the place to watch', with *thea* referring to the ambiguous gaze and ostentation/show discussed in Chapter 2. Schiller originally delivered his notorious speech to the Kurpfälzische Deutsche Gesellschaft in Mannheim on 26 June 1784, after being elected as a new member of this society. It first appeared in print the following year. At the time, it was still entitled 'What Can a Fine Permanent Theatre Truly Achieve?' Only when Schiller edited the manuscript for his Collected Works in 1802 did he rewrite parts of it and give it the new title, 'Theatre Considered as a Moral Institution'. Initially, it was above all a plea to the members of the Mannheim club to finance and support the subsistence of Dalberg's Mannheim theatre, and thereby also secure Schiller's own temporary employment there. An English translation is readily available at the Gutenberg Project link given in the previous note.
7 The references are to Schiller's own Karl Moor in his *Räuber*, to Molière's *Misanthrope* and lastly to the now rarely performed 'English' *Trauerspiel* by Edward Moore entitled *Beverley, or The Gambler*, which had seen numerous translations and adaptations for the German stage.
8 On the relationship between Schiller's and Hegel's aesthetics, see Kuhn [1931] 1966 and Böhler 1972.
9 Schiller discusses this aspect more fully in the third Letter. Elsewhere, including in the *Schaubühne* essay, he also complained about the 'inner emptiness' felt as a result of being

permanently 'bombarded by sensuality'. A concise discussion is offered by Marcuse [1955] 1987, ch. 9, 'The Aesthetic Dimension'.
10   Schiller's position here is not all too unlike Slavoj Žižek's attempt to understand why, first, communism turned into Stalinism, and, second, why in the wake of the fall of communism, rather than enjoying liberty, ethnic cleansing and civil wars swept across former Yugoslavia.
11   Adorno makes a similar point in his *Aesthetic Theory*: 'Ultimately, however, even in the most extreme refusal of society, art is essentially social and not understood when this essence is misunderstood' (Adorno [1970] 2002, 349).
12   Karatani refers above all to a phrase from Kant's 1766 essay on Swedenborg where he also already introduces the notion of the parallax that would later become central for Žižek's Hegel readings:

Formerly, I viewed human common sense only from the standpoint of my own; now I put myself into the position of another's reason outside of myself, and observe my judgments, together with their most secret causes, from the point of view of others. It is true that the comparison of both observations results in pronounced parallax, but it is the only means of preventing the optical delusion, and of putting the concept of the power of knowledge in human nature into its true place. ('Dreams of a Visionary Explained by Dreams of Metaphysics', quoted in Karatani 2003, 47)

4

The essence of the text and its actualisation: Leopold Jessner, the playwright's radical servant

A classical, well-known text, staged beyond convention, if not – at least for some – beyond recognition: *Regie* is often associated with the staging of an interpretive, even idiosyncratic 'directorial vision', which is frequently perceived as ignoring the playwright's intentions and overwriting the instructions scripted in the playtext. The moment this new language of a *Regietheater* that reaches beyond the 'silent speech' of realist and naturalist *mise en scène* was born can be exactly dated: 12 December 1919. That day saw the premiere of the first production by newly appointed artistic director Leopold Jessner (1878–1945) at the Berlin Staatstheater am Gendarmenmarkt. The grand nineteenth-century building by architect Karl Friedrich Schinkel (later destroyed during World War II) used to house, until the previous year, the court theatre of the German Kaiser. For his debut on this stage, Jessner chose *Wilhelm Tell*, Friedrich Schiller's final play from 1804, which once more revisited the topic of political struggle for liberty. Jessner's production became legendary, not least for the turmoil in the auditorium on the opening night (see Schrader and Schebera 1977). Right-wing anti-Semitic protestors, who had taken issue with the appointment of the Jewish Jessner to head Germany's foremost theatre in the first place, tried to disturb the performance. From the upper gallery, they noisily protested against the 'Jewish swindle' they saw in the director's radically anti-illusionist aesthetics. A verbose argument erupted between them and, in particular, the critics who were sitting down in the stalls, and the director eventually brought down the curtain mid-play. The actor Fritz Kortner, who by the age of just twenty-seven had already become a popular celebrity, on this night made his debut in Jessner's new ensemble in the role of the evil county bailiff Gessler. He remembers most vividly (and perhaps somewhat too extravagantly) in his 1959 autobiography what he had observed forty years earlier spying through the closed curtain:[1]

Siegfried Jacobsohn, the editor and theatre reviewer of the magazine *Die Weltbühne* … stood on his seat in the stalls and had a crescendo battle with the wildly spiteful parts of the gallery, who simultaneously discharged a shrieking orgy of insults against those up there who were enthusiastic about the production.

The fortissimo howling of this exchange of opinions raged from the circle down into the stalls and back, to and fro, back and forth. Julius Bab equally jumped on his seat and joined the shouting. Kerr put his hands over his ears while a reviewer from a rightwing newspaper yelled at him. …[2]

Florath [*the assistant director, PMB*] had slipped away and on his own initiative had the curtain opened again. This unexpected *coup* guaranteed a momentary silence. The spectators on stage, caught out by the sudden opening of the curtain, fled from the scene, to the amusement of the spectators in the auditorium. The performance resumed. I went into my dressing room. (Kortner [1959] 1979, 277)

Yet, as Kortner then entered the stage 'properly', in his role as Gessler, the protest erupted again. He was clad all in black, with red make-up on his face and a whip in his hand, and thereby presented the audience with an abstraction of diabolic evil. There was no trace of the recognisable historical character of fourteenth-century folklore and the historicist production tradition of Schiller's play. Moreover, Albert Bassermann, Max Reinhardt's former principal actor who played Tell, began the famous monologue in which Gessler's assassination is prepared, 'Durch diese hohle Gasse muss er kommen' ('Here through this deep defile he needs must pass'), speaking against the backdrop of a bare stage with no sign of any alpine scenery. Another riot broke out, fists were flying and proper fights raged through the auditorium.

Erika Fischer-Lichte rightly counts this controversial production, alongside Max Reinhardt's *Midsummer Night's Dream* of 1905 and Peter Stein's 1969 *Torquato Tasso*, among the three pivotal moments of German theatre history in the twentieth century (Fischer-Lichte 1993, 374). Its impact was felt by critics on the very night. Borrowing a proverbial line from Goethe's *Faust*, Alfred Kerr, an influential critical voice ever since he had championed Naturalist stage aesthetics some decades earlier, enthused in the *Berliner Tagblatt*: 'Here is a wonder, do believe it!' (quoted in Rühle 1976, 50) The Berlin theatre landscape indeed changed drastically: within a year of the *Tell* premiere, Max Reinhardt – theatre director as well as commercial entrepreneur and impresario, heading an international entertainment empire – retreated to Vienna, leaving the operations of his Berlin theatre business to Felix Hollaender, and two other local *Intendanten* also resigned. Reinhardt's friend, the writer Hugo von Hofmannsthal, saw no less than the doom of civilisation in Jessner's *Regie* style, describing it as an 'erosion of the higher German theatre culture … which calls into question everything that had been built up since 1770' (quoted 24). Reinhardt had, of course, marked the peak of the first generation who had built up *Regie* since 1770. Far beyond German stages, he produced work in London, and later recreated his signature *Midsummer Night's Dream* on film in Hollywood. His Salzburg Summer Festival symbolised the canonisation of bourgeois theatre. Dramatic texts, from the Greeks to Shakespeare and Schiller, had become a cultural capital and status symbol indicating *Bildung* (see Boenisch 2014a; P. Marx 2006a). Art had become a religion, and the theatre its temple for a cosmopolitan middle class for whom the stage was their 'moral institution'. The radical impulses behind Schillerian (and similarly Hegelian) thinking had turned into the acme of the 'German nation of culture'. Against this sedimentation of 'classical drama', Jessner's *Tell* paradigmatically heralded the critical force of *Regie*, and theatre at large. Challenging the ownership of the dramatic canon and disturbing its appropriation by the middle-class establishment of the German *Bildungsbürgertum*, he outlined an alternative mode of thinking *Regie*. His tenure as artistic director at the Gendarmenmarkt theatre between 1919 and 1930 prompted, more than anything else, what Patrice Pavis described as the 'second discovery of the *mise en scène*' in the 1920s (Pavis [1982] 2007, 53).

Reenergising *Regie* in response to the in every sense extreme cultural sensibilities following the historic shock of World War I, Jessner became the role model for the new 'dramaturgic director', as his dramaturg Heinz Lipmann described him in 1927 (quoted in Fischer 1932, 564). He inspired and mentored a new generation of directors. Most notable among them were Erich Engel, Jürgen Fehling, Erwin Piscator (whose radical 1926 production of Schiller's *Die Räuber* was staged at Jessner's Staatstheater, not his own Volksbühne) and Bertolt Brecht, who made his first journey to Berlin in 1920 just to sit in and observe Jessner's rehearsals. The latter two continued Jessner's explicitly political experiments in 'epic theatre', a term Jessner had introduced to their vocabulary. In this chapter, we will explore the formal, stylistic and also ideological parameters of this 'dramaturgic *Regie*', thereby pushing our conceptual modelling of *Regie* further towards the concerns of the present. Jessner's works mark the moment where the shared intellectual heritage of *Regie* and German Idealist thinking came full circle: in what I will term the 'actualisation' of the dramatic text, his *Regie* takes the form of Hegelian dialectic mediation and sublation (*Aufhebung*) of the play-*text* in play-*performance*. As we have seen in Chapter 2, this *Aufhebung* is itself a dialectic process of cancelling and suspending, on the one hand, and safe-keeping and pre-serving, on the other. Further, I will describe Jessner's *Regie* as inducing theatral play through effects of 'plasticity'. Here, I do not, for once, refer to the well-known concept of stage plasticity introduced by Meyerhold to the language of *Regie* (which would not be inappropriate for an analysis of Jessner's works), but rather refer to Catherine Malabou's Hegelian exploration of this term. For her, the concept of plasticity charac-terises Hegelian dialectic thinking (Malabou 2005). It is, precisely, the dialectic think-ing of Jessner's *Regie* that reveals itself in his explicit commitment to the playwright's work in the very face of his own radical 'actualisations' of their plays.

Jessner's 'new objectivity': the blueprint for *Regietheater*

The 1919 *Tell* was the first of Jessner's landmark productions of classical works, which also included his renowned Shakespeare productions of *Richard III* (1920), *Othello* (1921) and *Hamlet* (1927) (see Höfele 1992; P. Marx 2005).[3] He established his reputation in his role as head director of Hamburg's Thalia Theater between 1904 and 1915, after which he assumed his first artistic directorship, at the Neues Schauspielhaus in his East Prussian hometown of Königsberg. His eleven-year tenure at the Berlin Staatstheater eventually gave his innovative stage aesthetics widespread exposure. Furthermore, Jessner was involved in both the Bühnengenossenschaft, the German equivalent of the Equity union, and he headed the Vereinigung Künstlerischer Bühnenvorstände, the lobby organisation of artistic directors. In these dual roles, Jessner became instrumental in shaping the system of subsidised public theatre in Germany, which has been much envied ever since. When the democratic Weimar Republic replaced the Kaiser's Empire after World War I, Jessner made a crucial case for the old court theatres that had originated in the former small states before the unification of the German Reich in 1871 to be saved from privatisation, as many had proposed. He petitioned to instead run them by the new German Republic as the State's cultural provision for its citizens; for Jessner, theatre's 'true purpose' was to be a 'real common good of the public' (Jessner 1979, 52).[4]

Born the son of Lithuanian immigrants in Königsberg (today's Baltic Russian exclave of Kaliningrad), Jessner was a practising Jew as well as a committed socialist until his death. He began to work as an actor at the age of sixteen. Carl Heine, the director of the 'Ibsen Theatre' company with whom he performed at the turn of the century, encouraged his turn to directing, which led to his appointment as director at Hamburg's Thalia Theater after mounting only four productions.[5] It was the time Antoine composed one of the first manifestos written by a director about the now firmly established theatral practice, his 'Causerie sur la mise en scène' (Antoine 1903; Sarrazac 2005), soon followed by Edward Gordon Craig's notoriously emphatic advocacy of the director as 'the most important figure in the whole world of the Theatre' (Craig [1911] 2009, 9). Jessner picked up the heterogenic prompts of, on the one side, the realist-historicist-naturalist line of the Meininger, Brahm and Reinhardt, and on the other side the seemingly rather contrary directorial modernism of Appia, Craig and others. Jessner's approach radicalised the visual dramaturgy of the latter approach, precisely as he married it to the encompassing sensory experience provided by atmospheric *Regie* typical for the former tradition. But to ultimately fulfil the potential inherent in these variant experiments conducted by his predecessors, Jessner had to cut the umbilical cord. He explicitly positioned his own work against the radicalism of the modernist avant-garde and expressionist theatre (which Jessner is often unduly associated with in some theatre history books), while equally unequivocally rejecting the naturalist *mise en scène* and its authentifying illusion of *milieu*. Instead, Jessner claimed for his work the label of 'Neue Sachlichkeit' – 'new objectivity'. Choosing this term, he associated himself with the values of the post-expressionist movement of this name that had spread across the arts in the early 1920s. In his own words, his aim was 'to objectify what has come to be accepted as a programme. It all depended ... on the fusion of the newly achieved with the eternal validities of the stage' (Jessner 1979, 101).

As a blueprint for future *Regietheater*, Jessner's approach was characterised by that central paradox of *Regie*: he was ultimately committed to what he called, throughout the various stages of his career the 'idea of the play' or its 'central motif' (*Grundmotiv*). In Jessner's own words, he directed each play 'out of its inner self, exploiting its boldness to the maximum, and lifting it precisely thereby into the realm of the supernatural [*in das Gebiet des Übernatürlichen*]' (Jessner 1979, 102). The 'supernatural' he refers to here can best be understood as 'post-Naturalism': a *Regie* that no longer relies on spectacular magic nor on the surface 'truth' of the milieu. He interpreted the legacy of Schillerian liberty as a vital commitment to a theatre that defines itself, first and foremost, as a contemporary institution in the very sense of the German word *zeitgenössisch*: a companion or comrade, even, to the times. Jessner outlined this dual imperative as early as 1913, explicitly referring to Schiller's *Schaubühne* speech, which remained, as his biographer Matthias Heilmann expresses it, his personal 'magna carta' throughout his life (Heilmann 2005, 89):

> In order to grasp the artistic demands of his time, the director must not shut himself off from the world. On the contrary: if he wants to grasp the full value of theatre in the sense of the Schillerian 'moral institution', he must stand firmly in the world and must comprehend the politics of his own time. (Jessner 1979, 148)

This attention to the present circumstances of the production was further enhanced by the experience of World War I and its aftermath, and by the experience of leading a theatre during the allegedly 'Golden' period of the Weimar 1920s, when, in the Republic's capital, Berlin, Nazi brigades actively interfered with theatre productions, and when political as well as racist militant clashes and murders became a part of daily life.

Jessner saw the value of classical plays in the opportunity they offered to reflect on present concerns through the distant lens of the cultural memory and human legacy inscribed in the archive of canonical texts. In 'The Theatre: A Lecture' from 1928, the most sustained of his many insightful and articulate essays on theatre art, Jessner maintained:

> Any art which is not of its time, remains hanging in a vacuous space without any roots, and it will at its best have some superficial charm to offer. ... As far as so-called eternal works of art are concerned, their 'eternal', timeless effect results from their ability to give each time an appropriate resonance [*Was aber die sogenannten ewigen Kunstwerke betrifft, so besteht ja ihre ewige, d.h. zeitlose Wirkung gerade darin, daß sie jeder Zeit das ihr Gemäße zu geben vermögen.*] (Jessner 1979, 102)

The Hegelian necessity for mediation that attempts to bridge historical distance precisely by *not* obliterating the gap and unattainability of the past turns into an imperative. Jessner's great achievement was to tear the play's very impulse, its cry for liberation and liberty, from the save haven of convention and canonisation. It became sensible for the audience on the night that Schiller's play was here once more imbued with all its critical edge.

Jessner, for this purpose, never explicitly 'updated' the classics he staged, nor did he insert instantly readable contemporary references. He did not put Tell, Gessler or other protagonists such as Hamlet into modern suits. There was no actor dressed up as kaiser, and no actor wearing the mask of Trotsky to trumpet the parallels as seen in Erwin Piscator's later production of *The Robbers*. Such superficial updates would, for Jessner, obliterate the plays' central idea in much the same way as the elaborate historicism that conserved this pulsating core into obscurity. Instead, he relied on the dynamic of theatral play as the sole agent of his *zeitgenössische Regie*. Importantly, the act of theatral mediation always remained legible, as he never effaced the visibility of the other theatral triangle, either – of text, *Regie* and *thea*, which mirror the key vectors of theatrality, *semiosis*, *kinesis* and *aisthesis*. Jessner's direction exposed and worked with the very 'metatextual discourse' (Pavis [1982] 2007, 53) that arose within these triangles of theatrality. Far beyond interpreting or illustrating the playtext, his *Regie* thereby *actualised* it, in the fullest sense of this term: it used theatral play to turn the words and the fictional world of the play into actual action, into something that actually (and not only potentially) happens in the present moment. Theatre thereby acquired the currency and urgency suggested by the French term of *actualité*, meaning the news and events of the day. At the same time, Jessner remained committed to the unique idea of a play, which evokes the German meaning of actual, 'eigentlich': It expresses what is 'own' and therefore unique, relating to an essential core – an *Eigentlichkeit*/actuality that, as will become clear in the further course of my argument, refers to the text as well as to the *Regie* and the spectators.

Such actualisation can no longer be considered in terms of staging or producing 'the play', and indeed with Jessner it becomes doubtful whether there is at all any such totality of '*the* play'. The *Grundmotiv* is conceived as an ideal, universal core that – in a strictly Hegelian sense – always requires a concrete actualisation, introduced through the director's (and the production's) own contemporary perspective.[6] Conversely, canonical plays such as Schiller's or Shakespeare's acquire their universal cultural value not because they are 'beyond' concerns of the present day and somewhat untainted by our current pressures, but because they allow (we may even say: they *force*) each and every later generation time to rediscover themselves in the texts, and to reappropriate them as their own:

> But, Ladies and Gentlemen, there are, at the end of the day, neither classical nor modern authors. From a theatre perspective, the poet does not belong to any generation. There are contemporary poets who are one hundred years old, some who are fifty, others who are twenty. Shakespeare, Schiller and Wedekind are just as much spokespersons of today's generation as are the youngest authors. (Jessner 1979, 103)

Thus, 'at the end of the day', there was for Jessner no contest about the 'ownership' of the text, of the canon and of the work. Rather than perceiving conflicting claims to 'owning' the text between playwright and director, Jessner insisted on the director's very responsibility to actively assume this ownership and to then pass it on to the spectators, thereby evoking the sense that the play as an active cultural legacy belongs to them. This is his vision of genuine artistic accessibility, and the opposite of slavishly spelling out the scripted words and actions, while effacing any difficulties for one's audience. Making a text truly accessible means seriously committing to its universal core. Jessner therefore rejected any allegations, prevalent then as now, of being at odds with playwrights' work and their intention:

> At all times, the director has been made to look like the egomaniac who, against the sense of the poetry, creates only for himself; like the one who, irrespective of the work that is presented, stages a brilliant display of fireworks. ... The director, however, is today, in the era of new objectivity [*Neue Sachlichkeit*] more than ever, in the fullest sense of the word, the servant of the work. This is how it ought to be, and this is how it is. (Jessner 1979, 104)

He repeatedly portrayed the work of a theatre director as akin to that of the text's 'solicitor':[7] his task is to represent the interest of his client in the case and make representations to the authorities as necessary in this interest; the commitment reflects, above all, 'the requirements of the cause' (Jessner 1979, 147). On occasion, the client, less knowledgeable in legal matters, may be stuck with his own spontaneous interpretation of the law, and potentially even reject the lawyer's plea made on his behalf. Nevertheless, lawyer and client have the same mutual interest of persuading the authorities of their cause, which we can compare to playwright and director, who seek to persuade the audience as the ultimately 'judging' instance of theatre of their shared cause – the play.

This approach further highlights the essentially dialectic form of *Regie* from which Jessner's work gained its peculiar force and power. In the spirit of Hegelian *Aufhebung*, the distance between the text and his (or our) own present is not annulled in some pseudo-harmonious 'higher unity'. The effect of Jessner's production is, rather, reminiscent of Slavoj Žižek's materialist reading of Hegel, which visualises *Aufhebung* as a Moebius strip, and not in the popular image of an upwards spiral: sublation leads us back to the starting point, only we are now able to see it from a different viewpoint, which we are never able to synchronise, in one and the same moment, with the earlier, as it were, 'naïve' and unmediated perspective. Instead, we can only ever switch between both perspectives on the same object or reality, but in each case there remains a stain that reminds us of the other perspective, which in itself produces its own blind spot. The dialectic movement of mediation and sublation thereby installs what Žižek terms a 'parallax perspective' (see Chapter 7). Similarly, Jessner's *Regie* opens up such different, irreconcilable perspectives on the same object – the playtext. This dialectic actualisation of the text afforded by *Regie* turns the director from a *metteur en scène* into a 'metteur en contradiction', as Pavis quips in French (Pavis [1982] 2007, 53). *Regie* and Hegel's dialectic thinking thus share the same driving force: they are set in motion by contradiction, for Hegel 'the root of any movement and agility' (Hegel 1986c, 75). As the idea of the parallax perspective suggests, this is not the contradiction between a playtext's 'true intention' and its allegedly deviant, directorial 'subjective' interpretation: *Regie*, rather, actualises the inherent contradictions of the playtext, as identified from the point of view of a present-day sensibility – the point of view of the director, the actor, the audience. *Regie* stages this contradiction through the triangular interplay of the theatral energies, and it is the director's task, in his/her subjective singularity, to identify this contradiction inherent in the play's central idea – thereby establishing the vital relation between the present (actual) moment and the true (actual) universality of the text.

It is no problem that the *Inszenierung* relies on such a partial perspective embedded in present, 'actual' concerns. Rather, this actuality vouches for its artistic and aesthetic validity. Here, *Regie* realises another key tenet of the Hegelian/Marxist materialist approach as it maintains that the universal dimension – whether of a notion or of a play – will only ever appear 'as such' through a specific, particular and historical constellation, or in our term, through its 'actualisation'. It would thus be wrong to efface all traces of *Regie* behind the claim of 'truthfully' illustrating the words on the page. One can only arrive at (a text's) universal dimension if one does not obliterate the subjective particularity of the act of interpreting. As Catherine Malabou reminds us:

> Hegel's great originality is that he shows exactly how an interpretation that aims at nothing more than universality, that disallows any role for the singularity of the exegete, an interpretation, indeed, that refuses to be plastic, in the sense of both 'universal and individual', would be in reality particular and arbitrary. … Such a reading, even though envisaged as a model of exemplary 'fidelity to the text', is absolutely non-philosophical, and remains confined, as Hegel says, in 'ratiocination'. (Malabou 2005, 181)

This theatrical production of a playtext activates the historically situated forces of 'styles of thinking', bringing into play *kinesis* and *aisthesis* as well as (abstract, rational) *semiosis*. As a result, it is necessarily partial and contingent, but for this very reason it unlocks our access to the text in its 'actual' dimension – its 'sense', which is, with Hegel, precisely the 'sensory appearing' of the play's idea. Only the representative regime proffered the sense of a static, immutable meaning, reiterated by a mechanical artisanal representation. Within the aesthetic *dispositif* of art and philosophy, the individual 'actualisation' of the text becomes a vital part of a new claim for artistic truth, which is now understood as necessarily different and responsive to (our own) time: what is truthful and authentic is never the (abstract) playtext, but our own attitude and our commitment as interpreters to the contingency of our position – the 'truthfulness' is found in the inclusion, not the disavowal of the particularity and contingency of our viewpoint. Authenticity means admitting that the resolute subjectivity of our position as reader-director-interpreter is prerequisite for accessing the text's universality.

Regie thus operates between the Hegelian categories of abstract and concrete universality. If we elevate a specific, particular, yet inevitably arbitrary and contingent reading into the 'fixed' universal meaning of a play (while obliterating the contingent position of this very assertion), we affirm its 'abstract universality': the canonical text becomes an abstract, 'dead' work of art, solidified as a commodity that can be valued and owned as cultural capital. In concrete universality, however, the engaged position of the interpreter is never bypassed or erased: 'The true "concrete universality" of a great historical text like *Antigone* (or the Bible or a play by Shakespeare) lies in the very totality of its historically determined readings' (Žižek 2012, 359). The particular *Inszenierung* is a necessary stand-in for this 'true concrete universality': there is no central idea, no *Grundmotiv*, beyond the concrete, actual performance in the present, which is anchored to a specific moment in time. Rather aptly, Pavis prefers to conceptualise *mise en scène* as the 'concretisation' rather than the 'interpretation' of the playtext (Pavis 1998, 364). As Mark Fisher asserts:

> Tradition counts for nothing when it is no longer contested and modified. A culture that is merely preserved is no culture at all. … No cultural object can retain its power when there are no longer new eyes to see it. (Fisher 2009, 3–4)[8]

The proposed term 'actualisation' thus refers to a mediation which, as Hegel expressed it in his *Phenomenology*, points to a 'display of what is one's own in the element of universality, whereby it becomes, and should become, the affair of everyone' (Hegel 1986a, 309). The gist of Jessner's term *Sachlichkeit* similarly touches upon the Hegelian 'revelation of the collective within individuality and its work' (Jameson 2010, 67) – the collective universality he marked by the term Spirit.

Jessner's works are prime examples of how *Regie* as concretisation resonates powerfully with contemporary sensibilities and current contradictions without diminishing the universal dimension of the text into mere abstraction, nor into simple particularities. He had already proposed a 'concretisation' of *Tell* in 1913: 'I furthermore intend to portray *Wilhelm Tell*, this cry for freedom, this magnificent folk tale, as something other than a realist rural comedy' (Jessner 1979, 15).[9] Directing a play like *Tell*, for him, no longer exhausted itself in an 'abstract' representation of the play's plot *about* the abuse of power and an illustration of the struggle for freedom on stage. Instead, *Regie* had to stage this conflict through the, as it were, concrete means of scenic-theatral dynamics, translating it into a stirring 'sensible' experience. The dramatic, tragic intensity of the play, the stakes dramatised in the plot, thereby acquire their direct aisthetic theatral force: far beyond allowing the spectating public to just 'understand' the narrative, Jessner's production used the triangular theatral dynamics to make Tell's 'cry for freedom' available for the audience to sense. To achieve this effect, it no longer sufficed, indeed it would have been entirely counterproductive, to mount realist Swiss scenery on stage, or to put the actors in historical costumes, while reciting Schiller's lines word for word. Jessner radically decluttered the milieu of Brahm's productions, and he refrained from staging spectacular naturalist illusions in Reinhardt's mode. The sparse economy of theatral signs in his productions drew on the kinetic spatial dynamism of Appia's and Craig's visions, while championing a stripped-down and radically concentrated 'poor' theatre on an almost empty stage some decades before Brook and Grotowski. Jessner's *Regie*, as he himself asserts, 'does not try to affect sentimentality, but to touch the human core [*Sie will nicht an Sentimentalität, sondern ans Mark des Menschen greifen*]' (Jessner 1979, 102).

On the purely sensory level of theatrality, the spirit of the new Republic breathed through the Switzerland of the 1919 *Tell*, perhaps even the revolutionary spirit that at the time was spreading from the Soviet Union. Yet this 'concretisation' of the play's central motif and its universality necessarily remained contingent and subject to change, even within Jessner's own work. It is only logical that when Jessner staged *Tell* again, only four years later in 1923, his emphasis shifted from ruthless oppression that associated Gessler with the old kaiser towards the theme of liberation from foreign invasion: the conflict between Tell and Gessler now resonated with the French occupancy of the Rheinland and Ruhr area. The audience was offered a different view onto the same thing: Schiller's *Grundmotiv* was again resynced with the circumstances of the production situation. If fully understood in its Schillerian dimension, the play, precisely as play, must ever be in such a state of continual becoming. From the perspective of the spectating public, the ever-new actualisations of a play and its *Grundmotiv* also privilege, if not demand, an engagement with the play *as play*, and not as a cultural artefact or as a fictional world, with which one could identify, or with whose characters and situations one could feel empathy, rather than recognising one's own 'actual' situation through the 'parallax' perspective of (the) play. The true site of the play(-text) becoming play(-performance) is where the play's idea is thus translated into 'sensible' theatrality, which makes us see – according to the speculative logic of *Regie* – the past in the present, and the present in the past.

The term *Sachlichkeit* must therefore not be misunderstood as *mise en scène* dictated by the allegedly 'objective' surface of the words the playwright wrote, without any mediating intervention by *Regie*. Rather, it refers to the 'objective' analysis of its *Grundmotiv*, expressed by the dramatic narrative, and of its theatral force. From this angle, the playtext appears as one (literary) form given to the expression of a principal idea at the heart of the play, while the play-performance is a different, theatral form which renders the same idea sensible. According to the logic of *Aufhebung* introduced above: the text's theatral mediation brings us back to the same text from a new vantage point, which must necessarily appear as a partial distortion of the text. Yet, it is only this change of viewpoint that allows us to sense the play's universality concretely – mediated by the theatral dynamics of meaning, motion and perception. *Regie*, in this Jessnerian understanding, is the name for this subjective force of speculative mediation that sees itself in the service of this core idea, and which makes the playtext's sense concretely available to the sensory experience of the public. This process of actualisation at the same time induces reflexive distance – between the past of the play and the present of the performance, and also between the fictional narrative and the reality of the spectators' world – which in the strict Schillerian sense is the ultimate prerequisite for the liberty of human play.

Step-stage and 'Jessner speed': *Regie* beyond illusion

The most radical and most outrageously provocative innovation which the Berlin audience had to face on the evening of 12 December 1919 was, therefore, the mediated staging of political critique through Jessner's explicitly non-realist mode of presentation. The kinetic and aisthetic theatral dynamics were freed from their ties to historical, naturalist or spectacular realism. Theatre was ready for its (entirely theatral) quantum leap beyond representation. The semiotic meaning of the play was, in Jessner's work, released in a placeless symbolism of the vast and abstract spaces created by his designers, enmeshed in a play with light, shadow, darkness and monochrome colours. The acting, meanwhile, further emphasised an atmosphere of sensory expressiveness which prevented immediate recognition and avoided any visual, purely external assertion of established assumptions and expectations about the classic plays which Jessner staged. His productions gained their explosive impact precisely against their almost dematerialised background; they prevented the audience from directly recognising, immediately identifying with and affirming (or equally rejecting and dismissing) either a distant fictional world or a current, topical surface imposed on a play as its contemporary interpretation. The aisthetic link of the theatrical interplay generated a concentrated experiential focus which, purely through theatrical mediation, created an explosive short-circuiting between the 'there and then' of the play and the resonances of its idea in the 'here and now' of the performance moment: the distance inserted by the neutral, even generic geometric sets amplified the echoes and resonances in the present all the more, vividly demonstrated by the tumultuous eruptions around Jessner's *Tell*.

In his initial Berlin productions, the very motor of Jessner's *Regie* was the famous *Stufenbühne*, or 'step-stage',[10] which designer Emil Pirchan (1884–1957) kept reinventing in various incarnations. Sharing an approach similar to Bauhaus and other 'objective' art forms of the time, the steps and plateaus of Pirchan's sets no longer represented 'varying rooms and landscapes, but formed an abstract arena of mythic occurrences' (Jessner 1979, 99). They equally served the play's idea, becoming another theatrical equation of the *Grundmotiv*. Reviews of Jessner's Hamburg productions already testified to the director's talent to create dense atmospheres, describing him as an 'artist of moods' [*Stimmungskünstler*].[11] He then dispensed entirely with conventional painted scenery in his *Danton's Death* of 1911. Instead, there was a single set for the entire production: This first stage production of Büchner's play was performed in front of a single red curtain on a stage sparsely strewn with a few metaphoric props. The scenography mainly relied on salient colours and on the calculated use of lighting. This focused pictorial and kinetic evocation radically differed from the literal illustration that previously dominated the historicist and naturalist stages of a previous generation of *Regie*. Perhaps Büchner's play simply had to wait for Jessner's *Regie* to be staged. He embraced it as a play about the universal idea of revolution *as such*, not at all as 'history play' about the French Revolution. Through this 'central motif', he generated its concrete repercussions in the present.

Yet it was through his congenial collaboration with Pirchan, a trained architect who had designed commercial billboards before becoming head of the prop department at Munich's Nationaltheater in 1918, that Jessner ultimately became, in the words of Karl Theodor Bluth's contemporary account, 'the director who feels the space' [*der raumfühlende Regisseur*] (Bluth 1928, 18). In stark contrast to Brahm and Reinhardt, Jessner and Pirchan's abstract stage provided focus by refusing spectacle. Pirchan described his innovative approach as 'terracing of the territory' ('Terrassierung des Terrains', Pirchan 1949, 48): he arranged various levels, steps, angles, plateaus and platforms, which turned the stage space itself (and in particular the vertical dimension) into a performative agent. This forced the audience to come to terms with a direct and very sensory clarity that actualised the core idea of the play in a most precise

Figure 3 Spatialising dramaturgic relations of the play: the original model box of Emil Pirchan's 'step-stage' which he designed for Leopold Jessner's 1919 Berlin *Wilhelm Tell*. Courtesy of Theaterwissenschaftliche Sammlung der Universität Köln, Schloss Wahn.

way. Accordingly, Pirchan's set for the 1919 *Tell* made no more than a vague reference to the play's historical Swiss setting (see Figure 3). As mentioned, even the notorious 'hohle Gasse', the narrow passage in the Alps where Tell eventually ambushes Gessler, was indicated merely by curtains which showed an iconographic pictogram outlining mountain scenery. In Jessner's words, 'a single ridge of a mountain, mounted on stage in an *Über*-perspectival way, conveyed the *idea* of the Alpine world instead of its *illusion*' (Jessner 1979, 99; original emphasis). At the centre of the stage was a rectangle of steps that filled the entire width and left the fourth side open towards the auditorium. These 'steps' formed tiers around a central play area, offering an additional dynamic of vertical and horizontal levels in order to spatialise the dramaturgic relations of the play. In the background, monochrome curtains added to the concrete symbolism: green for the *Ruetli*, and red for freedom and Gessler's death. Curtains were also used to optically reduce the vast, empty set for more intimate scenes in Schiller's play. Throughout the production, simple theatrical signs indicated the *locus* of the scenes: Altdorf, for instance, was signified by an emblematic hat on a pole, rather than any realist hint of a pretty rural village.

This spatial framework, without wings and scenery, was then brought to life by a carefully conceived scenic rhythm that was to a large extent generated kinetically through the actors' movement. In Bluth's terms, the space had become, 'mathematically put, a function of the actors' (Bluth 1928, 18). *Tell* gives an instructive example of how Jessner created theatral dynamics through crowd scenes, the arrangement of groups, proxemic relations and the spatial contrast between groups and individual characters, between large scenes and intimate moments. Jessner himself outlines what he calls his 'architectural' approach to *Regie*, using *Richard III*, his 1920 follow-up to *Tell*, as his example, again with Kortner in the lead. Retrospectively, he described this production as a 'paradigm of the *programmatic* mode of representation', highlighting again *Regie*'s 'programme' of actualising the play's central idea (Jessner 1979, 99; original emphasis). It is well worth quoting at length to demonstrate how Jessner positioned his *Regie* against influential earlier productions by the Meiningers and Reinhardt:

> The play is well known. Its premises are: London, murders, execution, battles, court- and coronation receptions. The Meininger, in the [18]70s and 80s adhered to all this faithfully and mounted Westminster and the Tower of London on stage as they appeared historically. The battles were represented in accordance with the rules of the art of the battlefield at the time, and the coronation ceremony was brought on stage with all historic rites of the court protocol.
> Max Reinhardt's production transferred the turmoil of warfare behind the scene. Even before the War, the public no longer seriously believed in bloody *stage battles*. Blaring fanfares, clashing spears were meant to acoustically evoke the *illusion* of fighting. The court society and the coronation ceremony were all still represented using the means of the Meininger, yet no longer applying the style of painting of the [18]70s and 80s, but the impressionist mode.
> The new programmatic approach no longer demanded *illusion*, but the *symbol* of the representation. London and the Tower now became: a bloody red sky above a grey, fatefully rising wall – thereby the atmosphere of murder and execution as characteristics of the plot are transferred pictorially. Gloucester's coronation takes place on the terraced stage, which is entirely clad in red, the colour of blood. On the highest step stands the newly crowned king. At his feet, the court society is grouped, no longer as a historical representation of the court clique of the time, but signalling the symbolism, as a uniform, entirely ossified society in equally blood-red costume.
> The following battle scenes likewise unfolded on this terraced stage, *represented* by the beating rhythm of countless kettledrums behind the stage. Not in order to pretend the illusion of a real battle, but to render the *dynamic* of a battle in its uncanny tension. (Jessner 1979, 99f.; original emphasis)

Richard's final downfall was again actualised spatially with an emphasis on theatrical *kinesis*: Kortner tumbled down from the peak of the terrace steps, dishevelled and mad, and was then killed at the very bottom by the 'white knights' of Richmond's party (see Figure 4).

Writing in retrospect, Jessner described the scenic radicalism of his early productions, such as *Tell* and *Richard III*, as 'a systematic approach to rid the stage of the accidental randomness of illusionist decor, making it instead available – as a place- and timeless theatrical space [*Schauplatz*] – for a mode of representation that derives its laws solely from the innermost substance of the poetry' (Jessner 1979, 156). The immediate recognisability and easy consumption of familiar classical tragedies was prevented by the *Aufhebung* of representational illusion in a pictoriality that establishes a crucial dynamics between theatral *kinesis* and spectatorial *aisthesis*. Here we find the nucleus of a strategy of defamiliarisation that demanded a new, different

Figure 4 Sublating representational illusion in theatral dynamic: Emil Pirchan's design sketch for Jessner's *Richard III* (1920). Courtesy of Theaterwissenschaftliche Sammlung der Universität Köln, Schloss Wahn.

mode of looking from the spectating public. Jessner realised an actual 'retheatralisation' of theatre as he saturated the dramatic *semiosis* in his productions with the theatral energies of *kinesis* and *aisthesis*. In a sense, his approach was therefore 'postdramatic' *avant la lettre*: his was a theatre that no longer relied on the immanent 'dramatic cosmos' of plot and characters alone but rather sublated the drama in theatrality through the force of *Regie*. Crucially, for Jessner (just as for Brecht and later Schechner) this 'sublation' never entailed a need to decry the dramatic tradition as conservative and stale. On the contrary, its entire purpose was to reactivate its once vital energy, reminding us of that important connotation of the German term *aufheben*, of 'storing', 'preserving' and 'keeping'.

Jessner's *Regie* reveals such genuinely theatral strategies at every level. The scenographic principles we identified in *Tell* were echoed on other levels of his exemplary production. The actors did not deliver conventional portrayals of rural freedom fighters. Instead of embodying individuals and their psychological motivations and convictions (hence a *kinesis* hierarchically subordinated to *semiosis*), they exhibited symbolic, elemental *Ur*-types: against Gessler as personified devil, Bassermann's Tell, all in white, attracted almost all of the light on an otherwise very gloomy, semi-dark stage. Here, *aisthesis* supports *semiosis* as equal partner. The text of Schiller's play, meanwhile, was tightened, and even some of the most famous set-piece speeches cut, as demanded by the strict concentration on the 'central idea'. Furthermore, the theatral dynamics of performing and, in particular, the kinetic and aisthetic delivery of the text itself supported the pure symbolism in the (semiotic) service of the *Grundmotiv*. Whereas the designs by Emil Pirchan, and later by Caspar Neher (who would then famously go on to work with Brecht), added an appropriately non-realist 'universally objective' environment, Jessner himself continued to concentrate on the delivery of the text, what in German theatre is known as *Dialogregie*. Back in 1913, Jessner had maintained: 'I am a director of the word and not of the decoration' (Jessner 1979, 15). At this moment in his career, he had abandoned any 'theatrical' distraction around the text, any spectacular illustration typical of the 'Berlin Realism' that dominated stages all over Germany at the time. Theatre critic Julius Bab, who had himself worked as Jessner's dramaturg at Königsberg, emphasised this talent of the director:

> Jessner was in particular able to renounce, for his purposes, any splendour of decoration, and to a certain degree even the richness of the actors' performance, since he created his entire impact based on the speed, on the rhythmic structuring, the powerful arrangement of accentuation with which he orchestrated the dramatic dialogue. (Bab 1928, 78)

Jessner, in particular, invited his performers to exploit paralinguistic means, pushing for a genuinely theatral delivery of the text. The tempo, accentuation and rhythm of the language itself, as well as tone of voice, became principal theatral means at the actors' disposal. Jessner described speech as the actor's 'most accomplished instrument', and he considered the 'precision of expression' their pivotal task (Jessner 1979, 100).

Incorporating kinetic and aisthetic theatral dynamics into the very act of speaking allowed Jessner to create a style of verbal delivery far beyond the conventions of oratory rhetoric with its focus on triggering affective empathy. Far from simply 'spelling out' the text, the rhythmic quality of lines, the sonic and acoustic quality of words and the tonal intensities of individual syllables all contributed directly to an aisthetic presentation of the play's sense. In the service of this theatral delivery, even well-known scenes and speeches may be toned down or cut entirely. The guiding principle for the arrangement and delivery of the text, too, was 'objectivity':

> The clarity of the steps on stage was transferred to the word. Speech became disciplined to the extreme, concentrated and polished. ... As far as the language is concerned, it was entirely rid of any pathetic moment. ... The *objective* attitude of the word was the sole defined objective. Even the monologues ceased to be showpieces of rhetoric mastery, but their intention was to be no more than the transmission of the thoughts going through the mind. (Jessner 1979, 101)

This inevitably created unfamiliar challenges for his actors, who not only lost theatrical showpieces but were almost exposed in their bare theatrality, not unlike the later postdramatic strategy that turned performers into what Gerda Poschmann termed 'text-bearers' [*Textträger*] who deliver speech and textual discourse (Poschmann 1997, 296). There was no decoration on stage to hide behind, and no props to fidget with. Conventions of stage rhetoric were left behind, and the introduction of theatral qualities of speech invented a new dramatic 'spoken word' art which ultimately privileged the text in its ideal quality. Bassermann started playing Tell calm and quiet, yet as the performance continued, his delivery became ever more hurried and breathless, symbolising the devastating effect of Gessler's power over his character. This was even the case for some of the famous monologues, which were traditionally subject to declamation and stage elocution. As Günther Rühle noted, the audience could physically sense 'a man acting in self-defence' (Rühle 1976, 55), just by listening to the sound of Tell's speech. This is another example of how the *Grundmotiv* was translated onto every theatral layer. What eventually became known as 'Jessner speed' allowed (and demanded) not merely a well-rehearsed, quickfire delivery, but an almost instinctive play by the performers. It provided the performers with purely theatral means to charge the scene with a sense of aggression, beyond 'acting it out', shouting or emoting.

With regard to gesture, Jessner's theatral *Regie* design equally opted against illustration; instead of mimicking and redoubling, he again used purely theatral means that further added to the play's theatral actualisation. The actors' physical expression was reduced to a few precisely articulated gestures. The director's 1914 Hamburg production of Wedekind's *Marquis of Keith* was reportedly one of the first where he had the performers 'freeze' unless they were speaking: only the actor who had a line would move, while the others sat motionless, hands clasped in their laps. It is, however, essential to note that even in the midst of the surrounding setting and costumes in all their abstraction, and of the reduction to a few significant gestures, Jessner's productions were never described as stylised (as, say, the work of Robert Wilson), and they were remote from the expressionist pathos of urgency common at the time. On the contrary, and again not unlike Brecht's famous 'model productions' at the post-war Berliner Ensemble, Jessner's own defamiliarisation achieved an altogether more 'human' way of acting in its very renouncing of any fourth-wall realism and *milieu* decor, and this can be connected with the Hegelian principle of 'concrete universality'.

As much logical consequence as surprise, Jessner explicitly rejected fellow directors who used performers like 'pieces on a chess board, which are to be shifted according to the calculations of the director', and likewise dismissed *Regisseure* who prepare a concept 'on the desk without considering the individualities of their performers' (Jessner 1979, 145). Alfred Kerr concisely summarised the special 'Jessner effect', even in the programmatically bare *Tell* of 1919, by contrasting the abstract environment and the play with the performers bringing it to life:

> Here, a stylized Switzerland is experienced: a Switzerland without nature; a purely conceptual Switzerland; not a tangible Switzerland. Yet, Schiller's Switzerland is very much tangible. At least: the people talk like human beings. In the past, everything was the other way round: the scenic countryside was real and the characters unreal. Then rather today's approach! (Kerr 1981, 171)

A decade later, in 1928, Jessner himself looked back to his famous step-stage of the earlier productions as 'not so much an experiment, perhaps instead more a demonstration – necessary to assist in creating the style of the essential, the style of precision' (Jessner 1979, 99). At this point, the strict and ascetic style no longer seemed to be required, and his later productions of the 1920s reapproached more realist parameters. At the same time, he stressed that even then, his approach would 'draw its structure and its flavour still not from picture postcards, but from the sense of the representation [*Darstellung*]' (Jessner 1979, 101).

Viewing habits, expectations and the strategies and conventions of directing and spectating texts had for ever changed: *Regie* had emancipated itself from realist representation, and there was no innocent way back. To continue insisting on Meiningerian historicity, on Reinhardtian grand spectacle, had become an ideologically marked choice. At the same time, Jessner's work ultimately opened up the schism that would for ever set apart the theatre worlds of Continental thinking of *Regie* against pragmatic Anglo-American theatre production.

Jessner with Hegel: The plasticity of *Regie*

In his thought-through dramaturgic *Regie* with its commitment to a close study of the play's *Grundmotiv*, Jessner never relied on superficial updating or random associations. The exemplary 'actualisation' of the playtexts in his work points to the paradox at the heart of *Regie*: the director's work is certainly an active act of art, not simply reproductive imitation. At the same time, all 'meaning' is already there in the text – yet it requires actualisation and concretisation to become accessible and sensible, that is, to make sense. *Regie* therefore sublates the text, but contrary to popular cliché, it does not insist on a competing claim for authorship and authority that annuls the playwright. Jessner's explicit distancing from the rigorously individualistic aesthetics of expressionism emphasised that his was not a subjective art, which took its prompt from the director's inner genius, from his interpretation or 'concept'. Rather, *Regie* at its core is a paradigmatic process of mediation, which dialectically sublates the necessarily subjective approach and perspective in the 'concrete universality' of the *Inszenierung* that is the only 'actual' theatral manifestation of the text: the singular moment when the otherwise purely abstract playtext is actualised in its full semiotic, kinetic and aisthetic dimension. The *Inszenierung* is not a mere 'realisation' of an antecedent, hierarchically privileged (literary) playtext, and yet remains dialectically tied to this text.

The standard reproach that a director such as Jessner should have written his own play instead of labelling his work with the names of Schiller or Shakespeare thus totally misses the point. For both contrary forces, the text and the *Inszenierung*, only the 'third term' created through their dialectic mediation allows them to become more than their particular singularity: the dialectic process creates a dissensus by confronting text and production with different, mutually exclusive (particular) partitions of the sensible. Through this contradiction, text, *Inszenierung* and lastly we, too, as spectators become able to adopt a stance of distance. As we saw in our discussion of Schiller in Chapter 3, we should not understand the imperative of autonomy as a demand for the artist's obscure reclusion, but rather as insisting on this space that allows for self-distancing, for a detachment from one's own position.[12] *Regie* is, therefore, the ultimate realisation of Schillerian 'play' in its absolute commitment to ultimate liberty. It takes further what Hegel, discussing the dramatic form as synthesis of lyric subjectivity and epic objectivity, outlines as central mediating effect of 'the third mode of presentation', where 'the *objective* can be shown as belonging to the *subject*', and vice versa:

> This objectivity, which emerges from the subject, as well as this subjectivity, which is presented in its actual realisation and objective validity, is the Spirit in its totality, and provides as *action* the form and the content of *dramatic* poetry. (Hegel 1955, 935f.; original emphasis)

This innovative and rather delicate Hegelian 'double vision' which *Regie* applies to classic (and other) texts through spaces, voices and bodies can be directly linked with the notion of plasticity, which Catherine Malabou identified (alongside temporality and dialectics) as a 'point around which all the transformations of Hegelian thought revolve, the centre of its metamorphosis' (Malabou 2005, 13). The term, based on the Greek *plassein* (to model, to mould), re-entered Western European discourse prominently in the early nineteenth century, the time of the aesthetic regime, of Hegel and of the emergence of *Regie*. Signifying both the capability of receiving form and of giving, producing and even annihilating form (as in the detonation of plastic explosives), the notion of plasticity serves Malabou as a key to grasping the dimensions of Hegelian 'speculative thinking'. Similarly, Hegel described sculpture – or *Plastik*, in the newly emerging German word of the time – as key for understanding his ideal vision of classical Greek culture. He suggested we 'consider from the point of view of plasticity both epic and dramatic heroes and equally the actual statesmen and philosophers', all of whom he found to display 'this same plastic, universal yet individual character which remained the same both inwardly and outwardly [*diesen plastischen, allgemeinen und doch individuellen, nach aussen wie nach innen gleichen Charakter*]' (Hegel 1955, 664).

Plasticity thus points to the 'style of thinking' we similarly encountered in Schiller: for Hegel, it acts as a mediating term which we can relate to the dynamics between the three factors of theatrality in our context. Hegel himself notes that the 'plastic individualities' he perceives in his historical and mythological Greek role models give form to an 'embodiment of the spiritual [*Körperlichkeit des Geistigen*]' (664), hence effecting a form of 'sensible translation'. This reminds us of the integral dynamics between the semiotic and both *kinesis* and *aisthesis*, as essentially embodied activities of *thea*, and furthermore of the middle ground that Schiller accorded such crucial importance in the name of beauty and liberty. At the same time, plasticity points us to the core moment of perpetual movement which Schiller so elegantly emphasised through his notion of *play*, in the German sense of 'Spiel haben' in order to avoid getting stuck and static. Plasticity in its very term evokes such dynamic malleability of thinking that challenges fixed and stable positions. This stance against any form of one-sidedness becomes a crucial aspect that the Hegelian 'Spirit' aspires to: it can only fully actualise itself as 'in and for itself' after positing itself as its own other, thereby dissolving the fixity of its position. This contradictory tension is at the heart of self-determination (see Hegel 1986c, 561).

A similar aspect is evoked when Hegel suggestively describes, in the preface to his *Science of Logic*, how 'a plastic speech [*ein plastischer Vortrag*] demands, too, a plastic sense of receptivity and understanding on the part of the audience' (Hegel 1986b, 31). He contrasts the 'plastic speech' with the 'nervousness and distraction characteristic for our modern sensibility [which] allows for nothing else but to respond to more or less obvious reflections and the next best ideas' (31); again this resonates with the age-old reproach against *Regietheater*. Plasticity, however, points us to an awareness of how our own speech (or production) is moulded and given form (by the text), in the same way as our response elastically responds to contemporary life and our own concrete context and our issues. The (again, ideal) attitude of an audience that does not go straight off on a tangent but follows while 'calmly renouncing [their] *own* reflexions and ideas' (31) complements Hegel's scenario. This philosophical approach reveals the powerful and potentially radical force engendered by *Regie*, an aspect that often is forgotten in the day-to-day business of getting the curtain up on the night. Far beyond pragmatic producing or authoritative interpretation, *Regie* activates dynamic relations and dialectic processes between the triangular constellation of the text, the *Inszenierung* and the spectating public. This became clear in Jessner's elaborate aesthetic-political wager: theatre gains its socio-cultural relevance only by being *zeitgenössisch*, yet this must not mean conflating fiction and reality, past and present, art and life. *Regie* only works by 'plastically' mediating these distances, in order to present us with alternative constellations of the sensible (hence alternative configurations of the theatral forces of *semiosis*, *kinesis* and *aisthesis*), which then allow us to reflect, from this distance and through 'magic' speculative thinking, even more forcefully and productively on our own immediate issues and pressing concerns.

While Jessner was instrumental in inspiring the emerging work of his most important directorial protégés Brecht and Piscator with his dialectic approach, his own career and productivity was eventually exhausted in ongoing political controversies and anti-Semitic attacks against his person (he resigned from his post as artistic director of the Berlin Staatstheater in 1930, succeeded by the notorious Gustaf Gründgens, and went into exile in 1933, to the Netherlands, to Palestine and eventually the USA). Jessner never returned to Europe, dying at the age of sixty-seven in his Californian exile shortly after the end of the war in 1945. It should seem a most appropriate coincidence that the next *Regietheater* revolution in (West) German theatre arrived on the scene with another *Tell*: Hansgünther Heyme's scandalising 1965 Wiesbaden production. This new generation of the 1960s and 1970s, which included Peter Zadek and not least Peter Stein, who had been mentored by Fritz Kortner, fully implemented some of the most radical and productive innovations which had already been introduced by Jessner during the Weimar 1920s. He had thereby mapped out the terrain for the second major phase of *Regie*, which runs right up to the present day and the directors discussed in the second part of this book: Jessner pioneered *Regie* as an engaged and engaging practice that turns theatre into a political force by its very power of dialectic mediation, through its *mise en sens* of contradictions.

Notes

1. As Jessner's biographer Matthias Heilmann argues, some details of Kortner's much-quoted account contradict contemporary descriptions from reviews and other sources; further, there are no independent sources to confirm some of the details he provides, such as the trumpets blowing on Gessler's entry in a way reminiscent of Kaiser Wilhelm's fanfare. Heilmann remains sceptical about the documentary value of Kortner's account and suggests that he may have inadvertently embellished his recollection after four decades spanning the turbulent times of the Weimar Republic, Nazi Germany, World War II and emigration (Heilmann 2005, 147f.).
2. Julius Bab (1880–1955) was an important theatre critic in Weimar Germany who had previously worked as Jessner's dramaturg during the director's Königsberg years. Alfred Kerr (1867–1948) was another prominent reviewer.
3. Throughout his career, Jessner did not solely direct classics. On the contrary, he was particularly committed to giving exposure to new playwriting talent. At Hamburg, he championed the works of Ibsen and the emerging Frank Wedekind. His approach to Ibsen was, however, notably different from the milieu-based naturalism of the Brahm tradition. Jessner, in fact, had a particular penchant for tackling plays previously considered as unstageable, such as Ibsen's *Peer Gynt*, Wedekind's *Lulu* trilogy and not least Georg Büchner's *Danton's Death*, whose first stage production he directed in 1911.
4. Jessner's case for this consequential theatre reform is well documented in Hugo Fetting's collection of Jessner's writings (Jessner 1979, 52–60). Actively engaging in the work of the theatre union, Jessner likewise was a driving force behind the introduction of a standardised contract for actors that defined basic conditions of employment. Before his reforms, actors were rarely paid for rehearsals or in case of illness, and they had to provide their own costumes. Jessner also successfully lobbied for the founding of the first state-funded acting school in Berlin.
5. Heine, who had worked with Ibsen himself during the writer's days in Munich in the 1880s, took a distinctly different approach to Ibsen than Otto Brahm, who subsumed Ibsen into the new aesthetic paradigm of naturalism. Heine, and later Jessner, saw in him a modernist innovator. It was Ibsen's emphasis on the 'idea' that pushed Jessner beyond realist historicism and Naturalism. (See his lecture on Ibsen, Jessner 1979, 222–5.)
6. Jessner kept quoting the lines from Goethe's poem 'One and All': 'In re-creating the created. / Lest fossilise the animated. / Aye, active power, is manifest; / The non-existing actualizing.'
7. He thereby follows Alfred von Berger's *Hamburger Dramaturgie*, see Jessner 1979, 147.
8. A similar political stance characterised the cultural materialist tradition of the 1980s, which put forward radical 'concrete' alternative interpretations of Elizabethan drama to contest the appropriating 'abstraction' of Shakespeare by a Conservative Thatcherite elite (see Dollimore [1984] 2004; Dollimore and Sinfield 1985).
9. This envisaged production, proposed as part of his (unsuccessful) application as artistic director of Berlin's Neues Volkstheater, did not materialise, yet Jessner subsequently staged his first *Tell* at Königsberg in 1916 as a prelude to his Berlin production three years later.
10. Both in English and German, the *Stufenbühne* has frequently been referred to as 'stairs' or *Treppen*, a term which Jessner emphatically rejected as inaccurate in numerous lectures and writings (for instance, Jessner 1979, 99).
11. From a review in *Hamburger Fremdenblatt*, 9 April 1908, quoted in Müllenmeister 1956, 105.

12 Alenka Zupančič points to the prime example of Magritte's famous *Ceci n'est pas une pipe*:

> What is at stake here is not simply that art should not be able to use an element of reality (the factual), but that, if it uses such an element, it is no longer identical with itself – it begins to exist in difference to itself, and *as* difference to itself. This, and nothing else, is the fascinating meaning of Schillerian ideality. (Zupančič 2006, 207)

PART II
The theatral appearing of ideas
The thinking of contemporary Regie

5

The tremor of speculative negation: on *Regie*, truth and ex-position

Perhaps it is more than only a cliché, after all. Continental European 'directors' theatre' does stir up a lot of controversy with its productions of classical texts in predominantly non-realist settings that demonstrate a director's distinct interpretive grasp and stylistic signature – even in Germany itself. At least every other year some big debate about the cons (and, subsequently in defence, the pros) of *Regietheater* keeps the arts sections of the nation's media busy for a few weeks. In the autumn of 2005, when the Düsseldorf Schauspielhaus opened its new season with a *Macbeth* staged by the late Jürgen Gosch (1943–2009), all hell broke loose – on stage and off-stage as well. With lurid headlines, the local tabloid press denounced the alleged waste of taxpayer's money on the city's public stage, and even the more sober weekly news magazine *Der Spiegel* staged its part in the debate. It drove Joachim Lottmann, one of the country's post-unification pop literati, to see the performance. Even while confessing right in the first paragraph that he had no interest in theatre, he still went on to describe Gosch's production as 'disgusting from the very first moment', and expressed serious concern about its effect on the school classes in the audience. The writer contrasted his experience with the production of Wilde's *Ideal Husband* he attended on his *Spiegel* mission at neighbouring Bochum: There, at last, the actors (some prominent film faces and other celebrities) 'were allowed', as Lottmann phrased it, to portray 'proper characters', to speak, for once, a text not corrupted by contemporary slang and everyday parlance enforced on it by the director, and they played in proper period costume – all this allegedly 'true to the text'.[1] Since the 1850s, and hence almost since the beginning of *Regie*, most German attacks on *Regietheater* appeal to this fundamental category: the ideal of *Werktreue* and *Texttreue*, of being true to the work or text

(Prütting 2006; see also Balme 2008 for a critical reflection on the 'fundamentalist' ideology of the concept).

Five years before Gosch's *Macbeth*, in December 2000, a prominent heckler in the name of this much-invoked 'truth' made similar headlines across the German press: 'This is a decent play! One mustn't play it like that!' ('Das ist doch ein anständiges Stück! Das muss man doch nicht so spielen!'). As eagerly reported by the media, it was the City of Hamburg's dignified former mayor, Klaus von Dohnanyi, who jumped from his seat during the first night performance at the city's Thalia Theater and yelled these very words at the stage, leaving the auditorium and letting the doors slam behind him. Once more, *Regietheater* was taken to task. On stage that night was a new production of Ferenc Molnár's 1909 *Liliom*, which launched the career of the hitherto unknown Michael Thalheimer (b. 1965). Significantly, both Thalheimer and Gosch, two directors who represent two different generations of German *Regie*, both themselves frequently employed terms such as 'truth' and 'truthfulness' when discussing their work in interviews, post-performance discussions and on similar occasions. Their *Regie* thus offers us the opportunity to reflect further on the idea of a *theatral truth*, which seems at the heart of (m)any problems with contemporary European *Regie*. This chapter will explore how they exemplarily reappropriated the contested notion of the 'truth of the text', which had almost exclusively been enlisted by the opponents of *Regie*. During the previous reign of postmodern direction, the category of 'truth' would not be accepted as anything other than a momentary illusion, or as an ironic gesture. Gosch and Thalheimer thus represent an important shift in recent Continental *Regie*, towards a twenty-first-century 'new objectivity'. It transcends the 'classic' *Regietheater* aesthetics of the 1970s and 80s, of Peter Stein and Peter Zadek, with which Gosch had been associated. At the same time, it leaps beyond the 'de(con)-structivist' and 'pop' approaches, as they had prevailed in German theatre after 1989, most prominently associated with directors Frank Castorf and Thalheimer's contemporary Stefan Pucher (see Carlson 2009, 95–115, 181–93; on Castorf see Chapter 8).

Between them, Gosch and Thalheimer – who both trained and worked for many years as actors before moving into directing – were not only among the most controversial, but also the most successful German directors during the first decade of the new millennium, taking as a (not altogether objective) indicator their nominations for the Berlin Theatertreffen, the annual showcase of the season's ten best productions in German theatre, as selected by a jury of theatre critics.[2] In its emphatic seriousness, their reduced, minimalistic *Regie* points us towards an idea of truth which is not to be gauged by the 'accurate' correspondence with the original play, at the level of representation where every word in the text is spoken, each scripted action realistically performed and illustrated. This is the truth of *Werktreue* – an idea that resorts to values of the representative regime of arts, which was predicated on a timeless notion of metaphysical Truth, expressed by the artwork through symbolic representation. Yet, under the aesthetic regime, the Word was no longer automatically in the beginning, neither in the church nor in the theatre. As the development from Schiller to the historicist *Regie* of the later nineteenth century had already suggested, truth was no longer associated with mimetic repetition and adhering to given conventions. Instead, it became a matter of the artist's active mediation, of his or her negotiation of the theatral forces of 'scenes and senses', of *semiosis, aisthesis* and *kinesis*. It was seen as emerging from an engagement with the text, its performance and the public. As such, this aesthetic truth is contingent, yet not at all accidental. It is relational – related to both the text and its theatrical mediation through performing and spectating. We here encounter a notion of truth that makes the Hegelian transition from a metaphysical 'objective' truth and predicative logic towards dialectic, speculative thinking: a truth, which according to Hegel, necessarily includes our own position and perspective. His central argument against transcendental notions of truth, as they underpin notions of being 'true to the work', was precisely that our way towards the truth is always already a part of the truth itself, as he prominently suggested in the Preface to his *Phenomenology*.

Crossing the border of emptiness: Jürgen Gosch

Such a speculative truth, which no longer affirms what is given, but brings forth the inherent contradictions, must be unsettling and risk rejection. It is simply not compatible with 'entertainment', the commodity which the machinery of 'communicative capitalism' produces for purchase and consumption. Neither Gosch's nor Thalheimer's work discussed above delivered these goods and served their audience with 'fun'. In Gosch's *Macbeth*, in fact, any 'culinary' entertainment, in Brecht's term, was foreclosed from the outset. As the performance began, seven male actors, who between them shared all the roles, climbed up on stage from the auditorium, where they were seated in the front row, and undressed. They would remain fully naked for the remainder of the three hours that followed, played without an interval and with the houselights on. Over the course of these three hours, the set, initially almost clinically empty, containing only a few plastic chairs and tables and a huge white sail made of paper, was soiled and utterly destroyed (see Figure 5). In the end, a still life of a battlefield remained. The floor was covered with a gory, nauseating mix of flour (poured over Banquo as he was killed and making for a particularly powerful ghostly reappearance), the stage blood which the performers visibly squeezed from bottles during battle scenes and fights and juice and chocolate mousse that had served as human excrements in the carnivalesque witches scenes. The paper sheet was torn, the plastic chairs and tables smashed up. The brutality depicted in *Macbeth* has been the topic of many academic studies, yet rarely was it made so viscerally palpable and painfully true: a violent, but in vital counterpoints (not the least in the scenes with Lady Macbeth, here played by 'boy actor' Devid Striesow) also a grotesquely comical and poetic nightmare of a pre-civilised world, reigned over by human drives, aggression and bodily fluids.

Nudity and bloodshed also featured prominently in Thalheimer's controversial take on Molnar's play about the unemployed fairground worker Liliom and his relationship with the maidservant Julie.[3] He showed Liliom's suicide as bloody self-mutilation, in which this social failure almost fails again: a seemingly never-ending

Figure 5 A nightmare of violence made sense-able: one of the witches scenes from Jürgen Gosch's controversial *Macbeth* (Schauspielhaus Düsseldorf, 2005; set design: Johannes Schütz). Photo: Sonja Rothweiler.

butchery, where the still undead protagonist kept stabbing himself again and again over the course of many agonising minutes. Some spectators reacted with hysteric laughter, others left the theatre. The most controversial moment of the production, however, was an earlier (anti-)sex scene between the couple. It started as violent rape, yet Liliom failed to get an erection. Eventually, Julie, in her fateful loving compassion, gave him a handjob, after which he carefully cleaned her up with his handkerchief. A scene as gross as it was mortifyingly touching. Thalheimer turned the milieu study of the life of the lower classes (which Molnar suspends in the final half of his play, where he has God permitting Liliom to return to earth, sixteen years later, for one day only, to see their by then grown-up daughter again) into a both abstract and depressingly current visual and visceral confrontation with unemployment and with the frustration of the failing underdogs who find no place in society, who have no voice to articulate themselves and for whom violence at home is the sole means of expressing affection.

To dismiss his and also Gosch's theatre as merely obscene spectacle misses not only the deeply moving moments of tragedy articulated in their productions, but also overlooks the political and ethical engagement that is a vital motivation of their *Regie*. In his description of postdramatic theatre forms of the 1980s and early 1990s, Hans-Thies Lehmann already identified the 'withdrawal of representation' as an essential reaction of theatre to the everyday saturation with omnipresent media images (Lehmann 2006, 172). The stylised concentration and refusal to illustrate which we encounter in the *Regie* of Thalheimer and Gosch discloses an even greater *negative representation*, evoking the Hegelian notion of negativity introduced in Chapter 2. As first step in order to approximate anything akin to 'truth', their theatre empties the stage of all standard means of media representation. It rejects psychological realism, which Gosch deplored and considered as 'fake' and 'embarrassing to watch' (quoted in Kümmel 2009). It counters what Thalheimer denounced as the 'illustrated lie' of representation (quoted in Kalb 2009, 38). It is for this reason that their productions, at times ascetic, elsewhere lavishly stylised, seem to sacrifice the play. Yet, what they actually sacrifice is the play's smooth integration into the global 'cultural industry' and entertainment machinery of semiocapitalism. Its logic seeks to trigger identification and empathy through the realistic fictional *milieu*, localising the drama of Chekhov, Shakespeare or Hauptmann in past times and distant spaces, in order to avoid any recognition of the spectator's actual present and its pressing issues. This is, however, the 'truth' which Gosch and Thalheimer seek to evoke. Their *Regie* exemplarily responds to the omnipresent semiocapitalist call for 'interactivity' and instant communication with the power of negation: fully exploiting the Hegelian force of *Aufhebung* as conservation through cancellation, they withdraw the text from its ready availability and consumability. Thereby, they propose an 'analogue' exposition of truth in a digital age. Accordingly, Jürgen Gosch's late work, which he created during his prolific years before his death in 2009,[4] revealed a delicate, subtle and supple approach, anything but superficial shock tactics – even in the rough *Macbeth*. In the naked bodies, Gosch discovered the 'truth' of *Macbeth*. He compared the vulnerability and, as he describes it, 'naturalness' of the performers' nude bodies with the paintings of Lucian Freud, whom he much admired.[5] This Düsseldorf production brought Gosch back into the spotlight: a contemporary of Peter Stein from the former East Germany, he had worked mainly at the Berlin Volksbühne during the 1970s, before being expelled to the West after a controversial take on Büchner's *Leonce and Lena* in which he allegedly caricatured the regime of Erich Honecker, chairman of the GDR State Council.

For Gosch, and in different ways for the younger Thalheimer, a specifically theatral spatialisation became the condition for still reaching, shaking and penetrating our senses despite our over-saturation as a result of twenty-four-hour access to web-based media, social networks and other forms of digital connectivity. The uncovered, volatile as well as monstrous nude bodies in *Macbeth* were framed by a set that was as bare as the performers' bodies. It was designed by Johannes Schütz (b. 1950), whose sparse yet atmospheric spaces, extraordinary environments filled to the brim with emptiness, became a recognisable signature of Gosch's late *Regie* work.[6] Their 2008 collaboration on Chekhov's *Uncle Vanya* (premiere 12 January 2008, Deutsches Theater Berlin) and *The Seagull* (premiere 20 December 2008 as a co-production of Deutsches Theater and Volksbühne Berlin) was their most exquisite achievement. For *Vanya*, Schütz closed off the entire height and width of the Deutsches Theater's proscenium with a huge rectangular box, with no windows, no doors, no exits (see Figure 6). The solid walls were freshly plastered with clay for each performance so that they gradually dried during the evening's show. This gave the walls a distinct, earthy yellow colour that changed as the clay settled and dried, while at the same time gradually

Figure 6 Atmospheric environments, filled to the brim with emptiness: a scene from the final act of Jürgen Gosch's *Uncle Vanya* (Deutsches Theater Berlin, 2008; set design: Johannes Schütz). Photo: Iko Freese.

marking the performers' costumes, and filling the auditorium with its distinct, earthy smell. A step across the full width of the rear wall provided an opportunity to sit down. Only a few metres deep, the set leaned from the proper stage space into the auditorium, past the front boxes and front rows. It thus brought the action unusually close to the spectators, even to those seated further away. Within this stunning earthy cage of *Vanya*, a prototypical Chekhovian samovar in the first part and a tray full of the professor's pills and medicines remained the only significant props. Meanwhile, a small poster map of the African continent put up in the fourth act became the only element to decorate the bare walls. For their *Seagull*, Schütz opened up this box-set to the sides, so that only the massive rear wall remained. This time it was painted pitch-black, using real tar. At the beginning, two performers carried a huge stone through the auditorium onto the likewise empty stage and placed it right at the front centre. It was from here that Nina would deliver her performance in Kostya's play.

The same characteristic gesture of 'clearing the space', of precision, subtraction and reduction was continued through other aspects of Gosch's *Regie*. As a result, everything presented on this sparse, direct stage was prominently amplified: Astrov's bizarre, gigantic moustache, for instance; the odd blue-violet colour of the cord suit which Vanya wore along with trainers, as well as his quirky hat and glasses. Similarly, physical activity was minimised, yet again for this reason became even more memorable: Vanya's unsteady gait, his constant fatigue and yawning; Astrov's habit of scattering food around him, such as the stubs of gherkins he munched or the tails of sardines. Later, Elena would emulate precisely this idiosyncratic action as she spoke about the doctor. Within this space, Gosch allowed for realistic acting, even some old-style declamation of senior actor Christian Grashoff, formerly the GDR's closest equivalent to a Laurence Olivier, and here cast to play retired professor Serebrejakov in *Vanya* and Arkadina's brother Sorin in *The Seagull*. In the latter play, the character of Semjon Medvedenko, the teacher married to Masha, was expressed almost purely gesturally, through his chocolate addiction, while most of his lines were cut: he literally had no say. Gosch charged the empty environs through such simple and very concrete details, props and actions to a most powerful effect. In the delivery of the text, he also allowed for pauses and silences, for moments when nothing was spoken, when no one did anything – and these gaps became even more poignant.

The use of spaces and places within the box followed a similar logic of constraints and focalisation. Astrov, from early on, was assigned 'his' position stage-right. Vanya settled right in the middle of the rear step, where he remained for most of the time. Elena, the professor's younger, second wife, and to a lesser degree Sonja, his daughter from his first marriage and Vanya's niece, were virtually the only characters notably 'moving' and crossing the stage. In the final act of *The Seagull*, Kostya sat at the very front of the stage, tearing over the duration of the act page after page of a huge pile of paper, his own playscripts, while the rest of the household was simultaneously engaged in their joyful dinner and card games behind him. He was then the sole character to go off stage, behind the huge tar wall, from where we heard the sound of the gunshot. Except for Kostya's suicide, the box-set space in Gosch's 'Chekhovs' remained absolute: there was literally no outside. When towards the end of *Vanya* the other characters leave, and only he and Sonja stay back on the estate, sitting on the bench in the midst of their files and folders, the other performers remained on stage, turned towards the side wall stage-left, where they visible created the sounds of departing horses and coaches with coconut shells, rattles and bells. Everything in these performances was thus laid open, presented and never pretended.

Similar to Jessner's radical abstraction, Gosch's *Regie* established a relation to the text through reduction and withdrawal, hence through gestures of negativity. He only afforded the text a minimal 'plasticity'. By cutting out or painting over any scenic context and putting the performers into empty boxes, Gosch's performances approximated the laminar two-dimensionality of a relief. This effect most directly evokes Malabou's description of Hegelian plasticity introduced in the previous chapter, as receiving as well as giving form. The formal rhythm, kinetic body and aisthetic sensuality generated by these scenic spaces that were cleared of the logic of medial representation provided negative presentation. They offered in the static arrest of the play a grasp of the text's 'concrete universality', a physical, sensory grasp in the sense of the German word *begreifen*, which highlights the tactility of comprehension, which complements the plasticity of dialectic thinking. This theatrical situation thus bears the marks of what Alain Badiou calls a 'truth-event' (Badiou [1988] 2005a). Discussing Mallarmé's work, he argued that 'truth-events' emerge precisely from radical reduction, if not the negation, of mimetic realism as well as from the subtraction of any superficial expressivity. They take place right 'on the edge of the void' (Puchner 2009, 262); this certainly describes the spectators' position *vis-à-vis* Schütz's empty box-sets. These gigantic monochrome voids – the fertile emptiness of the *Vanya* stage, the material nothingness of the pitch-black *Seagull* environment – provided backgrounds for a Schillerian 'play' of and with the play(text): for the 'true' drama, the tragedy, to emerge.

Gosch frequently spoke of the inspiration he drew from watching his two youngest children play completely immersed and without inhibition in the playground. For his productions, he sought for a similar sense of pure, real play and the liberty it engenders. 'This is wrong, this is theatre', was the director's most common feedback in rehearsal. The ultimate reality – the theatral present – thus enveloped the presented performance and the fiction of Chekhov's plot and character at all times. It was made palpable, in every single moment. In its full ambiguity of showing and gazing, of meaning, moving and sensing, it guided the peculiar, playful encounter Gosch's *Regie* facilitated between characters, performers and the public. What most actors, just as others who met the director in his final years, remember most about the late director is – silence. By all accounts, Gosch remained a distant observer. He never got up on stage himself to demonstrate a scene. Instead he watched, mostly silent. He never aimed at 'fixing' a scene, solving it, finding a solution that could then be readily reproduced each night of the performance. His invitation, even demand, to 'play' resulted at times in excess: one may think of the nudity in *Macbeth*, but also of some (as the performers confirm) genuine brawls and scuffles, for instance between Trigorin and Arkadina in *The Seagull*. Their relationship was given a rather different dynamic through Gosch's casting choice. Corinna Harfouch as Arkadina showed a middle-aged woman full of energy, who entertains Trigorin as her 'toyboy' playwright-lover, who is the same age as her own son, the failing writer Kostya. In their scenes, the actors let a violence short of cruelty erupt, which is usually kept beneath the surface of Chekhov's text.

In his later years, Jürgen Gosch thus reinvented his approach to *Regie*. After his move to the West, he had become a constant presence at major theatres, yet towards the late 1980s his star gradually faded along with those of Stein, Zadek and other *Regietheater* protagonists. Gosch's tenure as artistic director of the Berlin Schaubühne, where he succeeded Peter Stein and Luc Bondy, ended only a few months into his inaugural season in 1987/88 with a catastrophic failure. His own debut production at this prominent hothouse of 1970s *Regietheater*, of all plays, another *Macbeth*, was condemned by theatre critics, while audiences left in droves during the four-hour show, and it was soon cancelled. Gosch resigned, and withdrew from German theatre for almost a decade, directing for Toneelgroep Amsterdam during this period. Here, he encountered a different approach to acting and performing that was formative for his late work. It seems ironic (or, maybe, necessary) that another *Macbeth* marked his comeback to German theatre more than fifteen years later.[7] 'My most confident times were my worst', Gosch said in retrospect (quoted in Wilms 2008, 114). He frequently referred back to a specific turning point. Working in Hamburg in 2002, an actor complained to him that the rehearsals had become an administrative act of organising the performance, making it 'weathertight' for the first night, while losing all courage to experiment and try things out (Gosch 2004, 91). The critique chimed with Gosch's own growing weariness of coming into rehearsal with his ready-made vision of the production. At this point, he made a significant last-minute change, just days before the opening night: all performers would be present on stage for the entire performance, whether their character was in any one scene or not – one of the devices that would, from then on, remain a signature of his late work. For his next production the year after, Shakespeare's *As You Like It*, Gosch made an even more radical decision: to go into rehearsal without casting any of the selected actors in a specific role. Instead, everyone, male and female actors alike, was allowed to try any role in rehearsal; it was agreed that the performers would be able to secure the role they wanted to play by showing the most effort and determination.

The resulting dynamics between the actors proved to be uncontrollable: after only four performances, the actors even refused to go on stage together again. Once more, a Gosch production disappeared from the playbills early, but this time to a productive effect. While being clear about the failures of this all too radical attempt, Gosch also cherished its value.[8] Once he found the congenial frame of Schütz's empty playing fields, these fostered, like some form of theatral test-tube, the mode of presentation Gosch sought: they allowed for play that was organic, in the sense that it was not cultivated, trimmed and harmonious, but resembled unconstrained wilderness and was in the process of constant growth. Going beyond conventions and expectations, it seemed akin to Eugenio Barba's idea of living 'scenic bios'. As the actors confirm, the peculiar energy of 'free play' in rehearsal carried into the run of these productions in the theatre's repertoire. Even after years of playing (at the time of writing in spring 2014, both *Vanya* and *The Seagull* are still in repertoire at the Deutsches Theater), actor Ulrich Matthes – who plays the lead role of *Vanya* – stresses that he still feels the reverberations from this way of rehearsing, 'that nothing has become fixed, but that you still relate to your acting partner anew, react in a new way. This openness, which Gosch somehow instils, keeps the productions so playful' (quoted in Behrendt *et al.* 2008, 100).

Importantly, this 'biotic' and playful encounter with the text integrated both performers *and* spectators, albeit in clearly distinct, designated roles. Gosch's late productions can indeed be described as a community together in play, maybe even a communion in the joint time and joint space of theatre. This common encounter is effectively facilitated – not on the basis of much-invoked 'interactivity', but because the boundaries between performance and audience are respected. The material box-sets of Gosch's Chekhov productions fully enclosed the performers, who entered *in communis* at the beginning and after the interval, via steps from the front row of the audience. They remained present throughout. In *Vanya*, those not in the present scene lined up in a row against the side walls, mostly stage-left. Some faced the wall, others watched the scene.[9] Between the acts, they changed the scene, and their costumes, themselves; each actor had their own little plastic box that contained all their props and costumes, and which was stored right underneath the apron of the stage during the scenes. The interplay of visibility, of looks, watching and averted gazes was even more prominently exploited in *The Seagull*, this play about theatre, as those who were not in the scene sat on the step at the back and very visibly watched the performance. And already in the earlier *Macbeth*, those actors who were not in the scene again took their seat in the front row and became audience, too.

The audience, meanwhile, was equally enveloped by this peculiar atmosphere of a community-communion. The effect was heightened by very concrete means.

Schütz's box-sets literally pushed the actors' play right to the front of the stage; his constructions, like the *Vanya* set, often spilled over the proscenium and covered the front rows of the stalls (see Figure 6 above). The houselights remained on for most of the performance, while Gosch's lighting designers also invented quite specific modes of lighting the productions. Both Chekhovs were lit frontally. Instead of the standard theatre lighting, one gigantic lamp, similar to a lantern in a lighthouse, was placed in the back row of the stalls, engulfing both the audience and the stage in a shared beam of (at times blinding) light, which projected long shadows against the walls of the *Vanya* box. In the second act of that production, the sleepless night, a carefully focused quadrant of light fell into the box from a spotlight in the dress circle, whereas the play's fourth act was solely lit with footlights, no longer from beyond the stage. Just like the set itself, this lighting – in all its evocative and emotive variability – did not directly represent (daylight, moonlight …) or symbolise anything: it was pure theatral play with the visceral, kinetic and aisthetic intensity of light.

Performing in these productions, as well as spectating them, shifted the attention to the ultimate present of the moment. This is confirmed by actor Ulrich Matthes: 'With Gosch, everything is totally focused on the moment of a situation. On whether it has a certain truthfulness, or, maybe a less grand word: whether it has reality' (quoted in Behrendt *et al.* 2008, 97). As a prerequisite for the emergence of these ultimately true and real moments, every detail in the situation had to be 'true' and 'real' in itself. During their eight-week rehearsal time for *Vanya*, the actors worked, from the start, in a mock-up of Schütz's set in its original dimensions, and rather than discussing intentions and interpretations, Gosch worked religiously through the text, starting with the first sentence of the first scene. Once they had come to the end of the play, after a few days or even weeks, they would start again from the beginning, again in full chronological order. Gosch would never rehearse a particular scene out of order, or repeat a scene. If an actor whose character was in the scene was unable to attend, the whole rehearsal would be cancelled. Gosch became close to being obsessive; the actors remember that during one rehearsal of *Vanya*, they waited for several hours for the design assistant to get the right sort of cheese, mentioned in a stage direction, from a delicatessen, as Gosch was unhappy with the cheese originally brought in from the theatre canteen. Another time, he rejected several bouquets of roses to find the right, perfect colour, and would not contemplate rehearsing the scene with some stand-in plastic bouquet. Once more, the actors had to wait – not unlike the typical Chekhov character. Truth would only emerge from direct simplicity and the objectivity of the 'silent speech' of things themselves, not from an intellectually devised concept imposed on them, and most certainly not from theatrical pretending.

In order to achieve the truthfulness he strove for, Gosch gave his actors great freedom, in rehearsal and even after the premiere. But he demanded ultimate commitment and expected that the performers abandon any reservations and inhibitions about 'playing'. According to Matthes: 'He calls on you to have the heart to do something, in every respect – emotionally, physically' (Matthes, in Kümmel 2009). The provocative nudity; the playful, at times even violent stage fights; the monstrous emptiness: as Gosch expressed it, 'there should be in every production somehow such a moment where one crosses a certain border. Where in all crassness and knowing that one actually must not do it, one transcends the limit' (Gosch, in Kümmel 2009). Importantly, he added: 'one cannot achieve such moments by mystifying, but only by using very concrete, very real means. It is in their sum that they can effect a certain tremor of time' (Gosch, in Kümmel 2009). Such a 'tremor of time' is characteristic for a Hegelian speculative truth that is based on immanent contradictions, and which 'counts in' the concrete actualisation (the reality of *thea*, of performing and spectating) in all its partiality: in this sense, *das Wahre ist das Ganze*, truth is the whole, as Hegel maintained (Hegel 1986a, 24). Such a dialectic totality is never ultimately fixed, but remains in a state of constant becoming; its name is play. Gosch's *Regie* facilitated this play by releasing the playtext into an empty void that was freed from mechanistic means of reproduction and instead predicated on strategies of withdrawing, reducing, clearing and cleansing to the point of clear and simple emptiness.

Dissecting the essence of the playtext: Michael Thalheimer

Praised by Hans-Thies Lehmann for his productive reinvigoration of the concept of tragedy for our age as 'one of the most brilliant talents in contemporary theatre' (Lehmann 2011, 87), Michael Thalheimer is perhaps best known for condensing classical plays to their compact 'pulsating core' (see Thalheimer 2008). While any plot line, scene, dialogue or even character which obscures a clear vision of this core, or 'essence' (a term the director frequently uses), risks deletion in his tightly composed productions, at the same time he remains almost religious about the text. Displaying the speculative dialectics typical of *Regie*, Thalheimer keeps stressing that although he makes some cuts, he never alters a line, adds other texts (as often happened in the German deconstructionist theatre of the 1990s) or even modernises the language:

> There is absolutely no changing or altering of texts in my work. I stay true to the texts. … My interest is to see what kind of frictions arise from working with texts from a hundred years ago, like Wedekind's, or from antiquity, almost two thousand years ago – to see what happens if such a text is used in contemporary times, as understood by contemporary people. Does that text still have currency and validity today? That is the essence, or aim of theater: to work with this friction within a text that has been around for a long time, and to see how it behaves, what that text can do, and how it can develop in contemporary times, rather than amending things from a contemporary perspective. There's also this pleasure in the original words. When you read Goethe, or Shakespeare, or Wedekind, the language is amazing and powerful if compared to contemporary language. There's also the way that writers have invented characters, the setup, the whole play; that needs to be respected rather than changed. (quoted in Levine 2007; translation amended)

Crucially, of course, Thalheimer contests the assumption that being 'true to the text' is achieved by both speaking every word as written down by the playwright and illustrating the plot and the prescribed actions literally and realistically. Speaking about his work, he instead repeatedly opposes becoming 'a slave to the text' to being 'true to the work' (see Levine 2007).

For Thalheimer, the true essential 'intentions' of the work are situated on a level beyond the scripted surface of the text. He conceives of dialogue, the plot and characters first and foremost as the dramaturgic expression of this underlying intent, which aims for a specific reaction from the audience. He believes, therefore, that the director's task is to make this emotional underpinning fully available to a contemporary audience's experience – especially where this runs against standard expectations and conventions, which only testify to the appropriation of the plays as 'cultural capital' and affirm the values and ideology of a middle-class *Bildungsbürgertum* spectatorship. Purely literal illustrations of a playtext, far from being 'truthful', according to Thalheimer, contain the explosive dynamics which are for him at the very heart of theatre:

> Only if we manage to seriously translate into our own present time the past emotional response, which Schiller, Goethe or Lessing created, only then are all the subsidies and the tax-payers' money justified. Theatre, for me, is the space for a debate that is poignant and that hurts. All those playwrights wrote their pieces back then on the verge of crying out loud, driven by rage and willing to provoke a response right there and then. And rage, breaking boundaries and crying out – that must still be today what it is all about! (quoted in Schütt 2004, 19)

Thalheimer, more often than not, manages to capture and amplify these tense dynamics which often lie dormant, especially in a well-known classic such as *Faust* or Hauptmann's naturalist plays, some of which were censored at their first production. There is hardly a Thalheimer production that doesn't touch a nerve. Not only has there been a remarkable concentrated silence in the auditorium at many of the performances I have attended, free from the usual coughing or rustling of sweetwrappers, but also these tensions (especially in earlier productions) frequently quite literally erupted, with audience members yelling at the stage and slamming doors, including the mayor of Hamburg. At the same time, I even witnessed initially unruly school groups in the audience getting drawn into the production, sharing a very affective aisthetic response to the radically abstract production values with other audience members.

Following the breakthrough success with the scandal-prone *Liliom* in 2000, only Thalheimer's fifth work as a director, he rapidly became a 'shooting star' in German theatre. He worked mainly at Hamburg's Thalia Theater (until 2008) and after that, like Gosch, at the Deutsches Theater Berlin under Bernd Wilms's artistic direction. There, he produced his seminal takes on Lessing's *Emilia Galotti* and the two parts of Goethe's *Faust* (see Boenisch 2008; van den Berg 2007). When Oliver Reese, his congenial dramaturg on these productions, was himself appointed artistic director at Schauspiel Frankfurt in 2009, it became Thalheimer's new home of choice, before he moved to the Berlin Schaubühne in 2013. At Schauspiel Frankfurt, Thalheimer and Reese continued their explorations of German classics with a strikingly sharp production of Schiller's *Maria Stuart* (2011), while also returning to their venture into Greek tragedy, which began in 2006 with the *Oresteia* at Berlin. They combined *Oedipus Rex* and *Antigone*, thus merging the Sophoclean myth of the House of Labdacus into a four-hour-long production (2009), where the two individual plays became logical companions, like the plays of the Aeschylus trilogy. This was followed by *Medea* in 2012. Throughout his career, Thalheimer has shown a particular penchant for modern classics: from *Woyzeck* (Thalia, 2003) to Ibsen (*The Wild Duck*, Deutsches Theater, 2008), Wedekind's *Lulu* (Thalia, 2004, shown in 2007 at New York's Brooklyn Academy of Music; see Kalb 2009; Levine 2007) and in particular German naturalist playwright Gerhart Hauptmann. Thalheimer staged his *Einsame Menschen* (*Lonely Lives*, Deutsches Theater, 2004), *Rose Bernd* (Thalia, 2006), as well as *Die Ratten* and *Die Weber* (Deutsches Theater, 2007 and 2011 respectively).

Thalheimer's audio-visual imprint is as distinctive and identifiable as Gosch's. Where the latter's approach was primarily marked by the self-dependent, thoroughly committed play of his performers energised by the motor of Schütz's empty yet grand spatial situations, Thalheimer's work is characterised by its meticulously calibrated rhythm, which is particularly enhanced through his long-standing collaborations with both set designer Olaf Altmann and composer Bert Wrede. Thalheimer frequently uses the notion of 'score' (*Partitur*), and of 'scoring the text' to describe their collaboration (see Boenisch 2008, 34). A characteristic feature is the delivery of dialogue in a way that fully exploits paralinguistic dynamics: varied in speed and pitch and accompanied by a strategic orchestration of silence and of moments where a sentence or line is interrupted by a pause mid-sentence. This rupture then shifts the sense radically. In his Hauptmann productions, even the Silesian dialect was turned into a theatral device that functioned as an aisthetic trigger. It was no longer used to authenticate the *milieu*, as by Hauptmann, but the artificial delivery aspired towards a 'speech before words', to use Artaud's famous phrase from *Theatre and its Double*. It never, however, fully relinquished the power of meaning. In Thalheimer's *Regie*, speech thus acquires a new visceral force and seems to interrupt the Derridean 'closure of representation'. Conversely, the stylised verses – whether from Greek tragedy or German classics – lose their poetic 'cushion' and gain a razor-sharp, explosive poignancy. In his *Oresteia*, the chorus, placed in the theatre's upper circle, became a pure, faceless voice. The only line from the concluding *Eumenides* part of the trilogy to be spoken in Thalheimer's production was 'Peace for ever'. As final chorus chant, it resembled more a cruel threat than celebrating a resolution. The careful work on paralinguistic qualities and the delivery of lines also paid off in *Maria Stuart*, where – as one critic phrased it – the two protagonists 'talk daggers, forged from a red heat flow of iambic verse' (Weinzierl 2011). This effect was aided by a clever use of echoes and reverb effects, created without transmitting the actors' voices via microphones as other directors do.

In this carefully calibrated 'acoustic score' – Robert Wilson's terminology seems pertinent here as well – the dialogue, via its paralinguistic dimension, becomes part of a larger texture. The other vital components are the soundscapes, the often aggressively loud music and at times violent sound effects arranged by composer Bert Wrede (b. 1961). They usually offer a constant acoustic backdrop to the entire production.

Precisely calculated and calibrated, Wrede's music blasts earsplittingly from the speakers at times, then wavers almost indiscernibly in the background as if coming from far beyond the stage. Often, he uses a well-known pop or rock song as 'theme' for a production. He extracts short samples, isolating atomic sound fragments, which he then loops. Only gradually do they build up to the recognisable song – as in *Maria Stuart*, where he sampled an aching metallic scratch along a guitar string as recurring sound effect that punctuated the production.[10] The music thus reinforces a formal 'rule' which Thalheimer has employed since his early productions: just as the sound develops in patterned repetition, variation and a gradual build-up, so do signature 'catchphrases' allocated to characters (in earlier work, such as *Emilia Galotti*, they were often hammered home somewhat through constant reiteration), and equally a characteristic gestural figuration or physical action that externalises a character's 'character' in a visual emblem. To use *Maria Stuart* as an example again: Mortimer's somewhat slimy manoeuvring between the rival queens and his involvement in plots on either side was here physicalised through convulsions and physical tremors. The character was thus portrayed principally by corporeal means. Similarly, in *Emilia Galotti*, Prince Gonzaga's love-sick state of mind, which set Lessing's deadly bourgeois tragedy in motion, and which took Lessing an entire act to plot, was condensed into a silent visual and gestural tableau that became the overture to Thalheimer's production, again orchestrated by Wrede's soundtrack.

The actors' bodies are the link between the paralinguistic rhythm, the gestural score and the spatial energy generated in the vast, geometrically organised, non-illusionist spaces. The latter are designed by Olaf Altmann (b. 1966), who has been Thalheimer's scenographer of choice since his first directorial work in 1997. On the surface, his sets seem very simple; most of them exactly fit the measurements of the specific theatre and its proscenium, making touring impossible. Altmann's cubes and boxes are at times reminiscent of Johannes Schütz's environs for Jürgen Gosch, yet they are more than just a container for the actors' play. Characteristically, Altmann's scenic arrangement sections off a rigorously confined acting space, usually right downstage, and a scenic space behind (or above/around) it. Some of his designs make use of the full depth and even height of the theatre's proscenium, others restrain or even cover up the stage opening entirely. Anything that happens within this pictorial space – such as the geometrically shaped paths, proxemic figurations or sightlines in *Emilia Galotti* or *Maria Stuart* – only serves to enhance a dynamic thrust towards the forestage as an energetic 'vector', to use Pavis's apt term. These sets do not so much serve a 'visual' theatre, as Klaus van den Berg suggested (van den Berg 2007), but rather have a direct physical impact on the performers. This was taken to extremes in Altmann's design for Hauptmann's *Ratten*, where the proscenium opening was contracted to a five-foot-high quadrant: a rat cage in which none of the characters was even able to stand up straight (see Figure 7). In his *Tartuffe* (Schaubühne Berlin, 2014), the action took place within a narrow cube which rotated very slowly in the vertical, so that the furniture – and with it, some actors – eventually hung from the ceiling. Elsewhere, he erected a steep diagonal on the revolve for Ibsen's *Wild Duck* which the performers had to climb precariously, and in the *Oresteia*, he positioned a very narrow forestage as sole space for the actors to perform in front of a gigantic

Figure 7 A pictorial space that has physical impact on the actors: Michael Thalheimer's production of Hauptmann's *Rats* (Deutsches Theater Berlin, 2007; set design: Olaf Altmann). Photo: Barbara Braun.

wooden wall that again closed up the entire height and width of the proscenium (see Figure 8). In its later variation for *Oedipus/Antigone* in Frankfurt, it even enwrapped the front rows of the auditorium to both sides.

At all times, the theatrical energy is thus propelled into the auditorium. This has an effect similar to Gosch's late productions, where all action equally took place at the very front of the stage. However, whereas Gosch preserved (and even heightened) an essentially realist kernel of (physical, gestural and vocal/paralinguistic) acting within the abstract surroundings of Schütz's sets, Thalheimer's performers are usually lined up right downstage. As a rule, they deliver all speeches, including the dialogues, facing the audience rather than their fictional partner of the conversation. At times the speeches are truncated by pauses, which allow for a brief corporeal tableau directed at or engaging with the partner in the fictional world. Most of the time, speaking and physical action remain separated. The pictorial reduction and isolation of action result in a precise focalisation. The defined corporeal gestures, concentrated physical figurations and the often oddly colourful costumes that stand out against the huge uniform material of the set with its wide even surfaces, whether made from blond natural wood, white fabric or simply an almost dark, entirely empty stage, all contribute to a powerful effect of kinetic plasticity. It is because of this plasticity that, for instance, the liquidity and viscosity of red stage blood, including traces from previous performances that notably mark the wooden stage walls of Thalheimer's Greek tragedies from the start, gain their punching, visceral impact (see Figure 8). This is not blood (or, in other contexts, sex or excrements) as component of a realistic representation, nor even as a strictly metaphoric or symbolic theatrical sign. Instead, a Badiouian 'truth-event' manifests itself, as statuesque performing bodies shout, whisper or rush through the text in rhythmical compositions that are reinforced by soundtracks of eternally looped musical fragments, and the simple pictoriality of the red blood and blood-stained bodies against the blond wood enhances the visceral and sensory intensity. It makes us feel and sense the theatrical truth of a 'real' tragedy

Figure 8 Propelling the theatral energy of a 'truth-event' right into the auditorium: Olaf Altmann's set design for Michael Thalheimer's *Orestie* covered the entire proscenium arch of the theatre with a flat, wooden wall (Deutsches Theater Berlin, 2006). Photo: Iko Freese.

beyond clichés and stereotypical patterns, thus evoking catharsis, even: precisely that which we so rarely feel as a result of being bombarded with most horrific news, images of brutality in films, rape and bloodshed on TV or in computer games. A truth that reaches beyond the plot of the play and its representation becomes sense-able.

More than the original: the subjective truth of the text

The concise abstraction and negative reduction of Gosch's and Thalheimer's *Regie* points us towards a different politics of truth and re-presentation. It outlines a notion of truth that, rather than waiting in the text to be excavated, opens up only in the very processes of theatral actualisation, in a typically Hegelian gesture of retroactive positing. The true Idea of the play emerges in, as Žižek puts it following Hegel and Lacan, its very *appearance as appearance* (*Erscheinung als Schein*, apparition). Against the Platonian dismissal of art as (secondary) copy of the (first) copy of the Idea that is material reality, he insists that the Idea requires this relational distance between reality and copy to appear. It hence emerges from another triangular relation field: 'the Idea is something that *appears* when reality (the first-level copy or imitation of the Idea) is itself copied. It is that which is in the copy more than the original itself' (Žižek 2012, 375; original emphasis). Following this perspective, I argue that the playtext must be 'copied' in performance in order to make its 'essential truth' appear. There is no other, 'original' substantial essence, no fundamental truth of the text beyond or before its 'appearing' in play (see also Chapter 6 below). The truth is, precisely, not in the play, but it is out there. As Jacques-Allain Miller expresses it in Lacanian terms, 'essence is this structure in which the most interior is conjoined to the most exterior in its turning' (Miller 2007, 17).

Thalheimer's and Gosch's *Regie* accordingly no longer delivers signs that depict situations and seek to authenticate a fictional situation. Instead, it ties together and relates the internal core of the play and the most external moment of the performance's ultimate present. It thereby actualises the appearance of the argument, the thesis, the problem and the Idea, which the plot of the play itself expressed as its first 'copy'. *Regie* makes tangible, as apparition, what is 'in the copy more than the original itself.' This surplus is no external addition, but rather the appearance of the immanent 'concrete universality' of the text. Following Alain Badiou, the sense of the play is therefore 'not a sign for something that lies outside its form' (Badiou 2006, 45). The 'truthfulness' of a performance thus cannot be measured through external comparison, either, not even with the playtext. It is a strictly immanent 'figure of consciousness', as evoked by Hegel in the Preface to his *Phenomenology*. As such, it must, however, acknowledge – be conscious of – the process of its own actualisation and enunciation, hence its own relation to the text. True 'fidelity' can only be measured against this consciousness of the unavoidable partiality of our own position and our involvement in the appearance of this truth. This is the true responsibility of *Regie* – to the truth and actuality of its own process.

The strong theatral form in the works of Gosch and Thalheimer, the gestures of withdrawal, reduction and negativity that characterise their work, exemplarily transcends mimetic mirroring, direct reference or pure illustration. It is far more than the expression or translation of the (thematic) content of the plot but a theatral engine to release the abstract truth of the text in performance, facilitating the coordinated 'concretisation' of this otherwise abstract truth through the theatral dynamics of movement, perception and meaning. This truth of the text is thereby afforded a specifically theatral presence, which is notably different from the effect of presence that underwrites the logic of representation. The latter relies, as Jacques Derrida argued, on the authority of an absent 'master' *outside* the field, who 'governs it from a distance' (Derrida 2001, 296). He describes Artaud's theatre of cruelty as an attempt to foreclose this distance and to produce instead a form of presence which Derrida calls a 'nontheological space' (296). In contrast to Artaud, and even more so to some of his followers throughout the twentieth century, Regie in the early twenty-first century no longer naïvely believes in achieving a 'triumph of pure *mise en scène*' by simply dispensing of the dramatic text. The truly 'nontheological' present is relational. As a third term that completes the theatral triangle of performing and spectating, the text remains vital, even a prerequisite for arriving at a position of distancing which is crucial in allowing for Schillerian play in its aspiration for true liberty. Importantly, this distance no longer suggests an outside perspective, the possibility of a critical overview from an objective distance that would similarly 'master' and 'govern' from the outside. Conventional spectating relations of understanding, empathy and identification as well as critical deconstruction had relied on precisely such a 'theological' (or, in simpler terms, ideological) notion of 'objective distance'. It is the same position that facilitates the consumption of spectacular commodities produced by the omnipresent digital media industry – the much-evoked 'freedom of the consumer', which could not be further from Schillerian liberty of play.

The finely calibrated stage arrangements of Thalheimer's and Gosch's productions engage in complex ways with the realisation of such different spectatorial relations in the theatral encounter between the text, the production and the public. As we have seen in this chapter, the theatral dynamics of their *Regie* permeate the entire, 'common' theatre space of stage *and* auditorium, emphasising the shared community in a shared time and space. The prominence of the spectatorial frame is erased and the marked border of the proscenium frame overwritten, thereby destabilising the position of 'objective distance' opposite and outside the performance. And still, the spectators remain 'counted out': our spectatorial position is always kept at its reflexive distance. This is, crucially, no longer the distance that allows us to own, know, command, direct and dictate the 'object to watch'. The voyeuristic gaze of appropriation and consumption is replaced with a spectatorial relation of pure *thea*, which involves both the positions of directing and spectating. Conversely, thus, a *Regie* committed to this immanent truth cannot be grasped by the standard idea of a 'directorial concept' that imposes itself onto the play. Rather, Thalheimer's and Gosch's *Regie* 'thinks' in purely theatral terms, as Hans-Thies Lehmann asserts:

> When this position of directing is again and again accused of 'conceptionalism', one has to counter that this concept is precisely one which attempts to block the merely 'conceptual'

(that can be so often found in merely imposed dramaturgic 'ideas') and instead emphatically articulates what can purely be thought in and through elements of the theatre. (Lehmann 2011, 94)

This emphatic embracing of 'theatral thinking' is among the most prominent aspects of a *Regie* that aims for the speculative truth of text, a truth that appears only in the triangulation of the text, its concrete actualisation and the spectating public. In order to describe the strategic thinking of a *Regie* that reduces, condenses, even withholds the text against conventions of medial representation and thereby aligns the force of theatral thinking with a different, speculative form of mediation, I previously proposed the term 'theatre of ex-position' (see Boenisch 2008).[11] It strategically 'exposes' the dramatic, inner intensities of a play that lie beyond the surface of words. Further, it 'exposes' the public to the physical and visceral, sensory experience of the text's particular energy. As a result, the classical texts themselves are brought out of their standard position within the canon, and become thus 'ex-positioned', too.

The notion of 'the truth of a playtext' makes sense only when it is thought within such a framework of ex-position, which asserts that this truth is inevitably *our* truth. This is not an invitation to free-for-all, do-what-you-like directing, but on the contrary implies our duty to be truthful, and take responsibility for our participation and intervention in the dialectic act of mediation. This radically asserted, 'exposed' particularity and subjectivity negates the assumption of 'objective' representation, and counters the myth of a 'simple', transparent and singular 'true' representation of a text. The director who poses as the text or playwright's humble instrument, who considers himself as 'simply staging' the text, without taking an interpretive stance, in fact commits the most violent intervention. The idea of entirely transparent and invisible representation obfuscates its own excessive traces, if not hubris, of a directorial position that seeks to speak for and act on behalf of the 'truth of the text' it defines in the first place. Truth is not accurate, exact, nor singular and objective. It is not a matter of 'knowing it all' and understanding. For this reason, and especially in the theatre, we should forcefully reject allegations that a subjective, 'interested' perspective *distorts* the truth. We should retort, with Žižek, that 'it is the allegedly "objective", "impartial" gaze that is not in fact neutral but already partial – that is, the gaze of the winners, of the ruling classes' (Žižek 1999, 137).

The 'true truth' of the text has its site in what Badiou calls 'subject language': in an engaged, subjective perspective that permeates 'objective' structures, an interested viewpoint which insists on its fidelity to the truth-event, and takes full responsibility for its own standpoint and intervention. In its ultimate partiality and partisanship, such an approach to directing texts reinstates the 'essential' visceral vitality (hence, the theatrical truth) of the play's idea, while it is always prepared to face the risk of error. As Gosch expressed it in his final interview: 'Only by unswervingly investing knowledge, shamelessness and the readiness to err, there will be hope for a pay-off' (quoted in Kümmel 2009). It is thus that the 'thinking of representation' that is *Regie*, according to Badiou, is 'truthfully' elevated to 'an event of thought' (Badiou 2005b, 72). *Regie* discloses itself as a process of thinking, comprehension and insight into the narrative and drama, and its truth: a truth that 'should not be the narrative of what happens, but the cognition [*Erkenntnis*] of what is true in it, and of what is true, it should comprehend [*begreifen*] what in the narrative seems a mere happening [*Geschehen*]' (Hegel 1986b, 260).

Notes

1 Lottmann (2006, here pp. 164, 167). See also the response by theatre critic Wolfgang Höbel (2006). More recently, in 2009, Lottmann's younger novelist colleague Daniel Kehlmann, son of the less prominent German director Michael Kehlmann, was invited to give the opening speech at the prestigious Salzburger Festspiele summer theatre festival. On this occasion, he held the country's *Regietheater*, from Piscator and Brecht to Thalheimer, to task for his father's failed career in theatre (Kehlmann 2009). One of the directors attacked in the speech, Nicolas Stemann, responded in another newspaper (2009).
2 Both of the incriminated productions were in fact invited to Theatertreffen. In total, between 2000 and 2010, Gosch was voted eight times amongst the selected productions, Thalheimer six times.
3 Molnar's play is best known internationally in its musical adaptation by Rodgers and Hammerstein, *Carousel* (1945). On German stages, the play and its main character were particularly remembered in the portrayal by the popular Hamburg *Volksschauspieler* Hans Albers (1891–1960), both before and after the Nazi regime. This gave Thalheimer's Hamburg production particular poignancy.
4 Gosch eventually lost his long fight against cancer in the summer of 2009 while rehearsing Euripides' *Bacchae*. In his final years, he worked frantically at various theatres all over the German-speaking countries, directing in this period alone more than twenty productions: classics as well as opera and contemporary plays, in particular premiering new writing by German playwright Roland Schimmelpfennig, which the latter wrote specifically for Gosch to direct.
5 Gosch used full nudity in several of his late productions, including some of Schimmelpfennig's plays. In his final interview, Gosch commented:

> Sometimes I feel that the performers' nudity, the body, was able to tell something about the things we are dealing with. I am, however, only able to ask male actors to undress. One can never ask a woman to undress. … From memory, the use of nudity has worked best in my production of Roland Schimmelpfennig's *Im Reich der Tiere* [*translated as* Animal Kingdom; *the German title, however, also cites the name of a popular German animal series on television; premiere Deutsches Theater Berlin 2007, PMB*]. There, human beings literally transform on stage into animals. One cannot but deal, in the sense of the word, with the nudity of the creature. (Quoted in Kümmel 2009)

6 Schütz was a student of Wilfried Minks, the revolutionary designer who had supported the *Regietheater* directors of the 1960s and 1970s. He had worked with Gosch several times in the past, yet only after their Düsseldorf production of Gorky's *Summerfolk* in 2003/4, which won Gosch the first Theatertreffen nomination after an interval of twenty-one years, would Schütz properly become the director's second permanent artistic partner, following the death of Axel Manthey in 1995, with whom Gosch previously collaborated as regular partner (see Thiele 2008).
7 Actor Ernst Stötzner performed in both productions: as Malcolm in the 1987 Schaubühne version, and playing multiple roles as witch, King Duncan and Macduff in the 2005 production.
8 The director restaged the play in 2007 at Schauspiel Hannover.

9   Ulrich Matthes commented on this peculiar continuing presence:

    It all developed very slowly and without any direction. Where we change, where we are, when we are not on, which props we use. The bizarre thing about it was that [Gosch] never – never! – told us how we were meant to stand on the wall; whether we were supposed to look at each other, what we should do. We are often asked in post-performance talks whether we are there 'privately', or 'in character'. That was something each of us has to feel or find for himself. (Behrendt *et al.* 2008, 96)

10 Wrede's website www.bwrede.de/ documents some of his work for Thalheimer and other German directors. The *Maria Stuart* 'theme' can also be listened to, www.bwrede.de/mp3/BUEHNE/MariaStuart.mp3, accessed 10 August 2013.

11 The notion of 'exposure' is, in a very similar sense, crucial within Mieke Bal's critical framework of 'cultural analysis' (see Bal 1996).

6

Seeing what is coming: on *Regie*, playing and appearing

It was an entirely impossible scene, or at least it should have been. There was a bed and two tables. On one table there were two old-fashioned telephones and a coffee cup, and on the other was a typewriter. Paper was spread across the tables and the floor. I counted thirteen chairs. And eight people, four men, four women, who were virtually undistinguishable as they were all dressed identically in black suits, with white make-up on their face, each wearing a moustache. One of them was lying on the bed, another typed at the desk, another drank coffee. The audience, seated in the auditorium of the Munich Kammerspiele, watched this entire scene from above. It was no optical illusion. For his 2008 theatre adaptation of Franz Kafka's *Der Prozess* (*The Trial*), which toured numerous festivals, including the Vienna Festwochen and the Festival d'Avignon, and won several theatre prizes, German director and set designer Andreas Kriegenburg (b. 1963) built this incredible out-of-joint set on a revolving stage that was suspended vertically. The tables, bed and chairs were mounted on a disk of dark wood, which turned slowly and perpetually. It was inserted within an oval cylinder which was cast of white plaster and covered most of the proscenium space. The performers climbed through this mobile space, also persistently on the move, carefully rebalancing their precarious positions against gravity, clinging to the chairs, the tables, the bed (see Figure 12). In the course of this production, the spinning disk tipped back, and the only light fell from high above behind this opening. It was no wonder that many reviewers and spectators interpreted the set as an eye watching the theatre spectators – the proverbial 'eye of the Law' in the German language, evoking the authorities that are constantly watching.[1] In the end, when K. died, the disk tilted back into its upright position, closing the eye, and closing out any light, cloaking the theatre in pitch-black.

Where strategies of ex-position, which were discussed in the previous chapter, emphasised their 'negative' distance, Kriegenburg's work stands exemplarily for a mode of *Regie* that unreservedly invests in theatral play. Yet at the same time, and crucially for the dialectics of *Regie*, his work foregrounds the same reflexive distance between the watcher and the watched which we had encountered in Gosch's and Thalheimer's productions. As spectators, we are drawn into the play, but are simultaneously kept at an unbridgeable distance. As it took some effort on our part to adjust our spectatorial sensory cognition to the spectacularly disorienting perspective of *Der Prozess*, we were confronted with our own activity of watching. And what we saw and experienced was palpably more than the 'signs' of the theatre image in front of us, in the old language of theatre semiotics. A kinetic and aisthetic surplus, triggered here by the perpendicular revolving set and the impossible perspective it introduced, took us beyond strictly functional and efficient representation. It engendered theatral play, an excess of scenes and senses, of seeing and sensing, which marks the very *limen* of representation. In Kriegenburg's *Regie*, this theatral excess becomes the principal agent for the actualisation of the play-text as play-performance. The moments of theatral playfulness open up an experiential plane of virtuality, in the Artaudian–Deleuzian sense of a potentiality pregnant with possibilities. It supports what philosopher Martin Seel calls an 'aesthetics of appearing' (Seel 2003). In his perspective, too, artworks never exhaust themselves at the level of artistic imagination or the creation of fictional worlds. The sensory investment and the kinetic encounter in the very moment of aisthetic 'appearing' (*Erscheinen*) cannot be separated and simply be bracketed off as (secondary) 'reception' of an assumedly 'finished' and closed work of art.

Artworks, for Seel, ultimately gain their 'sense' only as 'genuine events of appearing' (48). They foreground the moment of appearing, of *becoming* sensible, and hence of the core process of theatralisation that Erika Fischer-Lichte captures with her notion of 'the performative' (Fischer-Lichte 2008). Seel's position certainly resonates with the idea of theatre's 'emergent meaning', spawned by a self-generating 'autopoietic feedback loop' that is triggered in the theatral encounter of performance and audience, as posited in Fischer-Lichte's post-semiotic 'aesthetics of performativity' (39 and 138f.).[2] Importantly, the emphasis on playful appearing countervails the production as well as consumption of the performance as spectacular commodity – the production of a closed interpretation, a crafted staging and creative spectacle. Instead, *Regie* instigates a process of negotiation, in which performers and spectators likewise take part. Where the text is no longer 'mastered' by the authority of the director and his craft, neither performers nor spectators are able to renounce their individual responsibility of par(t)-taking in the play by simply 'serving', which would mean relinquishing or even delegating this responsibility to 'the Master'.

One can barely find a more pertinent example of such 'responsible negotiations' of a playtext that facilitate the playful appearing of well-known dramatic texts than the work of tg STAN. The Flemish 'theatre players' cooperative' (the literal translation for 'toneelspelersgezelschap', the 'tg' of their name), which formed in 1989, has never employed a director in twenty-five years. Frank Vercruyssen, Jolente de Keersmaeker (sister of prominent choreographer Anne Teresa, with whose company Rosas STAN collaborated on several productions), Damiaan de Schrijver and Sara de Roo, the four core members of the Antwerp-based company, form a collective of equals. With their productions of modern and contemporary drama classics such as Chekhov, Ibsen and the Austrian Thomas Bernhard, they continue a typically Dutch and Flemish variant of theatral 'collective creation' that never renounced the tradition of canonical drama, unlike the approach of 'devised theatre' which contemporaneously emerged in the UK (see Heddon and Milling 2006).[3] Instead, the canonical playtexts are brought into 'appearing' through the dynamics of theatral play, where surprising and contingent effects (events) of play emerge, which suspend the strict logic of authority and representation. Neither 'authorised' by the director nor entirely underwritten by the text, the play triggered by STAN's (and in different ways by Kriegenburg's) *Regie* thus always appears as something that is, to paraphrase a central Lacanian formula, 'more in the text than the text itself': it is not 'owned' or 'willed' as in the mode of representation. *JDX – A Public Enemy*, tg STAN's 1993 production after Ibsen's *An Enemy of the People*, demonstrated this unique theatral play in their work in a particularly pure and compact way.[4] It was performed on an empty stage in front of the theatre's bare walls. Without any props, the four performers shared all the roles of the play, apart from Frank Vercruyssen, who played only Ibsen's protagonist, doctor Thomas Stockmann, who discovers that the wells supplying the city's profitable spa centre are poisoned. Downstage right, behind a small table, sat a very visible prompter, often a well-known guest performer from another theatre company (see Figure 9). He or she read out Ibsen's stage directions and many of the speech headings. These were necessary prompts for the audience, too, since de Keersmaeker and de Roo in some scenes changed the character they were playing from line to line, at times even swapping them. Vercruyssen, in particular, fired off his text at breakneck speed, like a cascade of words. The playtext thus gained a kinetic materiality of its own.

Typically for tg STAN's performances, there was no fixed blocking; the performers were free to decide their actions in the moment. What happened on stage changed each night: the speed, the dynamics between the characters, the proxemic energy, even the entire mood of certain scenes. While it is certainly true of any performance, it was thus even more highlighted here that the playtext is necessarily actualised on each and every night. The performers, rather than representing characters, here functioned as the *Fremdkörper* that Schiller evoked in his experiment of the chorus: they introduced playful moments of contingency into this actualisation. As they negotiate the text in the very moment of its mediation, rather than repeating and 'executing' fixed directorial decisions, a genuinely theatral 'free play' is realised. As it includes the spectators as well, it anchors the playtext's universal dimension within a local, individual and particular context, without needing to make any overt references. As Damiaan de Schrijver notes:

> We try to get the dust off the texts without 'updating' them, because that already happens merely by speaking them on stage today. No, you really don't bring a text into the present by putting gel in your hair, wearing jeans and putting on sunglasses. At the end of the day, it is always about looking for and finding words and meanings that you yourself wouldn't

Figure 9 The playtext brought into appearing: Stijn van Opstal of fellow theatre company Olympique Dramatique as guest prompter in *JDX – A Public Enemy*, tg STAN's 1993 production of Ibsen's *An Enemy of the People*. The photo was taken at the anniversary revival of the production at Antwerp's Monty Theatre, where the production had premiered two decades earlier, in March 2014. Left: Damiaan de Schrijver as Mayor Peter Stockmann. Photo: tg STAN/Tim Wouters.

have been able to come up with. The fantastic thing about being a theatre player is to be able to give a voice to all these words, even if you don't agree with them. (Aerts 2014)

In 1993, *JDX* resonated with the political climate after the landslide victory of a racist party in local Antwerp elections. Twenty years later, the production had lost little of its political urgency, of its 'companionship' to the times in Jessner's sense. As the contemporary references were not locked in an act of representation, but instead emerged from the situation of theatral play, *JDX* offered to its 2014 audiences the same space to join the play with fresh associations about political events of today.

A similar strategy was at work in *Zomergasten*, tg STAN's production of Gorky's *Summerfolk* (2010). The play's get-together of a group of hedonistic intellectuals who feel that something must happen, but who instead decide 'rather not to act' and keep talking and dining in their *dacha*, the sumptuous new summer home in the countryside, was equally full of open, playful contemporary resonances. The 1904 pre-Revolution play became a reflection of their as much as of our own self-inflicted powerlessness as intellectual *datchniki* who merely keep musing about political developments instead of taking action. De Schrijver explains the company's approach thus: 'You share the insight good writers have had and you try to put that across to the audience so that they have a better understanding of your motives and of the complexity of society' (in Demets 2004). Importantly, neither Ibsen nor Gorky's (in Hegelian terms) 'abstract universal' fiction or our own 'particular' current world of the twenty-first century collapsed. Instead, in its theatral play, tg STAN's performances made us 'look awry' at the dramatic fiction as well as at our reality. Taking Brechtian defamiliarisation to a further level and applying it to the theatre event as a whole, this strategy of exposed, self-reflexive theatral play makes strange *both* the well-known dramatic narrative *and* our immediate present-day world, including our very act of spectating.

As a result, the coordinates of the text appear from a new perspective, and the playtext is opened up for a fresh kinetic and aisthetic experience that reverberates with our own present. This was certainly true for the audience who watched *JDX* in 1993's Antwerp, yet also reflected the experience of watching Kriegenburg's *Prozess* or his production of Goethe's *Stella* (Schauspiel Frankfurt, 2011). Here, he established a new, genuinely touching relation to the excessive sentimental pathos of Goethe's drama through the very distance afforded by theatral playing.[5] Similarly, tg STAN's *Nora* (their production of Ibsen's *Doll's House*, 2012) managed to rid the familiar drama of standard preconceptions and expectations. The production allowed for the domestic tragedy of *both* Nora *and* Torvald to unfold. It again genuinely moved the audience as the final door slammed, leaving Helmer (again Vercruyssen in the lead) alone on the bare stage. Such affective impact on the spectator in the work of tg STAN and Kriegenburg results from an encounter with the playtext that throws the spectator right back on their own realities as theatre spectators. The direct flipside of the playful excess of appearing is the heightened reflexivity that is triggered by a dialectic play of and between realities, which decentres any fixed, one-sided perspective. In the live interaction between stage and auditorium (Fischer-Lichte speaks of the unique 'co-presence'), the two central factors of *thea* – of ostentatious performing and of sensible experiencing – are intensified and become far more than functional means towards an end (of meaning, interpretation, spectacle or another reified product of performance-making). Mediated by the theatral forces of movement, perception and meaning, both the performers' and the spectators' own sensory perception and experiential response are directly reflected, or better, projected into the text: this is the condition of its aesthetic appearing, which is orchestrated and 'put into (the) play' by *Regie*.

Capturing the reality of theatre: tg STAN

tg STAN's work resists any urge for illusion and stage realism. Typically, there are no illusionist sets, no period costumes, no attempts at realistically rendering the fictional world on stage. Frank Vercruyssen describes one of the central agreements of the collective as 'the decision that you don't let reality escape from stage' (in Winnacker and Peters 1999). As spectators of their performances, we likewise never escape from our own realities. While Kriegenburg typically maintains the conventional spatial separation between stage and auditorium, even escalates it to a puzzling confrontation as in *Der Prozess*, tg STAN often directly break through it. In *JDX*, they notably played towards the audience. In *Berenice*, their 2005 production of Jean Racine's 1670 tragedy, which tg STAN created with their long-term friends Forced Entertainment's Cathy Naden in the lead role, the audience was even seated on little stools right on the stage, in the middle of the action, with actors at times taking a seat next to us. Yet even here, as we were spatially 'immersed', our role remained clearly that of the audience: we were invited to take on and really *play* this role, consciously and thereby reflexively. As de Schrijver put it: 'In the end the audience is a player too. That is what we always say: we can never play without the audience as a player' (in Winnacker and Peters 1999). Yet this does not result in the much-evoked equation of theatre and ('real') life; the fictional world and the present of the performance are far from conflating. The performance remains marked as a special situation of *thea*, as serious play clearly distinct from everyday reality, while at the same time the sense of a boundary between reality and fiction becomes fluid and porous.

Not unlike Jürgen Gosch's work discussed in the previous chapter, the houselights stay on throughout many of their productions. Usually, the production begins as soon as the audience enters the auditorium. In *Zomergasten*, for instance, the spectators came from the foyer into a pitch-black space, where we were met by the performers, who were equipped with torches and led us to our seats. In *Nora*, lead actress Wine Dierickx – a member of fellow company Wunderbaum, and one of the many guests whom tg STAN regularly invite – walked through the theatre while the spectators were arriving, chatting informally in her role as Nora, pointing out the new leather sculptures the couple bought for their living-room, complimenting a female spectator on her dress and enquiring about the earrings, while also commenting on Torvald's suit, as Frank Vercruyssen walked across the stage. In some productions, there is a seamless fluidity around the start of the actual play. As *Nora*, which was co-produced with Portuguese and Norwegian theatres and included Portuguese actor Tiago Rodrigues as another guest in the cast, was performed in English throughout, the initial talk in local Flemish and the following switch into English resulted in a more notable break. Watching (especially as a Flemish audience) Flemish actors perform a play in English with Flemish surtitles again heightened our own spectatorial reflexive distance from the performance, while foregrounding the text as material. The effect resembled the prompter's presence and their announcement of Ibsen's scene instructions in *JDX*.

The time of this unconditionally playful actualisation of a text is the present of the performance, further multiplied by its intersection with the space-time of the fictional world. While no longer disappearing behind a fictional world, these theatral worlds of presentation still make no claim beyond their eventual actuality. Certainly, the performers do not appear in their everyday clothes in the 'here and now' of the real twenty-first-century theatre evening. The sets, which with the passing of twenty-five years are no longer just bare but now typically consist of an assemblage of found objects, mostly from second-hand shops and antique markets, where the costumes are also sourced, create a sense of time difference without obeying the representational law of period accuracy. In *Zomergasten*, the set evoked a ship. Ropes were hung from the rigs, as were some exposed theatre lanterns, blurring the line between nautical and theatre rigging (see this book's cover image). According to the core principle of tg STAN's *Regie*, we were faced with an undecided openness, an ambiguous evocation of *both* a decidedly non-illusionist presentation of a play *and* at the same time a finely calibrated symbolism that activated poetic playfulness even more effectively – without any space for spectacular magic, escapism and pretence of illusion, hence for (old-style) 'theatricality'. In *Zomergasten*, not even the music (which, as so often with STAN, included some recognisable pop pieces) was played via the theatre's sound system, but came from a battered stereo on stage (presumably another acquisition from the charity shop), operated with the remote by Vercruyssen in his role as engineer Pjotr Suslov.

A further characteristic of their work is that all performers remain present on stage throughout. In *JDX*, a spotlight marked out a small central playing area and those performers not in a scene remained seated around chairs and tables at the rear of the stage, drinking water, smoking and always watching the performance. In *Zomergasten*, the actors not in the scene set up the next scene on stage or took down the set elements from the previous scene, thereby creating a constant hustle and bustle through the aisles of the theatre, shifting furniture, ladders, chairs and other props and set elements to and fro in a permanent flow of activity and work. This restless theatral activity functioned as a backdrop (as 'action-scape', to invent this term) to the verbal *raisonnements*, the chit-chat and long monologues that make up Gorky's drama; its action contrasted with the phlegmatic stasis of his characters. This strategy of counterpoint – reasserting the rationale behind Schiller's 'chorus' – 'counters' the playtext with (theatral) play. It facilitates the play's appearing as reflexive *Erscheinen*, which asserts an absolute autonomy of play, in the Schillerian sense: it makes us sense the past through the present, and the present through the past.

The autonomous character of theatral play against the laws of theatrical representation is most notably asserted by tg STAN's unique casting. *JDX*, like many of their early productions, was played by the company's four performers (see Figure 10), and recently, *Nora* was similarly performed by a cast of just four (see Figure 11). Even *Summerfolk*, with its many roles, was still only acted by a company of nine, again including the usual guests from fellow companies. Typically, all actors will perform

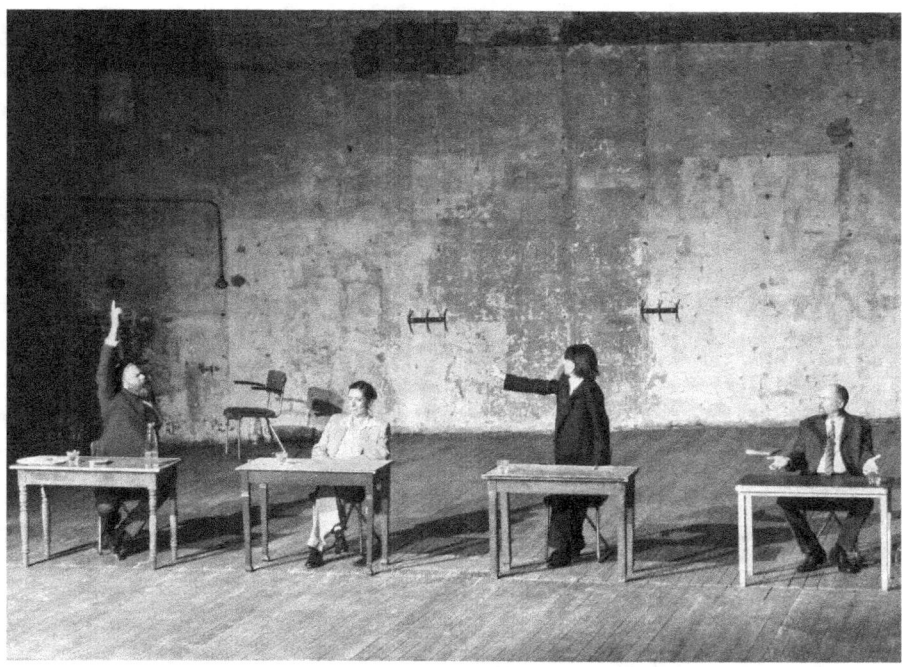

Figure 10 Resisting illusion and stage realism: the public assembly scene of Ibsen's *An Enemy of the People* in tg STAN's 2014 reprise of their 1993 breakthrough production, *JDX – A Public Enemy*. From left: Damiaan de Schrijver, Sara de Roo, Jolente de Keersmaeker and Frank Vercruyssen. Photo: tg STAN/Tim Wouters.

multiple characters, except for a few central characters (such as de Keersmaeker's Varja and de Roo as Olga in *Zomergasten*, Dierickx's Nora, Vercruyssen as Thomas Stockmann in *JDX* and Torvald in *Nora*). No attempt is made to hide this. The actors invent some paralinguistic idiosyncrasies for the characters, or individual signature gestures or a corporeal habitus that soon becomes clearly recognisable. Simple means allow them to switch effortlessly between roles from one line to the next. A small change in the hair, putting on some glasses or just throwing on a jacket suffices, as with Damiaan de Schrijver in his double role as Councillor Peter Stockmann and Captain Horster in *JDX*, or with Vercruyssen in *Zomergasten*; he even manages a dialogue between his various characters in an exquisite scene. Similarly, in *JDX*, de Keersmaeker and de Roo perform between them the characters of Stockmann's wife, his daughter Petra and the journalists Hovstad, Billing and Aslaksen. In a central scene in the newsroom, where they all meet, each performer takes one response in the dialogue, so that the speech headings read out by the prompter remain the sole orientation. As a result, the performers become explicit mediators of the text. They speak the text as text, in a matter-of-fact, neutral way that does not seek to suggest a specific meaning *behind* the words. Our own spectatorial attention fully focuses on

Figure 11 Negotiating the text in the moment of play: in tg STAN's *Nora* (2012), as in all their productions, performers remain on stage throughout, watching the scenes they are not in as bystanders. From left: Frank Vercruyssen, Jolente de Keersmaeker, Wine Dierickx and, observing from 'without', Tiago Rodrigues. Photo: tg STAN/Magda Bizarro.

the reality of each word, not on the fiction it conveys. The actors, with their bodies and their action, become agents of the theatral mediation of the text: the very process and the machinery of creating the theatrical fiction (including the characters) becomes prominently exposed, rather than being disavowed as under the regime of representation.

The characters are thus literally outlined through the text. Without any 'internalisation' of the dialogue, but by merely presenting it as utterance, the productions avoid the 'theatrical emoting' of love, anger or critique that is scripted in the text:[6]

> We're not interested in an actor's virtuosity, as it is often restrictive. For instance, speaking angry words in an angry tone becomes a limiting pleonasm. Chekhov's Ivanov is a sad man. We think it's much more interesting not to emphasise his sadness but rather, by lending him a comical or cheerful attitude, to provide ourselves with a wide range of possibilities between the two extremes; and, by the same token, to restore the character's complexity. The more so because Chekhov's characters are not realistic, but they personify certain concepts. Our starting point is the fact that the audience isn't stupid and doesn't necessarily wish to be told what to see and what to think. Broadening its scope is more exciting. (Firmin-Didot 2005)

As audience, we are never made to forget that in front of us are actors at work: they are playing with the text, playing for the audience and playing in the here and now of the performance situation. Their 'liberty of play' also allows for mistakes, for instance when a character is suddenly addressed with the actor's real name, when the actors in *JDX* confer with the prompter about the text, or when the performers in *Nora* throw in a quick comment in Flemish. Some of these mistakes may be deliberately 'built-in', most happen accidentally. Tg STAN refer to the tradition of Flemish painters (who also fascinated Hegel) of hiding, in their paintings, consciously designed effects that break through the illusion, such as a painted tear on the canvas. For the actors, these moments become important as 'rhythm variations' which 'increase the emotion tenfold, while allowing one to keep one's distance' (Firmin-Didot 2005).

This reflexive distance remains the crucial aspect of the play inherent in *Regie*. It is important for both performers and spectators. Crucially, this distance again no longer suggests a position on the 'outside' of the text, a bird's-eye view or any such position beyond (and, hierarchically, 'above') the frame of the play. It is, rather, a strictly immanent reflexivity which induces distance and thereby splits the present moment from within: in Hegelian terms, it is a 'speculative distance'. This unique speculative moment of presence acquires a quality that goes beyond Brechtian 'showing' (*Zeigen*), as it has become a staple of the modern actors' toolkit. It likewise differs from its incarnation in postmodern performance practice, paradigmatically analysed in Philip Auslander's discussion of the Wooster Group (Auslander 1997, 39–47), where the actor's 'persona' was superimposed on the character and served as central focaliser for the audience's relation to the drama. In this self-conscious and self-assured reflexivity, however, the 'excess' of play remained external, and was mainly associated with the 'knowing' performer's (or director's) vantage point. The text, its world and characters were thus destabilised from this external position that, for instance, sought to disclose the text's disavowed ideological implications. Yet, in presuming and affirming such an alternative critical standpoint from which the text could still be championed, albeit in an alternative, different and critical way, this approach inadvertently reiterated the classical gesture of the modern, enlightened subject. Whereas the hierarchical dominance of the *playtext* as 'big Other' policing the theatral performance may thereby have been decentred, the critical subject took its place as principal authority centre-stage.

The explicit lack of a singular director-figure in tg STAN is a persistent reminder of this ideological trap. The actors, to paraphrase Hegel, 'remain by themselves in their otherness' as characters. In their reflexive play, acting (and, conversely, spectating) means putting oneself at risk, in line with Jürgen Gosch's assertion quoted in the previous chapter. Negotiating the appearing of the play in its inherent ambiguities and contradictions, the actor's performance of a character comes close to Hegel's assertion (in the *Aesthetics*) that the portrait of a person can be 'more like the individual than the actual individual himself'; a claim which Robert Pippin, fittingly in our context, described as Hegel's 'near-Kafkaesque' statement (Pippin 2005, 289; see Hegel 1955, 786f.). Against conventional psychological representation, tg STAN present the character as text – hence, as embodiment of a 'style of thinking', energised by the immanent theatrical dynamics of movement, perception and meaning. Such (dis-)play of 'theatrical thinking in process' (and not: psychology) requires a different preparation to the usual production work. Most of tg STAN's rehearsal time is spent around the big wooden table in their headquarters, a loft-space warehouse in the harbour district of Antwerp. Here, all members of the collective sit together and spend the greater part of their time closely studying and discussing the playtext. While they express as much commitment to the essential 'truth' of the text as Gosch or Thalheimer (see Chapter 5), Vercruyssen notes:

> [T]here is an initial distance between us and the text. We always thought that we have to respect the text and speak the text as it is, but we cannot deny the fact that we do have a language. So we fit the text to our mouth and that forces us to translate everything. (In Winnacker and Peters 1999)

He points out that even the translations of well-known English, German and French plays are always in Dutch – the official standard language, and not in Flemish, with its different vocabulary, pronunciation and great regional variations, especially between West and East Flemish. When preparing a play, the company – who speak Dutch, English, French and German, and who perform many of their productions in several language versions – get their hands on as many editions and translations as they can find. Comparing virtually every sentence, they compile their own adaptation. Noting that many translations tend to make decisions with quite a significant impact on the meaning and interpretation of a play, their versions try to capture the resulting ambiguities and differences as far as possible, rather than making decisions. This mode of working can be foreign for observers and even guest performers. As Jolente de Keersmaeker comments, 'others are mainly concerned with the question, "What is the emotion we are going to throw at the script?". If you ask them why a sentence occurs in a particular place in a script, or what something means, they are stuck for an answer' (in Demets 2004).

This close work on the text fosters an intimate knowledge of every single line, each word, even. It takes up most of their rehearsal period. The company will only start working on the floor once they get into the actual performance space, a few days ahead of the premiere. Vercruyssen anecdotally reveals that even many of their friends never come to a first night, since they cannot bear the tense atmosphere of these very first performances, as they threaten to explode out of sheer theatral energy. As a rule, tg STAN arrive at no more than simple agreements, which they compare to traffic rules – the actual 'driving' can then only be done in the company of an audience, and in response to their responses:

> Reproducing the same movements by rote, without any surprises, robs them of the slightest spark of life. That's why we only define a framework for the staging, what we call the 'traffic': maybe we'll decide to keep mostly standing in the first act and to try to sit down more often in the second act. Then each of us adds his or her natural choreography to these preliminary guidelines. For instance, in a dialogue between lovers keeping a certain distance may seem more appealing, as it keeps intact the desire to move closer to each other. But all these rules are low-key and should never become a system. Breaking them can bring a new vitality to the performance. (In Firmin-Didot 2005)

In tg STAN's work, *Regie* discloses its very nature as process, not structure: a process that engenders fluid mobility, which seeks to avoid 'getting stuck' in one single dimension or position. This aspect of *Regie* can be linked with the (Žižekian rereading) of the much-debated Hegelian notion of 'Absolute Knowing', which has been subject to the same misreading as *Regie*: it has likewise been accused of (directorial-dictatorial) absolutism. Žižek, however, emphasises an understanding linked to the notion of 'absolving'. An 'Absolute Knowledge' of the text, such as the one tg STAN arrive at through their almost academic study, enables a gesture of absolution – of 'absolving' the text, that is, of releasing it in the very act of play. The thorough intellectual grasp of the playtext does not necessarily entail its unfettered dominance that conquers text and audience alike with the power of the director's authority. As Žižek asserts, 'the Hegelian dialectical process is in fact the most radical version of a "process without a subject", in the sense of an agent controlling and directing it – be it God or humanity, or a class as a collective subjective' (Žižek 2012, 405).

Can the same not be said about the process and the thinking of *Regie*? It does not seek to control or dominate the text, but it releases the text at the concluding point of a dialectic process (in Hegelian terminology: it 'externalises' the text). Žižek's reading stresses that this point at which the dialectic process arrives is not alienation but

> the highest point of dis-alienation: one really reconciles oneself with some objective content not when one still has to strive to master and control it, but when one can afford the supreme sovereign gesture of letting this content go, of setting it free. (Žižek 2012, 405)

For Žižek, this process of 'letting go' is what the Hegelian 'absolute' is about: 'Absolute Knowing' points to something that is not just a 'relative' knowing that brings external criteria and standards to the text. As mediation, *Regie* cannot be but an imposition, yet it thinks the (play-)text as absolute, as 'absolutely' self-authorising its play-performance. This articulates the responsibility of *Regie* very clearly: it protects the text from any external cause that seeks to underwrite (the) play (whether truth, beauty, ethical goodness or the director's political critique and deconstruction), and instead guarantees that the 'authority of play' remains absolute. This responsibility of *Regie* was (even *avant la lettre*) so elegantly symbolised by Schiller's 'wall' metaphor in his 'chorus' essay, with which he expressed this ambiguous demand of absolute autonomy. tg STAN are one of the purest examples for this central principle at the heart of the dialectics of *Regie*.

Giving the text its spaces and bodies: Andreas Kriegenburg

The difficulty with this position is of course that any *Regie* that truly subscribes to this value – following Schiller, one may call it 'absolute liberty' – has to take a position of *not* owning the play, of *not* exercising ownership and authority *over* the text: true play (like true liberty) cannot be authored and directed, otherwise it merely becomes the representation of play. Only the play itself can authorise the play, and not the *auteur-*

Figure 12 An entirely impossible scene: the slowly turning revolving stage, suspended in the vertical, designed by Andreas Kriegenburg for his stage adaptation of Franz Kafka's *The Trial* (Kammerspiele Munich, 2008). Photo: Arno Declair.

director. Žižek's take on Hegelian 'Absolute Knowing' can help us break this deadlock. Pavis has coined a beautiful term that equally captures this 'absolution' of the playtext in the liberty of theatrical play: in his wordplay, *Regie* turns a text into a text that is 'émis en scène', emitted and released into the scene (Pavis [1982] 2007, 22).[7] This is literally true for Kriegenburg's at times spectacular 'é-mise', where the remarkable sets afford scenic life (in the sense of Barba's *bios*). They give body to the performers' play, complementing it as focaliser, and elsewhere literally setting their physical dynamics in motion, as with the revolving vertical Kafka-'eye', or the diminished wooden box erected on the intimate Frankfurt Kammerspiele stage for *Stella*, which barely allowed the actors to stand up straight. This physical corporeality of Kriegenburg's spaces is directly linked to the pronounced physicality of acting, which we find in his work, too. Valery Tscheplanowa, who played the lead role of Stella in his production, notes: 'We don't play characters, but spaces, in which we are.'[8]

The corporeal expressivity of Kriegenburg's *Regie* is not at all psychologically grounded. Actor Marc Oliver Schulze notes, 'One borrows a character.'[9] The director never supplies his audience with identifiable characters 'like us' in situations 'we know', and which we can equally easily identify with – hence with objects we can understand, command and consume. Instead, we encounter in his works moments of theatral appearing, where the text is released from its ideological baggage, from what appears to be known and established. Its characters unfold into the theatrical space, and the drama is opened up beyond hermeneutic, interpretive and intellectual meaning, allowing instead for a playful discovery of its sense. Casting is a very crucial factor here. In *Der Prozess*, Kriegenburg multiplies the 'K' characters who also play all other roles. Similarly, in *Herz der Finsternis*, his stage version of Joseph Conrad's *Heart of Darkness* (Deutsches Theater Berlin, 2009), six performers share Marlow's narrator role, often in a choric way, and they also play all other characters – except for Markwart Müller-Elmau, who plays Kurtz throughout, only to then allow for a magnificent ploy when Müller-Elmau eventually becomes Marlow in the final scene after his return to England, standing at Kurtz's grave. With some exceptions (such as *Stella*), the names of the performers are often stated without allocations to roles and characters in the programme booklets for Kriegenburg's productions.

The principal agent of these moments of 'absolute' theatral play in Kriegenburg's work is, however, the kinetic work of his actors, as is evident from the often demanding physicality of many of his productions, not least when actors perform while negotiating a vertically suspended stage space, as in *Der Prozess*. Kriegenburg ascribes this concentration on physical acting to his formative years in the regional GDR; away from the metropolitan centre of Berlin, the actors' physicality was the only resource at his disposal to create what could elsewhere be expressed using a lavish set (Kriegenburg 2008, 150). The director, who trained in pantomime during his adolescence, refers, above all, to Buster Keaton, describing him as 'one of the central artists as well as philosophical cosmographs of the last century', and as 'the earliest and most emotional influence, which has remained with me for the longest time' (Kriegenburg 2011, 6). His predilection for the sadness of silent slapstick and the bittersweet and tender humour of films by Jacques Tati and Ari Kaurismäki inspired the at times acrobatic, elsewhere pronouncedly vulgar physical play with objects, or even the entire set. The performers' physical play vitally contributes to another consistent strategy that characterises Kriegenburg's *Regie*: his calculated use of counterpoints. In particular, he sets explicit kinetic and aisthetic counterpoints of banality and vulgarity against the serious tone of well-known classics, or the overboard emotional exaggeration in a play such as Goethe's *Stella*. In his recent work, these counterpoints are instrumental in creating a typical tragi-comic tone, a melancholic atmosphere and a manifest spirit of neo-absurdist existentialism. Kriegenburg has thus notably moved beyond his early productions that resonated with Frank Castorf's steam-hammer bashing of the bourgeois establishment, Eastern and Western alike, along with its cherished values such as the canonical plays.[10] Today, his *Regie* is distinguished by its playful use of counterpointing, which responds to the playtext at hand. Notably, Kriegenburg almost never uses contemporary pop references, physical slapstick or everyday gags in his work on contemporary plays, especially not in his productions of contemporary German playwright Dea Loher, whose works he regularly premieres. Here, on the contrary, he often introduces modes of pronounced theatrical speaking, explicit declamation or other presentational devices from classical tragedy, in order to create a dynamic counterpoint to the represented present-day fiction.

Confidently calibrating the theatral energies of movement, perception and meaning that are at his disposal within the vivid 'scenic body' of his stage spaces, Kriegenburg even tackles complex narratives, such as Kafka's *Trial* or Conrad's *Heart of Darkness*, precisely by going beyond the purely semiotic logic of representation alone. Conrad himself thematises the inadequacy of language to capture and represent the intensity of Marlow's experience in the Congo jungle station, which is run by the notorious Kurtz. In a famous passage, the narrator addresses us as his interlocutor:

> Do you see him [Kurtz]? Do you see the story? Do you see anything? It seems to me I am trying to tell you a dream – making a vain attempt, because *no relation of a dream can convey the dream-sensation, that commingling of absurdity, surprise, and bewilderment in a tremor of struggling revolt, that notion of being captured by the incredible which is of the very essence of dreams.* ... No, it is impossible; it is impossible to convey the life-sensation of any given epoch of one's existence, – that which makes its truth, its meaning – its subtle and penetrating essence. It is impossible. We live, as we dream – alone. (Conrad 2009; my emphasis)

Whereas the well-oiled machinery of spectacular theatricality might stage such 'incredible dream-sensations', it is the imaginative, playful theatrality of Kriegenburg's *Regie* which makes them sense-able in all their 'subtle and penetrating essence', without failing 'its truth, its meaning'. In a similar way to Conrad's use of a character-narrator, Marlow, to frame the story and emphasise the act of story-telling, Kriegenburg also strategically emphasised and exposed the theatral presentation as it generates the stage illusion. As in tg STAN, we saw performance *at work*.

In *Herz der Finsternis* sounds such as the waves of the sea were visibly produced by the performers with a plastic carrier bag and a microphone, and they created the noises of the jungle with a didgeridoo-like tube, some bamboo sticks, buckets, nails or simply by stomping their feet. To render palpable the absurd, surprising and bewildering moment which Marlow speaks about in Conrad's narration, Kriegenburg, in this production working with his long-term collaborator, designer Johanna Pfau, built gigantic puppets that filled the height of the proscenium and were somewhat reminiscent of the famous statues on Easter Island (see Figure 13). They descended from the flies the moment Marlow's crew arrived at the infamous 'central station'. These puppets stood in for the black slaves in the narration; they got beaten up and whipped, while the performers who operated their heads and limbs via long poles uttered cries or elephant-like howling. At a different point during the performance, the audience was directly included in this theatral creation of play; a rare instance in Kriegenburg's work. As Marlow's boat got attacked upon their arrival, the performers – who watched through binoculars made from empty toilet-roll cardboard from the rig-like ladders that closed off the full height of the proscenium towards the auditorium – defended themselves by blasting air through some toy cannons right into the auditorium. Meanwhile the entire house had filled up with white fog, so it became ever harder for the audience to see the stage while one was repeatedly hit by the air pressure, which functioned more as a startling than a truly painful aisthetic involvement.

Together, the actors' physicality and the striking stage spaces emphasise theatral autonomy. In an interview, director Andreas Kriegenburg stated about working with his 'alter ego', set designer Kriegenburg:

Figure 13 A poetic counterworld that makes palpable the sense of a text: Andreas Kriegenburg's adaptation of Joseph Conrad's *Heart of Darkness* (Deutsches Theater Berlin, 2009; set design: Johanna Pfau). Photo: Arno Declair.

Neither of us has an interest in the direct illustration of reality. We try to blank out the surface of the reality, in which we live, and instead to devise in a self-contained closed space a creative, poetic counter-world, in which it becomes possible to turn an emotional reality into a memorable experience. The space does not need to allow for rational decoding. The power of the images unfolds precisely because nothing can be ultimately explained. (in Burckhardt 2009, 100)

With this genuinely playful approach of his *Regie*, Kriegenburg was instrumental in attuning German audiences to a theatre aesthetics distinct from the psychological realism or the pronounced expressionism that had dominated the stage ever since the generation of Peter Stein and Peter Zadek broke through in the 1960s. The director hailing from the East German region honed his unique way of working, unencumbered by either West German *Regietheater* realism or the post-Brechtian doctrines that reigned at the major (East) Berlin theatres.

Dramaturg Marion Tiedtke, who has worked with Kriegenburg regularly since the 1990s, astutely summarises seven key characteristics of his *Regie* (Tiedtke 2011). It is worth quoting her concise analysis in detail, as it usefully charts key tenets of contemporary *Regie* at large:

(1) The dominance of verbal expression is counterbalanced by awarding the corporeal expressivity (the nonverbal level) equal status.
(2) To psychology he adds the approach of choreography, unmistakably inspired by modern *Tanztheater*, above all by Pina Bausch.

(3) The principle of 'fidelity to the text' (*Texttreue*) is replaced by the principle of textual collage, in order to extend the contextual references of the work, and to allow a negotiation of present events by means of the scenic examination of the text.

(4) The director's authority to arrange the production is counterbalanced by artistic freedom in the actual performance: spaces for *extempori*, for free improvisation of an actor on a theme of the playtext, or on an aspect of their character, are a vital aspect of each production. Night after night, the actor has to fill anew this thematically defined free space both with life, and with his own words. Therefore, moments of unsecured free play remain within the fixed course of action.

(5) Psychological realism, which competes with cinema, is replaced with the quest for an original aesthetic world of the theatre....

(6) The dominance of acted emotion is replaced with instances of play that express this emotion, or it is expressed through musical soundscapes which underscore the text. Emotion is relayed, as in cinema, in line with the music.

(7) The closed character dramaturgy is opened up, and modes of acting are switched all the time: The actor is both character and commentator in one, and may jump between identification, distance and commentary. (Tiedtke 2011, 112f.)

Rather than revealing itself through an apparent, identifiable visual signature as in the work of Gosch and Thalheimer, Kriegenburg's style of *Regie* thus reveals itself through a set of formal characteristics that underpin the structuring of the theatral dynamics of an enhanced *semiosis*, *kinesis* and *aisthesis*. As core principles of his *Regie*, they enhance the vitality of theatral play. The director then further adds to this effect by introducing, not unlike tg STAN, but less extreme, a number of strategies that undermine the persistent systemic demand to deliver a 'product' to be reproduced on stage night after night. Kriegenburg, too, conceives of the audience as player, affirming our 'lead role' as well as our responsibility as spectators, rather than as immersed 'co-actors' of participatory theatre (see Alston 2013). We are positioned in the ambiguous position of spectating we have repeatedly encountered: both drawn in and yet distanced, both in a fictional world and yet in our own reality, both in contemporary life and yet in a fictional historical place, both emotionally involved and yet constantly reflecting. The audience is thus forced to negotiate and to 'interpret', in the very sense Rancière outlines in his essay on *The Emancipated Spectator* (Rancière 2009b, 22).

To emphasise this aspect, Kriegenburg's *Regie* carefully crafts the framing of the performance event. Performances rarely, if ever, begin with the lights going down and the first line of the text being spoken. Instead, spectators are gradually positioned, often through prologue-like scenes, which begin as soon as the doors open, again reminiscent of strategies in STAN's work. *Stella*, for instance, started with some very physical, improvised, often silly commedia-style routines; clownish games with a piece of biscuit, a long scarf and a jumper and a pianoforte. This prologue took place in front of a bare wooden construction that initially closed off the stage frame of the intimate Kammerspiele theatre at Schauspiel Frankfurt. The construction (again designed by Kriegenburg himself) was vaguely reminiscent of a travelling players' cart, befitting the beginning of Goethe's play, where Cecilie arrives at an inn with her daughter Lucie. At one point, the actors leaned against this wooden front wall and it collapsed backwards, so that they fell back with the wall into a small room, of which the wooden wall now formed the floor. Through this 'Alice in Wonderland' effect, audience and performers were eventually transported into Goethe's 1776 'play for lovers', in which the former wife unknowingly meets the woman for whom her husband, Fernando, once left her, the eponymous Stella, who has herself since been abandoned by him as he was unable to forget his first wife. The exaggerated slapstick of the comedic prologue served as a first counterpoint to the no less exaggerated pathos of Goethe's early play. Elsewhere, Kriegenburg started *Judith*, Friedrich Hebbel's biblical adaptation from 1840, with a similar prologue (Deutsches Theater Berlin, 2011). Performers in contemporary clothes painted a back wall, chanting 'I am Judith' in choric synchronicity, while the words 'I am not a terrorist' were projected onto the stage alongside a collage of contemporary news images. The atmosphere was thus charged with references to contemporary political fundamentalism and terrorism. This wall then collapsed, too, again indicating the start of the play proper. The director repeatedly used variations of this spatial device, a collapsing wall, or elsewhere the iron fire curtain, to separate an added, often improvised prologue (or epilogue) as a framing counterpoint to the actual play. It further contributed to our spectatorial reflexive involvement, to our distanced engagement, to our own play with the play.

Just as Kriegenburg's *Regie* surprises the spectators, most powerfully in his *Prozess*, and creates effects of a certain experiential imbalance that provoke our sensory alertness, he also surprises his actors, working explicitly against routine, habits, conventions and, above all, against expectations and one-dimensional, false clarity. As Lisa Stiegler, who played Lucie, the teenage daughter, in his *Stella*, confirmed: 'From a certain moment nothing has been planned or blocked. So far no two performances have been the same.' And lead actor Marc Oliver Schulze commented, 'You become very alert to what is happening in the present performance.' Both gave examples of things that had happened spontaneously on the night of the performance.[11] In *Stella*, only basic agreements were made and only the added prologue and the initial act were more thoroughly set out and blocked. Consequently, not only do the actors in Kriegenburg's productions act in the absolute moment of play, but the stage manager and the sound engineer may also adapt cues, or amend the volume of the soundtrack in order to react to the dynamics of the performance, especially in order to counter lifelessness and lack of play. Kriegenburg emphasises his belief that the single most central value in collaborating in theatre is the personal responsibility of everyone involved in a production. Neither actors nor backstage crew should ever merely become 'servants of my scenic vision' (Kriegenburg 2008, 140), nor should a director just calculate effects which may please the audience. In the director's work, everyone should instead only ever do what they truly and genuinely want to do, thereby expressing Kriegenburg's take on *Regie* as intimately associated with the values of Schillerian liberty:

> This is very important. It is associated with the idea that, in addition to what I want to tell, it is important for the spectators to experience a utopic space of free human beings. The actors do what they have developed in rehearsal together with me, yet now they have taken ownership of it. They don't do it in the performance for me, nor for the spectator, but they offer their own experience for us to watch, to witness, to feel. (Kriegenburg 2008, 146)

If there is a directorial concept behind Kriegenburg's productions, it is thus not the director's, but is a collectively owned concept, developed and discussed with the performers at length during the rehearsal period.

Rather surprisingly for the playful atmosphere of his productions, Kriegenburg's work is not at all based on improvisation, which is virtually absent as a strategy from his rehearsal work. Not unlike tg STAN's preparation around the big table in their office, there is a lot of sitting, talking and discussing in his rehearsals, too. What he terms 'scenic playing' (*das szenische Spiel*) is debated, outlined, talked through and agreed upon. The director emphasises that his prime approach to a text is based on emotional response and is focused on what he describes, using a somewhat old-fashioned German term that is hard to translate, as 'Wesenhaftigkeit' of the drama and its characters, its 'intrinsic character' or 'essence of being' (in Burckhardt 2009, 99):

> Rehearsing is actually an oddly pragmatic process. For a start, it is not about whether we stage the play historically or in modern dress, or in which environment we stage it, but whether we shall do so quickly or slowly, emotionally engaged or cold. (Kriegenburg 2008, 140)

Kriegenburg seeks to avoid starting rehearsals with any 'scenic thinking', as he calls it, any concrete idea of what should happen on stage and how the production should look. Instead, he works from the unique atmospheric character of a text, which he then tries to capture and communicate through the means and strategies of his *Regie*. Working on *Der Prozess*, for instance, Kafka's language appeared to him as if dressed in a very formal suit; its highly composed eloquence never seemed to consider even taking off the jacket, or even undoing a button (Günther 2010, 12). Accordingly, the eight 'K' characters in the production all wear old-style black suits. During rehearsals for *Stella*, Kriegenburg and the performers responded to the highly emphatic and at times rather overblown pathos of Goethe's language by establishing a central rule: when speaking the text the performers were not to stand up. Instead they had to sit, lie down, crouch or crawl across the floor as they spoke. This again supported the central principle of counterpoint. And the actors were again at liberty to vary this basic agreement every night. For this production, Kriegenburg worked with a small ensemble of new actors, with whom he had not previously collaborated and who were also new as an ensemble at the beginning of Oliver Reese's artistic directorship at Schauspiel Frankfurt. Given this situation, Kriegenburg spent the first weeks of rehearsals just learning and practising the tango with the cast. Later, they watched a range of movies by Russian director Andrej Tarkovsky, a visual prompt which British director Katie Mitchell also used when creating her Dostoevsky adaptation ... *some trace of her* (2008). Kriegenburg, however, never attempted to visually recreate the films' imagery. He used the movies merely as another atmospheric and emotional stimulus to inspire his actors' play of Stella's desperate love triangle. Only once the short rehearsal time began to come to a close did they eventually turn their attention to the play itself, to its sentiments and pathos. By that time, however, the performers had acquired, and were comfortable using, a physical language of exalted passion which they had encountered when dancing the tango, which allowed them to render the highly emotional states of their characters other than by simply 'acting them out' psychologically.

What actors and other collaborators comment on most about rehearsing with Kriegenburg – in addition to noting that a lot of time appears 'wasted', with informal conversation, laughter and many silly jokes – is that there is constantly music playing in the background, but not the soundtrack actually used in the performance. Kriegenburg uses it partly to create an atmosphere and to stimulate certain moods, but above all, as he says, to protect his actors and to avoid awkward silences. For him, the music makes the exposed vulnerability of everyone involved in the rehearsal room bearable. When he creates work with his regular performers (some of whom, like his lead protagonist Natali Seelig, have been working with him since the 1990s), he barely does any rehearsal runs and the final on-stage rehearsals (which, unlike the Anglo-American theatre system, rarely take the form of public previews in German theatre) are usually the first time actors no longer just talk through a scene. Kriegenburg comments: 'I know that the actors go through a painful, thoroughly exhausting process in each performance. They do not have to suffer just for me in rehearsal. I want them to save all their energy for the final dress rehearsal and then for the performances' (Kriegenburg 2008, 142). He is adamant that theatre requires the presence and emotional response of an audience to generate the full affective intensity that is at the heart of his *Regie* and that therefore the work on his *Regie* can only be properly completed in the actual performance situation.

The appearance of the future(s) of the text

The liberty of play exemplarily embraced and fostered by the *Regie* of Andreas Kriegenburg and the tg STAN collective opens up a playful 'style of thinking' that dissolves both the closure of a drama's fictional illusion and its historic distance, while importantly also countering the strictly functional domain of efficacy and marketability that elsewhere permeates all levels of our everyday globalised societies, including the entertainment industries. Instead, we are 'presented' – in the multiple senses of this word – with theatral play that heightens the virtual potentiality of the playtext. Brimming with energy and playful liveliness, it emanates what German phenomenologist Bernhard Waldenfels, in another context, described as 'signs of life below the threshold of meaning' (Waldenfels 2010, 70). Discussing the medial effect of images, Waldenfels analysed how paintings by Goya and Bosch evoke a palpable unease that inevitably challenges our spectatorial engagement. They demand some form of response, and require us to position ourselves through our acts of spectating. These signs, therefore, bring us to life, as they induce an implicit reflexive engagement, before any intellectual interpretation comes in. In Kriegenburg's theatre as well as in the productions by tg STAN, similar effects emerge through interplay of the theatral forces of *aisthesis*, *kinesis* and *semiosis*. Situated on the very threshold between presence and representation, these elements of play afford even well-known classics with the plasticity of the dialectic process, which is characterised, as Catherine Malabou outlined, by the contradictory operations of 'the seizure of form and the annihilation of all form, emergence and explosion' (Malabou 2005, 12). The temporal and spatial coordinates are multiplied, annulling the logic of coherent factual or fictional representation. The fixity of the scripted text is dissolved (or, 'absolved', in the sense introduced above). The particular resonances of the present moment resonate with the universal dimension of the playtext.

All these multiple and opposing forces generate the energetic vitality that underpins the true freedom of play(ing). It eventually introduces a third temporal dimension of time to the temporal multiplicity of the past (of the playwright as well as their fictional narrative) and the present (of *Regie* and the moment of performing and spectating). The purely binary tension is intensified by a gesture into the future. Seel's notion of 'appearing' already hinted at this third dimension. *Regie* thus instils into theatre performance both a retrospective and a prospective dimension. This becomes particularly tangible in the playful theatricality of Kriegenburg's and tg STAN's work. Malabou distinguishes this moment of surprise, inherent in the notion of an event in its becoming, from the ordinary notion of future; playing on the difference between *avenir* and *futur* in the French language, she describes it as *le voir venir*, 'to see what is coming'.[12] One could not better capture the attentive atmosphere fostered by the *Regie* work discussed in this chapter. Through this projective moment of appearing (each of the performances will necessarily be different, as a result of their formal composition), *Regie* dialectically sublates the rigidity of the playtext, and eventually breaks through the closure of representation, the transcendental metaphysics of presence, which was challenged not least by Derrida (who was Malabou's teacher).

The playfulness at work in the productions of tg STAN and Andreas Kriegenburg gives full meaning to Derrida's statement that 'play is the disruption of presence' (Derrida 2001, 369). Where *Regie* uses (in particular, rehearsal) strategies that are not merely pragmatically geared towards fixing a reproducible product(ion), it gives the canonical playtexts their future, as they will continue to be staged in ever new ways 'to come'.[13] Through exploring, studying and carefully investigating the texts, *Regie* creates points of beginning, which then allow for true Deleuzian repetition in the performances to come: ever-new beginnings, which depart from the same starting point, but take different paths each time. 'Interpretation', then, can no longer mean grasping the one reading waiting in the play – an assumption that follows the Platonian pattern of the Idea and its reproduction, which the standard concept of the 'type'/'token' argument in aesthetic theory wrongly imposes on *Regie*. On the contrary, *Regie* makes performers and spectators (and directors) discover the appearing of a sense of the playtext that is only 'emitted' through reflexive, performative play. We should thus invert our usual perspective: instead of reducing the potentialities of the dramatic text to the actuality of its singular *mise en scène*, *Regie* plays with the traces of potentiality at the very core of the actual playtexts – 'beneath the threshold of meaning', as it were. Opening what appears to be a closed system, *Regie* – far from being a secondary instrument of medial representation – is thus a process of theatral thinking that restores the ambiguous, contradictory, unseemly 'styles of thinking' (in

Schramm's term; we may of course also evoke Rancière's 'partition of the sensible' to the same effect), whose spectres and shadows split the text from within. It does so by asserting the play's 'absolute liberty'.

The structure of *Regie* follows in this very sense a movement parallel to the Hegelian dialectic process, as interpreted by Žižek.[14] According to Hegel, by going through the triadic movement of the dialectic process, the thing is said to 'become what it always already was'. Traditionally, this has been understood as an assertion of a closed and contained system, similar to the idea of theatre directing as actualising in the production the text's inherent potential that is 'always already there'. For Žižek, however, Hegel's thinking emphasises that only in the dialectic process does the thing *become* what it 'always already was'; his reading highlights the very process of becoming: precisely the emergence of appearing, rather than the pre-existing essence. In precisely this sense, Hegel's core proposition of 'retroactive positing of the presuppositions' reverses the direction: this apparent 'essence' only ever emerges through processes of mediation, sublation and actualisation, and is, strictly speaking, not there without such a process.[15] Hegel thereby becomes, for Žižek, 'the ultimate thinker of autopoiesis, of the process of the emergence of necessary features out of chaotic contingency, the thinker of contingency's gradual self-organization' (Žižek 2012, 467) – and hence, of course, an invaluable inspiration for the thinking of *Regie*. Supporting an 'aesthetics of appearing', of *voir venir*, *Regie* facilitates play in which *the* play *becomes* what it always already was. As we saw when discussing Hegel's notion of 'Absolute Knowledge', the necessarily subjective manifestation of *Regie* does not add anything external in its process of actualisation and concretisation. As an immanent, and strictly reflexive and speculative force, it makes the play's internal excess available through the theatral dynamics of motion, meaning and perception. The Lacanian approach describes this as 'non-All' (*pas-toute*): the text is never complete in itself as a substantial essence, but only in this substance *plus* its contingent excess 'beneath the threshold of meaning', of *essence (truth) in appearing (play)*, in the retrospective (*nach-träglich*) perspective Žižek accentuates with Hegel. This is precisely why the play of *Regie* in this Continental tradition of thinking (which is a thinking of representation and its problems and limits) produces an appearing of, say, Ibsen or Goethe, which is inevitably 'more Goethe than Goethe itself', to use Žižek's preferred expression, or in which there is 'more *Nora* than in *Nora* itself'.

Notes

1 It appears that the visual eye metaphor was not deliberately intended by Kriegenburg. He had in mind the awry black-and-white world of silent movies and some of the historic amusements of Munich's annual Oktoberfest fairground and beer festival, such as the 'Devil's Wheel', a large spinning disk where the operator tries to knock off the participants through varying the speed and throwing other obstacles at them. This historical amusement dates back to the time of Kafka's writing and Buster Keaton's movies. Further, the set and overall visual aesthetic of this production were inspired by Kafka's own drawings, which were reprinted in the programme book. Some of these drawings indeed appeared like design sketches that proposed such a suspended, revolving disk.

2. Fischer-Lichte sees contemporary theatre as providing 'the opportunity to explore the specific function, condition, and course of this interaction [*between actors and spectators, PMB*]. The job of the director [*the German original, however, crucially reads: 'Aufgabe der Regie ist es...', PMB*] lies in developing relevant staging strategies which can establish conditions for this experiment' (Fischer-Lichte 2008, 40, and 2004, 61).
3. Their role model was Dutch collective Maatschappij Discordia (literally, 'the discord company'), formed in the early 1980s around Jan-Joris Lamers and Matthias de Koning, the single most important radical theatre company in Dutch theatre during the 1980s. Collectively staging classical plays by Shakespeare and Chekhov, while also promoting contemporary authors such as Peter Handke, Thomas Bernhard and the Dutchman Gerardijan Rijnders, Discordia was the long-term in-house company of Amsterdam's then influential Felix Meritis arts centre. Discordia instilled the idea of collective creation, the core ethos of their work into an entire generation of young performers, while pushing them beyond realism and encouraging them to trust the reality of theatral play. Other companies who follow this tradition as collectives without a director are De Roovers and Dito Dito in Flanders and 't Barre Land and Dood Paard in the Netherlands. Discordia's de Koning supervised the graduation productions of the future members of tg STAN, while they were students at the Royal Flemish Conservatoire. He then became their principal mentor during their early years as a company, also performing in several of their productions.
4. The production was counted among the ten most important Flemish theatre productions of the twentieth century by the Belgian newsmagazine *Knack*; in 2014, it was revived on the occasion of the company's twenty-fifth anniversary.
5. tg STAN also produced *Stella* in Dutch (Kaaitheater Brussels, 1999) and English versions (Mousonturm Frankfurt, 2000), reducing Goethe's play to a duet of the two actors Sara de Roo and Steven van Watermeulen.
6. tg STAN even theorised acting theory in performance, staging Diderot's famous essay on the 'Paradox of the Actor' (famously written in dialogue form) in their 2001 piece *du serment de l'écrivain du roi et de diderot*.
7. Pavis first used this phrase in the French original of *Theatre at the Crossroads of Culture* (Pavis 1990, 30).
8. Tscheplanowa speaking at a post-performance talk which I attended at Schauspiel Frankfurt on 17 March 2011.
9. Schulze speaking in the post-performance talk, see previous note.
10. Kriegenburg worked as director at the Berlin Volksbühne even before Castorf took up his notorious leadership of the theatre in 1992. Following his apprenticeship as a joiner at the local theatre of his hometown Magdeburg, Kriegenburg made a foray into directing. His 1991 *Woyzeck*, created at the Volksbühne, was the first production by a theatre and a *Regisseur* from the former GDR invited to the annual Berlin Theatertreffen. For years, however, his work was patronisingly rejected by (West) German critics (for a contemporary account, see Ricklefs 1994). Kriegenburg then moved beyond the ironic gestures of the post-*Wende* pop-theatre, emblematically represented by the Volksbühne style of the time. He left Berlin in the mid-1990s, and worked in Hanover from 1994, subsequently in Munich and, from 1999, at the Burgtheater Vienna, during which period he managed to emancipate himself in the critics' eyes from his 'GDR stigma'. In 2001, he rejoined *Intendant* Ulrich Khuon, with whom he had previously collaborated at Hanover, becoming head director at Hamburg's Thalia Theater and later moving with him to Berlin's Deutsches Theater in 2009. Today, Kriegenburg is also a renowned *Regisseur* in opera; he created an acclaimed masterpiece with his version of Wagner's *Ring* cycle, conducted by Kent Nagano, at the Staatsoper Munich in 2012.

11 Stiegler and Schulze in the post-performance talk, see note 8, above.
12 According to Malabou:

> 'Voir venir' in French means to wait, while, as is prudent, observing how events are developing. But it also suggests that other people's intentions and plans must be probed and guessed at. It is an expression that can thus refer at one and the same time to the state of 'being sure of what is coming' ('être sûr de ce qui vient') and of 'not knowing what is coming' ('ne pas savoir ce qui va venir'). As a result, the 'voir venir', 'to see (what is coming)', can represent that interplay, within Hegelian philosophy, of teleological necessity and surprise. (Malabou 2005, 13)

13 The objective of Malabou's Heideggerian–Derridean deconstruction of Hegel is, of course, to arrive through Hegel's future at Hegel's future: through the future in his philosophy at an assessment of the future potential of his philosophy.
14 I here follow Žižek's reading in 'The Limits of Hegel' (Žižek 2012, 455–504).
15 Žižek seeks in this change of direction between *a priori* and *a posteriori* reasoning Hegel's crucial departure beyond Kant.

7

The intermedial parallax: on *Regie*, media and spectating

Our spectatorial attention and reflexive experience of *Scènes uit een huwelijk* by Flemish director Ivo van Hove (b. 1958) was particularly foregrounded and intensified. His stage adaptation of Ingmar Bergman's 1970s TV series *Scenes from a Marriage*, which the director created in 2005 for Toneelgroep Amsterdam, the foremost Dutch ensemble company he has been leading as artistic director since 2001, multiplied the story's protagonists.[1] The couple of Johan and Marianne was here played by three pairs of actors in different age brackets. On entering the theatre, the audience was equally split into three, and each group led on to a different part of the theatre's main stage, which was separated into three triangular sections. The set by Jan Versweyveld (b. 1958), van Hove's permanent collaborator since his very first performance piece in 1981, showed three contemporary interiors with modern furniture that are characteristic for his designs. They provide an often reduced, at times minimalistic frame for elements of reality, as in a notorious 1991 production of O'Neill's *Desire under the Elms*, where van Hove and Versweyveld populated their stage with living cattle.[2] In *Scenes from a Marriage*, each space – a dining-room, a living-room and the bedroom of the couple's flat – was inhabited by one pair of actors. In the course of the first part of the four-hour performance, the three groups of spectators moved from one space to the next to watch three scenes from the couple's marriage: Johan and Marianne witnessing, during their own honeymoon period, the painful breakdown of some friends' marriage during a dinner party; their own marriage turning into dull, everyday routine, which causes Johan to start his love affairs; and Johan eventually packing his bags to leave Marianne for a younger woman. The order in which the spectators saw these scenes, however, depended on which of the three groups they were allocated to. The actors repeated the same scene three times in a row, and the

Figure 14 Heightened realism, counterbalanced by the heightened reality of theatre: Hugo Koolschijn (front) and Roeland Fernhout (behind the window) as two of three 'Johans' in Ivo van Hove's *Scenes from a Marriage*, after Ingmar Bergman's TV series, where three scenes were played simultaneously (Toneelgroep Amsterdam, 2005/2011; stage design: Jan Versweyveld; the image was taken during the 2013 performance at the London Barbican). Photo: Jan Versweyfeld.

spectators were kept aware of this repetition. From all three rooms, doors led into a central space in the middle of the scenic triangle (see Figure 14). It contained a TV, a stereo, a fridge and a table, on which all props were placed and around which were seated the other actors who were not in the scene. Windows allowed the audience to see into this space, and also to catch glimpses of the other rooms through windows on the opposite side. The audience, therefore, also witnessed moments from the scene(s) they had already seen, or which they were still to see. Additionally, the heavy curtains that separated the three spaces on the theatre stage were not entirely soundproof, so that the audience heard moments from the other scenes, sometimes muffled in the background, sometimes rather clearly and loudly, especially during the couples' various quarrels and arguments.

After the interval, the set had disappeared and the stage was no longer divided up. The spectators now encircled a central (largely empty) playing area, again sitting on the actual theatre stage. Here, all three pairs of actors were present. Sometimes, the same scene was simultaneously played in three different versions, for instance the couple's bitter fight about signing the divorce papers. At times, the couples even interacted with each other, changing their configuration of different 'Johans' and 'Mariannes' for certain moments. Their final, reconciliatory and somewhat melancholic meeting at a later point of their lives was the only moment to be played solely by the couple who acted their separation scene in the first half (in the 2011 reprise of the production they were played by original cast member Hugo Koolschijn and Janni Goslinga). *Scenes from a Marriage*, which van Hove described as a favourite among his own works and which, partly with a new cast, has remained in the company's repertoire for a decade, reveals a characteristic aspect of his *Regie*. On the one hand, the acting of his exquisite ensemble of actors is superbly realistic, evoking the close-up proximity of the cinema screen. Van Hove refers to Peter Stein and Patrice Chéreau, whose work he saw during the 1980s, as formative inspirations. On the other hand, this heightened realism is regularly counterbalanced by an equally heightened emphasis on the ultimate reality of the theatre situation, an element which van Hove absorbed from the 1980s performance art scene. This careful calibration of realistic dramatic representation and postdramatic means of presentation creates the intriguing and intense effect of his works: a precarious, undecided ambiguity between realism and reality which fosters a sense of liminality. Not least, the emphasised theatral framing, as in *Scenes from a Marriage*, prevents both the spectators' identification with characters and their outright immersion into a fictional world. The effect of immediacy, the stated aim of psychological realism, is undercut; neither are spectators kept at the distance of gazing voyeurs. Van Hove's productions thus make audiences aware of their involvement in the play, of their own theatral negotiations – their acts of spectating (see Boenisch 2012). Paradoxically, this reflexivity amplifies our affective engagement with the fictional situation, such as the breakdown of a couple's marriage, precisely because of our heightened awareness of our own reality: what we see ultimately really affects *us*, not just *them*.

A similar experiential uncertainty distinguishes the work of van Hove's Flemish compatriot Guy Cassiers (b. 1960).[3] The opening moments of his celebrated four-part staging of Marcel Proust's epochal *Recherche du temps perdu* (2002–5) straightaway short-circuit fictional representation and theatral presentation.[4] The spectators read the words 'Piano music' projected on a screen. They heard, however, a violin, played by a musician visibly positioned on stage. As the performance developed, the audience kept reading about the 'knocking on the door', 'steps on the pebbles', even the 'blush on his face' or 'her eyes' – but these sensory impressions from the novel likewise only ever appeared as text projections. The actors spoke, their voices amplified through headset microphones, while the screen showed live-feed close-ups of their faces, alongside other images, such as well-known paintings. Rather than representing characters and action through dialogue (the format of 'dramatic theatre' of the representative regime, as seminally outlined by Peter Szondi, see Szondi [1956] 1987), the text was here presented *as text*. It was turned from the expressive declamation of speech acts into declarative 'acts of speaking'. No attempt was made to hide the complex set-up of audio-visual technology on the almost bare, dark stage, which was otherwise defined by very few prominently positioned colour accents, such as the performers' costumes and some isolated objects, props and sculptural set-pieces. Instead of presenting a coherent fictional totality, the separated media streams of voice, image and the actors' actual performing bodies, which the audience sees on stage, somewhat perforate the illusion of the plot and its characters. Watching the

Figure 15 Ambiguous pluralities perforate the semiotic texture of Guy Cassiers's *Proust* (2002–5, Ro Theater, Rotterdam; design Marc Warning/Kantoor voor bewegend Bild). His multisensual *Regie* emphasises the materiality of theatral mediation and creates an experiential uncertainty in the act of spectating. Photo: Ro Theater/Pan Sok.

famous love affair between Swann and Odette in *Proust 1*, for instance, the spectators noticed Swann's pixelated jacket on the screen above the stage; at some point, however, one realised that this was not at all an effect of a low-resolution projection, but that these pixels were really printed on his costume. In part 3, a live feed projection of one of the salon scenes imperceptibly changed into pre-recorded footage; it took the spectators a while to realise that only one Marcel was wearing a scarf (see Figure 15). As the scene went on, the characters on stage began to watch the screen themselves.

The film continued the scene they were in, while the characters/performers on stage still continued to speak the dialogue, thus dubbing the images. Throughout Cassiers's *Proust*, there were moments of similar friction between what the audience heard, what we saw on stage and what we read or watched on the screen. The theatral presentation never seamlessly gelled with the fictional representation.

A theatrical surplus arose from the gaps, traps, detours, blanks and ambiguous pluralities that emerged in the semiotic texture. This excess contributes to an effect which Flemish dramaturg Marianne van Kerkhoven aptly described as 'multisensual' character of Cassiers's *Regie* (orig.: 'multizintuiglijk', in Colson 2005, 134). No longer representing and authenticating a fictional reality, his *Regie* alerted us to the technical materiality of the mediatisation and the theatrical presentation in front of us. This asserted our own reality as theatre spectators. At the same time, this multisensual framework equally challenged the performers. They began to sense a split between their body on stage, the projected image of their face and the sound of their voice transmitted over the speakers (see Boenisch 2007, 127f.). By supplying the live media with the image of their face and with their voice, as well as operating them on occasions, they acted primarily within the space of theatrical presentation, rather than inside the represented fiction. Notably, this 'distancing effect' of multisensuality no longer relied on the juxtaposition or interplay of 'new' media (the screens, cameras, the manipulated audio track, etc.) and the 'old medium' of the stage (the presence of the actors, their bodies, etc.), as the standard formats of 'multi-medial' performance do. Instead, it integrated conventional tools of theatre with the elaborate projection and editing techniques. As a result it foregrounded theatrical mediation as a reflexive process.

Pushing beyond established conventions and relations of performing and spectating, Cassiers's *Regie* thus emphasises the specific theatral reflexive relationality – between text and production; actor and character; stage and audience; theatre and world. His multisensual mode of visualising, spatialising and embodying dramatic (and other) texts, and similarly van Hove's multiplication of spectatorial perspectives, lead to a 'fundamental recalibration of traditional dynamics between stage and audience, to the effect that the separation between the factual reality (of the actors and spectators) and the fictional worlds (of characters and the plot) is substantially challenged' (Boenisch 2007, 121). Making actors and spectators alike persistently aware of their inevitable complicity with processes of theatrical mediation, such strategies of *Regie* evoke central mechanisms of intermediality, 'an effect created in the perception of observers [*and equally performers, PMB*] that is triggered by performance – and not simply by the media, machines, projections, or computers used in a performance' (Boenisch 2006, 113).

In the work of both directors discussed in this chapter, the reflexive intermedial loop crucially depends on a rigid dramatic framework; this persistence of dramatic characters, plots and narratives in both van Hove's and Cassiers's work has been dismissed by some critics as outright conservative. Such formal criticism overlooks, however, the intermedial interplay of the conventional dialogic play with the exposed audio-visual mechanics in Cassiers's productions, or with the porous theatrical realities in van Hove's. Through blurring the borders between representation, presentation and presence, their *Regie* develops a major strategy of postdramatic theatre further, where the 'dramatic cosmos' (Hans-Thies Lehmann's term) is no longer positioned *vis-à-vis* the spectators, affirming them in their position outside and opposite, as 'the other' of the performance. Instead, the spectators are 'counted in' by means of the theatral (and above all aisthetic) dynamics activated by *Regie*. They become explicit addressees of the text, having to position themselves and relate to the performance. They are no longer able to 'consume' a cultural commodity. This enhanced self-reflexive engagement triggered by the multisensual and intermedial *Regie* of van Hove and Cassiers prompts what Alain Badiou, in his *Rhapsody for the Theatre*, calls practices of 'intermission': out of the immanent gap implicit in *thea* – as showing and gazing – emerges a momental interval when the audience can see and experience itself *as audience*, instead of disappearing in the anonymity of a consuming mass (Badiou 2008, 209). In these moments, we encounter ourselves as gazing subjects and experience ourselves as spectators – not because we enter the fictional world (as in the current vogue for immersive theatre), but because *the fiction itself enters the theatre*: as we literally begin to 'watch us watching', it dramatises our subjective engagement with the world (see Boenisch 2014b). This effect relies on the formal mechanics of what Slavoj Žižek, drawing on the Lacanian interpretation of *anamorphosis*, describes as the logic of the parallax: the 'constantly shifting perspective between two points between which no synthesis or mediation is possible', which he goes on to compare to the opposed sides of a Moebius strip: 'although they are linked, they are two sides of the same phenomenon which, precisely as two sides, can never meet' (Žižek 2006b, 4; see also Boenisch 2010a). This purely formal, relational and reflexive confrontation with our own acts of spectating reveals the central ethical and political stakes of *Regie* today. They go far beyond the thematic layers of a dramatic text and its critical interpretation. *Qua* its unique force of *thea*, theatre can become a unique occasion in which we relate to our self, to our other side we can never meet, and in which we thereby reflect on involvement and our responsibility as a subject in our (twenty-first century neoliberal, etc.) world.[5] Theatre finds itself at a crossroads between delivering the game of the, to use Rancière's term, 'stultifying' money-spinning global entertainment industry, or 'offering a model of orientation by affording distance in order to support our attempts to map our own position', as Schramm noted on the role of theatre in the seventeenth century (Schramm 1990, 212).

Zooming behind the mirror of the world: Ivo van Hove

The moment has become famous: about half an hour into Ivo van Hove's *Romeinse Tragedies*, his 2007 production that merged Shakespeare's three 'Roman tragedies', *Coriolanus*, *Julius Caesar* and *Antony and Cleopatra*, into a six-hour performance without interval, the first scene change took place. The spectators had just witnessed

Figure 16 Looking behind the mirror: the audience seated on stage in Ivo van Hove's 'Roman tragedies' (Toneelgroep Amsterdam, 2007; set design: Jan Versweyveld). The distance his spectating arrangements afford allows the audience to zoom in and zoom out of the play simultaneously. This photo shows a performance at the Avignon Festival, 2008. Photo: Jan Versweyveld.

Caius Martius' return from his successful battle against the Volsci, as neon working lights were switched on, stagehands began to reset the scene and some 'muzak' was played, as in a shopping mall. Next, a female voice addressed the spectators through the theatre PA system, welcoming us to today's performance: 'the stage is now open', we were told. The audience was invited to get up, cross the magic frontier of the fourth wall and take a seat on one of the many sets of sofas which were spread across the stage, surrounding two central platforms and the downstage playing area. Jan Versweyveld's set was reminiscent of a modern-day hotel lobby or airport lounge, while costume designer Lies van Assche dressed all performers in present-day, dark-toned professional business attire. On stage, the audience was not only able to get a prime view of the play but a bar and a food stall also awaited us, next to a reading corner with the latest newspapers and magazines, and even computers that offered free access to the Internet, also connecting spectators to the show's online message board. These 'service areas' surrounded the stage, alongside desks for the make-up and costume assistants, and workspaces for the video designers and the two musicians, all of whom did their work unconcealed from the audience (see Figure 16).

Over the course of the hours that followed, the audience was able to move freely between stage and auditorium. We could watch very close up on stage, or from a distance in our usual seats in the auditorium.[6] We could also 'watch live', as several remote-control cameras as well as another camera, operated by a camerawoman in the midst of the on-stage action, captured the events. The footage was broadcast on a huge cinema screen mounted above the proscenium, and on numerous monitors scattered not only across the stage space but also outside the auditorium, in the theatre foyer and even in the toilets. Meanwhile, large-screen plasma TVs on stage (less visible for the on-stage audience) projected a montage of current news images, from Barack Obama to war images from Iraq, while occasionally switching to 'live interviews' with the historical-fictional political leaders of the Shakespearean plays – such as the chief Volscan warlord Aufidius in *Coriolanus* – who were interviewed by a female broadcaster and responded to her questions with their lines from Shakespeare's text. Further, an electronic LED text display mounted underneath the cinema screen above the stage provided the audience with information on the historical background of the plays (on the Volsci, Coriolanus, the wars, etc.), and with details of the production ('three hours to Caesar's murder'). It also broadcast some of the messages entered by spectators on the online forum, and relayed news headlines of the day, from updates on real-world war zones to football results.

The resulting effect is familiar by now: as spectators, we were not transported into a Shakespearean theatre world remote from current event and affairs; 'here, not all the world is a stage, but the stage is all the world' (Coussens 2008, 4). Typically for van Hove's productions, of Shakespeare as well as modern plays, and of his preferred US twentieth-century dramatists from O'Neill to Hellman in particular, the spectators never face a historicist *mise en scène* of Rome in Caesar's time or of early twentieth-century America. His productions are, in Jessner's sense as discussed in Chapter 4, ultimately *zeitgenössisch*:

> Because I live today, I read a text with the knowledge of today: the knowledge of what I've read, what I've seen, my personal experience and what happens in society. Of course, as a director you have to understand a text from its time, but to simply restore and try to make a text work in the way that it worked it the nineteenth or even in the twentieth century is useless, I think. Theatre has the capacity of talking about today, and that's the only sense theatre makes for me. ... In the theatre, we should reflect, but that's a much slower process than what happens every day in newspapers, magazines, or television shows. Of course, the current war in Syria is terrible. You can say this on stage and we all agree, but we all agree anyway. So it's much better to stage, for example, *Troilus and Cressida*, and show the consequences of war, and allow us to reflect. That's what theatre is for, and not to represent reality. I like to quote the line by Harold Pinter from his lecture for the Nobel prize that the theatre should look *behind* the mirror, and not *into* the mirror. (van Hove, in Boenisch 2014c, 53f)

In his 'Roman tragedies', for instance, the prominent focus on media representation allowed van Hove to emphasise political oratory, especially in *Coriolanus* and *Julius Caesar*, while also showing a political trajectory from the transformation of an oligarchy in the first play, via democracy in the second to globalised dominance resulting in Octavius' autocracy at the end. Resonating with today's female political leaders from Hillary Clinton to Angela Merkel, ambitious Octavius was here played by actress Hadewych Minis. The battle scenes, in many historical plays a guarantee of theatricality, were rendered solely acoustically, as the two musicians launched a fearsome battle of loud, penetrating drum-beats while stroboscope flashes haunted the otherwise dark space. The only battlegrounds we saw were on the TV screens, while the combatants were (like contemporary politicians) not personally engaged in battle; they were shown rushing around, having crisis talks and managing the fighting. The world of the play, however, never simply collapsed into our reality. Critic Evelyne Coussens rather describes the resulting effect as 'zooming out and zooming in simultaneously' (Coussens 2008, 4).[7]

The realistic portrayal of characters, which we similarly have encountered in *Scenes from a Marriage*, was interwoven with political topics that resonated on multiple levels. The same 'zooming out and zooming in' then applied to the audience's spectatorial engagement, too. Sitting on stage in the midst of the 'Roman tragedies', our very being in the moment overlapped with the represented world of the performance. At the same time we were always confirmed in our role as both theatre spectators and as members of today's public. Whether we followed the heated debates in *Coriolanus* between the plebeians and Caius Martius while huddled on a sofa watching a TV screen and munching some noodles, or read the day's papers and checked our emails while Caesar was assassinated and Brutus and Antony gave their famous speeches, we were constantly confronted with our everyday habits of viewing, spectating and using media, and of participating in world news and private issues. This spectatorial tension imploded the representational closure and gave the normally transparent medium of theatre a prominent reflexive focus, which we have now repeatedly encountered at the heart of contemporary *Regie*. The two perspectives of our engagement – which mirror the theatral logics of representation and presentation – could no longer be brought into a single, consistent focus at one and the same time. Corresponding to the logic of the Žižekian parallax perspective, the spectator was able to either 'zoom in' on Shakespeare's plays, with the excess of theatrality (most notably, other spectators sitting on stage) remaining an irritating spot in their perception, or one reflected on this awareness of 'watching ourselves watching', whereby the persistence of dramatic representation with its characters and the story of the canonical play likewise prevented the seamless coherence (and thus supremacy) of the reflexive spectatorial position: 'We do not have two perspectives, we have a perspective and what eludes it, and the other perspective fills in this void of what we could not see from the first perspective' (Žižek 2006b, 29).

Even for those who made the choice of remaining in the auditorium, the very presence of the other spectators on stage triggered such an experience of a 'parallax perspective': despite being seated in the traditional auditorium space, one was no longer able to 'neutrally' observe the performance and 'consume' a totality of representation from an objective distance. Those sitting on stage became the vicarious public who reminded us constantly that we were equally part of this frame ourselves, of the very reality we were watching. The spectator *is* the perturbing parallax distortion. Even when we believe that we are observing 'objective reality', we always also encounter ourselves in this reality. We are therefore always also responsible for this reality. Marking such an inclusion of the subject of perception in the perceived, Lacan famously maintained that 'the frame is in my eye, but I am in the frame' (for a detailed discussion see

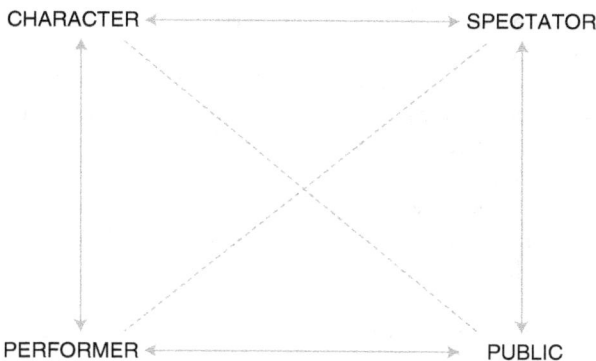

Figure 17 The 'theatral square' illustrating the relational network of theatre performance.

Miller 2009). Usually, this presence of the observer in the object (and thus ultimately, the Hegelian collapse of subject into the object) remains purely virtual – not in the sense of artificial digital fictions, but of Deleuze's idea of the Virtual as potentiality that is yet undecided and pregnant with all possibilities, with which the devout anti-Hegelian, as Žižek never tires of pointing out, came close to Hegelian terms of true actualisation of the potentiality. We thus encounter another crucial relational dynamic that energises what we may call, borrowing liberally from Schramm, 'the magic square of *Regie*' (see Figure 17). Even before having recourse to the text and its specific content and interpretation, *Regie* maps out a relational network between four key parameters in the form of a Greimassian semiotic square: on the one side, there is the axis of the actor and his/her character. On the opposite axis, there is no longer simply 'the spectator', but instead we find a structurally no less complex and shifting relationship: between 'the spectator' and what I have just termed 'the public'. The 'opposite number' of the character is 'the spectator' as audience member; this relates to their formal theatral function. But in the corner of the square the corresponds to the position of the actor, there is also the 'real' spectator: the member of the public, living in a specific society and context. In different ways, van Hove's and Cassiers's productions highlight the necessary balance of this 'public' dimension of spectating, which never leaves reality in the cloakroom. Yet, this 'public' position is all too often effaced, which of course supports the neoliberal hegemonic ideology of the consuming subject.

German dramaturg Carl Hegemann, a former collaborator of Frank Castorf, the late Christoph Schlingensief and others, developed this crucial point saliently. He stressed that theatre vitally relies on a dynamic relationship between *all four* of theatral agency's defining positions:

> Theatre stops being theatre at the very moment where the actor alone stands on stage and acts him- or herself, or performs anything, but it equally stops being theatre in the very moment where only the character is present on stage: then we are in cinema. The presence of all elements of the theatre convention – theatre visitors and spectators on the one side, and actors and characters on the other side – and their interaction are the crucial and specific element of theatre. (Hegemann 2011, 80f.)

Where *Regie* toys with the very limits of this theatrical square, it will manage to sublate the reality of performing as well as the reality of the performance. In 'Roman tragedies' – as in *Scenes from a Marriage* and many, if not most, of van Hove's productions – we are exemplarily addressed as audience *and* as public, and we see both the actor in performance and the performance of a character. The resulting parallax perspective stresses the ultimate sameness of the realities on either side of the stage; there is no hierarchy between a 'fictional world of the drama', the world on stage with its tricks, technology and machinery and our 'real' world outside and beyond the theatre. Such topology is pure ideology:

> [W]hat really accounts for the [staged illusion] is not this machinery as such but the frame which delimits the 'magic' space of the stage from the 'ordinary' reality off-stage: if we want to explore the mystery of the illusion by going backstage, we will discover there exactly the same ordinary reality as exists in front of stage. (The proof is that, even if the backstage machinery is totally visible, as in some theaters, the staged reality is still generated.) What counts is that one part of ordinary reality is separated from the rest by a frame which designates it as a magical space of illusion. We have one and the same reality, separated from itself (or, rather, redoubled) by a screen. (Žižek 2012, 374)

Reminiscent of Leo Bersani's 'relational aesthetics' (far more than Bourriaud's considerations of the same term in the name of 'widening participation'), this intermedial stance of *Regie* thus stresses the crucial aspect of 'sameness in difference'. It forces us to negotiate our common-nality with the world, rather than providing a distanced position opposite (and outside) it, which is the ultimate position of the 'alienated' capitalist consumer (see Bersani 2010).

The reflexive, intermedial way of experiencing our own acts of spectating should, therefore, also be clearly opposed to the postmodern, self-absorbed, narcissistic self-reflexivity that knows no horizon beyond itself, and equally to the limitless self-confidence of deconstructive criticality which deconstructs everything – apart from its own position. Instead, it is this reflexive stance that echoes Žižek's important rereading of the Hegelian passage from consciousness to self-consciousness, outlined in the *Phenomenology of Spirit* as a response to (and against) the Kantian transcendental approach: for Hegel, the very inability to put ourselves at a 'safe distance' from reality was no longer the limitation, but precisely the *condition* of assuming subjectivity, and thus (political, cultural and other) agency in the world. The Kantian problem – that all 'objective' content we experience is put there by the subject itself – is for Hegel, as Žižek continually stresses, the solution:

> This, then, is the status of the Self: its self-awareness is, as it were, the actuality of its own possibility.
>
> ...
>
> Our knowing is irreducibly 'subjective' not because we are forever separated from reality-in-itself, but precisely because we are part of this reality, because we cannot step outside it and observe it 'objectively'. (Žižek 2012, 348, 389f.)

From a theatral point of view, the reflexive relationality of *Regie* toys with the same impossibility of an objective viewpoint and its subjective sublation. It thereby continues to be characterised by what, according to Sam Weber, caused Plato to condemn theatre 2,500 years ago – that it 'haunts and taunts the Western dream of self-identity': 'Theater, in short, is that which challenges the 'self' of self-presence and self-identity by reduplicating it in a seductive movement that never seems to come full circle' (Weber 2004, 7–8).

This parallax of the 'reduplicated' spectator characterises contemporary *Regie*. Its reflexive confrontation with our acts of watching exposes the fantasy of a stable, objective and detached viewpoint from the outside that would unify perception and synthesise it into the one true meaning. It thereby introduces a split *within* the spectator – a 'split spectator' who exactly mirrors the Lacanian 'split subject'. Van Hove's work demonstrates exemplarily that this intermedial fold is purely formal. It does not, for instance, result from the thematic resonances of Roman and contemporary US warfare, but it is situated in the spectators' aisthetic experience: we experience ourselves as subject *and* object of spectating at the same time and we hit the impossible moment of encountering our own subjective gaze as spectators as object in the performance. It is precisely as a result of this parallax view that *Regie* most powerfully leaves the representative regime of art behind: rather than *representing* the impossible viewing position for us to watch and interpret, *Regie* uses theatral dynamics as its means by which to write right into the performance the incommensurable positions of spectating and our negations of the collapsing boundaries between the subject and object of the performance. As a result, we see and experience *both* fiction and reality from a minimally distant perspective.

Desubstantialising self-consciousness: Guy Cassiers

The 'multisensual', media- and image-based *Regie* of Guy Cassiers achieves a similar parallax effect through different means. First and foremost, it emphasises (almost to the degree of isolating) the semiotic, symbolic and imaginary exchange between stage and spectators. While the exactly calculated dramaturgy of Cassiers's *Proust* strategically extracted plotlines, motifs and characters from the multi-volume novel, the production still went notably further than other stage or screen versions, which mostly concentrated on the narrative strands themselves. Instead of streamlining, redoubling, or simply illustrating the action of the plot, Cassiers's *Regie* used essential theatral means to connect the representation of dramatic fiction with central themes of the novel, such as the question of the reliability of memory and the adequacy of language. These aspects of Proust had rarely been transferred to the stage or screen before. The visual and other mediatised information functioned like a permanent commentary on the dialogue and the dramatic narrative, offering – not unlike a voice-over in film – a counterpoint to the narrative representation, supplementing its meaning and framing the spectatorial perception. Watching the performance thus became 'a semiotic *rite de passage* corresponding to the apprenticeship to signs the narrator of Proust's novels underwent' (Boenisch 2007, 123). I here alluded to Gilles Deleuze's analysis in his dissertation on *Proust and Signs* where he maintains that the *Recherche* is not about finding the lost past, nor even about the much invoked sensuous remembrances that cannot be expressed in words, such as the infamous madeleine cake, the Vinteuil sonata or Vermeer's image of the *View of Delft*. It is, Deleuze argued, in fact 'based not on the exposition of memory, but on the apprenticeship to signs' (Deleuze [1964] 2000, 4). Cassiers staged the theatrical equivalent to this apprenticeship. The pluri-vocal and pluri-focal multisensuality of his *Regie* made the 'dematerialised signs of art' described by Deleuze experientially available: signs which cease to function effortlessly, which disrupt any coherent and unified efficiency of medial representation through the very substance of the semiotic material, producing instead 'the absolute and ultimate Difference' (41). Cassiers's Proust cycle therefore did not cohere in purely semiotic terms, as measured against the novels' plots (their 'content'), but it offered equivalents to the kinetic and aisthetic experience of reading the novels and to their central formal and structural concerns and challenges.

Cassiers continued with further large-scale projects, such as his *Triptych of Power*, a trilogy of plays on Hitler, Stalin and George W. Bush, which opened his tenure at Antwerp's Toneelhuis in 2006. He also turned to opera, directing his controversial *Ring* cycle, co-produced by the Teatro alla Scala in Milan and the Staatsoper Unter den Linden in Berlin (2010–12). Simultaneously with the latter, he created the trilogy *De Man Zonder Eigenschappen*, based on Austrian author Robert Musil's unfinished novel *Der Mann ohne Eigenschaften* (*The Man without Qualities*, 1930–42). He then started a Shakespeare cycle, with *Hamlet vs Hamlet* (again with playwright Tom Lanoye), and *Mcbth*, a music theatre adaptation of 'the Scottish play' created with composer Dominique Pauwels (both created in the 2013/14 season). With these recent works, Cassiers's *Regie* completed a transition which can be described, in Hegelian terms, as a step from 'conscious reflexivity' to 'self-consciousness'. His Proust cycle was an exemplary illustration of the starting point, where he used audio-visual technology, in particular, to create a theatral 'subjective camera' perspective, corresponding to the point of view of the narrator or a fictional character as articulated in the novel. This strategy, in all its multisensual effect, still relied on what Deleuze described as the signs of sensuous impression, which for him remain 'material signs'. They do not yet arrive at what Deleuze but also Proust, Cassiers and even Hegel variously refer to as 'the essence' of signs, or their 'essential understanding'.

Recent productions, in particular the Musil trilogy, went further and offered a theatral experience of the 'negative subjectivity' that is at the heart of Žižek's critical philosophy. Exploiting the theatral parallax, these productions allowed the spectators a 'confrontation with the nothingness of our selves that enables our subjective engagement with the world' (Boenisch 2014b). This crucial leap in Cassiers's work became tangible in a small-scale work that followed the *Proust* tetralogy. *Hersenschimmen*, after J. Bernlef's 1984 novel, translated into English as *Out of Mind*. It opened in March 2006 and brought to a close Cassiers's tenure at Ro Theater. The novel's protagonist, the ageing Maarten Klein (played by senior actor Joop Keesmaat, who retired from the stage with this role), suffers from dementia. Caringly looked after by his wife Vera, he increasingly loses his grip on the everyday reality around him. The novel is narrated in the first person, in a synchronic, chronologic stream-of-consciousness mode. Bernlef's readers become gradually aware of odd gaps and inconsistencies, and, ultimately, see the narration disintegrate: Over the course of the final pages, the novel collapses into syntactic fragments. Seeing the world through Maarten's eyes, the readers come to empathise with his perspective, but they also have to cope with an increasingly unreliable narrator, as Bernlef refrains from offering any corrective, distanced narrative voice. It is obvious that this short novel is the stuff Cassiers's theatre is made of. His adaptation, however, continued a shift in his own work that had become evident in the concluding part of the *Proust* cycle: going beyond the novels and drawing on *Monsieur Proust*, the published diaries of Proust's housekeeper, Céleste Albaret, this section eventually turned the novels' narrator (referred to throughout the playscripts as 'Proust', in distinction to 'Marcel', the novel's first-person protagonist) himself into the protagonist.

The experience of reading Bernlef's novel and that of seeing Cassiers's production remained distinct from the start. Cassiers added an external mediating framework, which allowed for a more distanced perspective and a spectatorial experience from without. The spectators were kept in the standard spectating position opposite the dramatic action. Very cleverly, then, Cassiers used his multisensual audio-visual set-up no longer as an epic, narrative device, but as a theatrical lens that – purely externally – synced Maarten's mind with the audience's spectatorial perception. Cassiers exploited practically the metaphoric short-circuit between the world-making power of the mind and the world-making power of theatre. As a result, the intermedial gaps that the spectators of Proust still experienced as a staging of the novel's form and its concerns, now radically concerned the audience's own negotiation with the materiality and mediality of theatre: the spectators themselves became the subject of the 'subjective camera' point of view.

In its first section, *Hersenschimmen* incorporated and exploited (or rather: repossessed and repositioned) theatral conventions and traditions that had hitherto remained remote from Cassiers's *Regie*. They were crucial to establish the reflexive spectatorial parallax. The untypically realistic set included wooden tables, chairs, doors, shelves, stairs and even an actual dog on stage. This illusionist space of realism (similar to the realist kernel in van Hove's work) was contained within an exposed frame that was elevated to the middle height of the stage. It could easily be read as a stylised apartment, but at the same time it also replicated a picture- or screen-frame on stage. Within this frame, three (frameless) screens initially showed a realist representation of windows opening onto an idyllic winter landscape with falling snowflakes, created through pre-recorded projections of a real exterior space. These screens soon began to double up as both literal and even more so metaphoric 'windows to the world' from Maarten's own deteriorating perspective. In monologic episodes live images of the actor's face were superimposed onto the realistic landscape projection. As narrative devices, the 'window screens' now offered a view into Maarten's mind, showing his perceptual irritation, isolation and growing seclusion. They rendered the broken linearity and incoherence of the narrator's narrative from the novel by means of jump-cuts, fast-forwarded pictures and loops, additionally aided by increasingly disconcerting electronic sound effects. The realist illusion was further distorted by digital video effects, such as blurred and fuzzy pictures, incoherent red-green shadows of the images, delay or pixelation. Eventually, the outside

Figure 18 Incorporating the fractured parallax into the theatral texture: Guy Cassiers's adaptation of J. Bernlef's novel *Out of Mind* (Ro Theater, Rotterdam, 2006; design: Marc Warning). The realistic interior gradually disappeared and dissolved, creating a theatral equivalent to the protagonist's dementia. Photo: Ro Theater/Sjouke Dijkstra.

landscape disappeared entirely and was replaced by dark negative images of trees and forests (see Figure 18).

Crucially, Cassiers went further to show the disintegration of a mind, projected by means of his multisensual media set-up. Eventually, in his *Hersenschimmen*, the entire theatrical frame that served to exteriorise Maarten's worldview equally disintegrated over the course of the performance. The early scenes with Maarten, his wife Vera and with Phil, the female nurse who moved in with the couple to care for them (and their, in Cassiers's production, real dog who was on stage), were still realistically played. Gradually, however, the theatrical machinery was used to irritate and disturb the spectators' perception. There were, for instance, scenes when the two women talked to Maarten, yet the audience only heard what they were saying (again, all speech was relayed via microphones) through speakers placed behind the set in the huge stage space, thereby creating a far-away echo and a muffled, reverberating acoustic effect. Maarten's simultaneous monologue of trajectories entirely of his own was meanwhile clearly audible through the main speakers. The audience was thus put in a position that emphasised their own aisthetic perception in the theatre, a position no longer corresponding to a narrative position in the novel. Towards the end, as the syntax falls apart in Bernlef's writing, on Cassiers's stage the set with its furniture and windows imploded, too. The back- and side-drops that had initially framed the illusionist living-room collapsed. At this moment, the projection of Maarten's face that had previously appeared on the three 'window screens' was projected as one huge magnification across the entire proscenium, before eventually dissolving into flickering lines and pixels of 'white noise'. The spectators were left facing Maarten, who was sitting on a chair in the middle of the raised platform, surrounded by nothing but the bare scaffolding, which allowed the spectators a clear view into the backstage area. Neither Maarten's mind nor the theatre machinery produced any more realities and worlds. And even this bare set eventually disappeared as the dim lights went down, leaving only a single spotlight which illuminated Maarten's head exactly in the middle of the stage; the performance's concluding image.

From representing a theatral reality, which gradually lost its organic coherence by being turned into an artistic bricolage of heterogeneous signs that disturb the representative order of causality and linearity (paradigmatically in the first three parts of *Proust*), Cassiers's *Regie* had thus moved towards incorporating the distortion and the fractured views of the multiple, incompatible parallax perspectives into the very texture of theatrical presentation. Instead of blending the spectatorial perspective with the character's or narrator's perspective and thereby evoking compassion and sympathy for Maarten's distorted view as an Alzheimer's sufferer, Cassiers's *Hersenschimmen* demanded that *qua* intermedial parallax, we negotiate with our own distorting act of watching, as the theatrical frame – and not just the represented fiction – disintegrated. This development of Cassiers's *Regie* follows to a certain extent the trajectory of Deleuze's argument in between his early and late discussions of art, literature and cinema, which, as Slavoj Žižek has extensively shown, differ from the popular 'Deleuzianisms' of the Guattari-inspired molar territory in *Mille plateaux* (see Žižek 2004). In his texts on Proust and Carroll, and again in his late books on film, Deleuze grappled with what he terms a 'desubstantialisation' of affects. He interrogated instances in these works where affects, such as boredom or love, were no longer attributed to individuals (persons or characters), but instead permeated the texts (and films) as free-floating event: as immaterial, depersonalised, 'desubstantialised' affect. Deleuze celebrated the art of cinema as 'Sense Event' that liberates affects, as well as the spectatorial gaze and the experience of time from their attribution to a specific subject: as incorporeal effects of material causes they were only retroactively attributed to positive entities. Žižek famously described this 'logic of sense' as the logic of 'Organs without Bodies', as opposed to the well-rehearsed Deleuze–Artaudian topos of the 'Bodies without organs', where virtuality engenders the emergence of bodies as pure becoming. The film image acted for Deleuze as a 'sterile' surface for such becoming. Žižek further illustrated Deleuze's argument by pointing out a similar 'desubstantialisation' of affects and desire in Hitchcock's films. He reminded us of some well-known shots, which appear to represent a subjective point of view, relating to a specific character, yet a closer look reveals that they are from an entirely imaginary perspective. They are only retroactively, precisely through their misreading as a subjective point of view, reassociated with a specific character. According to Žižek's Lacanian perspective, such a mistaken identity is not 'wrong' but instead reveals the fundamental truth about human 'negative' subjectivity. In a similar way, the perspective staged in *Hersenschimmen* is, even beyond desire, the placeholder for our own cognitive process of spectating. The production staged the very process of desubstantialisation of the symbolic as well as affective order.

Cassiers's *Regie* thus inscribed the spectatorial gaze as multisensual, yet desubstantialised viewpoint right into the texture of the performance. It cuts the 'objective' distance, and instead 'reterritorialises', to use the Deleuzian term, the subjective spectatorial gaze in the object that is being watched *qua* the parallax, reflexive dynamic force of *thea*. The spectators (their gaze, affects, desires) are fully absorbed within the 'sterile' (or, with Schiller, autonomous) structure of signs. It also arrests the movement of the drama in a pure abundance of text in its virtuality of appearing (the Deleuzian 'becoming'). As a result, in Cassiers's productions, there is, corresponding to the Derridean formula, 'nothing beyond the text'. The playtext and, in *Hersenschimmen*, even the entire apparatus of theatrical illusion appear as 'sterile surface': they become 'pure form', in its virtual (theatral) potentiality *before* the 'suture' of representation. *Qua* its kinetic, aisthetic and semantic dynamic, this dense textuality resists a coherent, causal and symmetrical totalisation within the horizon of representation. Cassiers therefore exposes his spectators to a dis-integrating multiplicity of the 'appearing of signs' – a perpetual excess of contrasting, confronting and complementing streams of mediatised information. His *Regie* privileges neither speech nor visual information, neither represented plot nor present action. The resulting effect ties in with the Lacanian–Žižekian assumption that instead of 'the (one) message', the one 'true meaning' which the spectator needs to reveal, there is, on the contrary, always *too much* meaning that is appearing: as a result of the excess of symbolisation and mediation there are *too many* parts that no longer add up to 'one'. The usually bare stage of his productions highlights this in an even sharper way; *Hersenschimmen*, meanwhile, stages this process in its reverse direction, culminating in dark nothingness.

As spectators, we are here no longer positioned as observers or even voyeurs opposite a text and a fiction that, as it were, happens without us, and we remain 'unseen'. The opposite is the case: the desubstantialising effect of the sterile surface of theatral textuality presents us with another instance where the artwork, as it were, watches us and reverses the spectatorial gaze. The resulting reflexive relation to ourselves as spectators emphasises our 'subjectivity' in the Hegelian–Žižekian 'negative' sense: the 'desubstantialisation of affects', and the absorption of both the show and gaze of *thea* within the sterile density of the theatral texture generated by the mediatised streams of signs on stage, makes this 'negative subjectivity' sense-able. This *Regie* no longer creates a spectacle for our distanced, 'secret' gaze of the consumer, not even for the sympathetic, compassionate 'enlightened spectator'. Instead, it radically demands that we confront ourselves as gazing subjects by exploiting the formal gap of the 'split spectator' introduced earlier in this chapter and by refusing a coherent, singular and 'subjective' position of spectating in parallel to the subjective position of enunciation within the symbolic order of language that bestows individual identity on the subject:

> [I]n pronouncing a word, the subject contracts his being outside himself; he 'coagulates' the core of his being in an external sign. In the (verbal) sign, I – as it were – find myself outside myself, I posit my unity outside myself, in a signifier which represents me. (Žižek 2007, 43)

This logic of the 'subject of the enounced' mirrors the logic of the 'subject of the audience', which likewise coagulates its individuality 'as one' in its spectatorial position outside and opposite the object that is being watched. This safe position of an 'objective distance' is undermined by the parallax perspective of theatre, which – according to the model of the 'theatral square' outlined above – always insists on the dialectic friction with the 'public subject of spectating' that is situated in the present, material reality of the situation. The resulting tension confronts our spectating with our own absolute, pure, and immaterial, 'sterile' self that spectates. It thus forces us to 'tarry with the negative', with the negative condition of our own subjective agency. It thereby demands our responsibility and almost forces us to actively repossess our task of spectatorship, precisely out of the ruins of any symbolic and imaginary order staged in *Hersenschimmen*.

Regie and the response-ability of spectating

The *Regie* of Guy Cassiers and Ivo van Hove stands exemplarily for contemporary negotiations with digital technology and audio-visual media machinery that puts these means in the service of the dialectic force that is (artistic) mediation. Their at times minute realignments and refractions of the theatre space and of spectating conventions thus contribute to the prominent debate on 'spectatorship'. Jacques Rancière rightly challenged, in *The Emancipated Spectator*, the widely assumed binary of a 'passively' consuming spectator and an audience getting 'actively' up on their feet. As he aptly demonstrated, many 'interactive' performances fail in the crucial task of challenging the underlying dominant 'partition of the sensible' that distributes the power of being heard and being seen. Instead of actually emancipating the spectators, such performances create even more 'stultifying' theatre experiences; the audience may no longer be seated in conventional arrangements, yet nevertheless 'what the spectator *must see* is what the director *makes her see*' (Rancière 2009b, 14; original emphasis). Following Rancière, the true emancipation of the spectator must mean fostering, without any reservation, the spectators' own intelligence as individual interpreters 'plotting their own paths in the forest of things, acts, and signs that confront or surround them' (17). Such a commitment invokes the key demands Schiller associated with the ultimately human activity of play, discussed in Chapter 3. The liberty of play affords critical distance in its insistence on ultimate autonomy, inefficiency and disfunctionality, thus by taking a distance both from the hegemonic political order of spectating and, as individual subject, from the streamlined integration into the collective of the spectating public. For Rancière, genuine emancipation will kindle in the spectators 'the power each of them has to translate what she perceives in her own way, to link it to the unique intellectual adventure that makes her similar to all the rest in as much as this adventure is not like any other' (17).

Such individual acts of 'par(t)-taking', in Rancière's understanding of this term, evoke, and indeed provoke, our individual spectatorial 'response-ability', as Hans-

Thies Lehmann famously expressed it with reference to an aesthetics that insists on 'the mutual implication of actors and spectators in the theatrical production' (Lehmann 2006, 186). In the epilogue to his seminal overview of new forms of theatre-making developed long before the advent of digital communication and the all-pervasive social mediasphere of the present that is at the heart of what Jodi Dean calls 'communicative capitalism', Lehmann already located the principal political potential, and even duty, of theatre performance precisely in its insistence on a relationality between the production and the consumption of meaning:[8] in its emphasis not only on our ability to respond, but on our obligation of 'respons(e)-ability' from which we, as spectators, must not step away. The *Regie* of van Hove and Cassiers exemplarily addresses the intelligence of the Rancièrian 'interpreter' as it takes its duty of mediation seriously, in its fullest Hegelian sense of *Vermittlung*: as necessary intervention of dialectic sublation, as theatral 'intermission', according to Badiou's term introduced above. This becomes evident where their work goes beyond simply using contemporary digital media technology on stage, and instead *misguides* and *misuses* not least our own spectating conventions, while at the same time relinquishing its own desire of authority. This prompts our reflexive awareness of media and of the processes of mediation, as Boris Groys emphasises:

> Media show themselves only if and in so far as they frustrate, shift and deconstruct the individual intentions of their users. If they would transmit these intentions absolutely adequately, their works would remain non-observable, structurally concealed. (Groys 2011, 9)

As he continues to assert, it is in the very encounter of these faultlines of media – which correspond to what I describe as inter-medial effects (Boenisch 2006) – that 'media have to be mediated by a subjectivity that takes upon itself the role of mediator of the media' (Groys 2011, 9). For Groys, this is the role which art has come to play since its entrance into the *dispositif* of modernism. I see here the structural position of *Regie* as theatral 'playing space' of mediation and subjectivisation. It ultimately asserts 'the Real of spectating', according to Žižek's insistence that

> the 'Real as impossible' is the cause of the impossibility of our ever attaining the 'neutral' non-perspectival view of the object. There *is* a truth, and not everything is relative – but this truth is the truth of the perspectival distortion *as such*, not a truth distorted by the partial view from a one-sided perspective. (Žižek 2012, 47f.; original emphasis)

This reality of the parallax could not be further from contemporary obsessions with authentic reality and 'real people' that pervade media, and many forms, practices and discourses of theatre, too.

Against the use of media content to fill the lack that is subjectivity (as 'pure self-relating negativity', Žižek 2012, 174) on an imaginary level or even through merely providing the one point of closure outside, in the coagulated 'point' of the spectator, the *Regie* of van Hove and Cassiers exemplarily outlines a theatre that asserts the empty position of spectating. It asserts and even expands on the symbolic representations offered by canonical texts from a range of sources. Yet, at the same time it realises an effect – expressed above as the ultimate density of the text – that is equivalent to the crucial shift from representation to presentation which Dieter Henrich already charted in Fichte's idealism:[9] the mediation of these texts brings us back to the self, but *against* the much criticised 'metaphysics of presence', as its 'presentation' now is disclosed as an effect of mediation. The reappropriation of canonical texts in this form of *Regie* thus escapes the strategies of 'deconstruction', or the label of 'postmodern'. The point of 'postdramatic theatre' – and hence its name – was precisely such a new investment in classical 'texts' in the widest sense of the term. Around the turn of the millennium, we witnessed such new, serious explorations into cultural histories and traditions, including all their 'baggage' and critical legacies, which Pavis described as 'the return of text and new writing of the 1990s' (Pavis 2013, 15).

Against the postmodernist challenge, deconstruction and dissolution (and, perhaps, even disavowal) of the founding gestures of a white, Western, male, bourgeois modern Enlightenment culture, we have more recently seen – in philosophical, political and aesthetic debates – a strategic 'post-postmodern' dialectic sublation of the postmodern deconstruction of modernity. I see the 'return of the canonical text' as a theatral form of such 'post-foundational' critique, as Oliver Marchart described it (see Marchart 2007).[10] This approach will still dissect any positing of a transcendent totality, universality or essence as a symbolic stand-in for the 'absent ground' of subjectivity and any social agency. At the same time, however, the 'weakening of ground does not lead to the assumption of the total absence of all grounds, but rather to the assumption of the impossibility of a *final* ground' (Marchart 2007, 2). In contrast to postmodern *anti*-foundational thought, such post-foundational thought thus does not outright reject this masking, but activates it in its productivity. The notion of 'contingency' to describe the (necessary) stand-ins that ground subjective agency as social being and critical 'response-ability' has become a prominent marker of these 'post-foundational' reconceptions of the 'negative ground' (see Butler *et al.* 2000). As moments of 'intermission', the parallax force of *Regie* strategically – through performative and theatral force – posits a reconfigured, contingent ground. It stages parallax disruptions of the saturated symbolic field of digital media representation by allowing acts of contingent, individual encounter – above all, encounters with our own spectatorial complicity and responsibility. They become the starting point for tackling, and merely coping with, the present reality of, in Žižek's words, our 'living in the end times' (see Žižek 2010). From this purely formal politicity of the parallax perspective, we now turn towards approaches of *Regie* which not only implicitly, but on their very surface seek to counter the encompassing global logic of 'communicative capitalism', which has turned art, and theatre, from an ideological, superstructural field beyond the economic base into a most prominent site of 'creative work', 'immaterial labour' and thus the exploitation of what Marx termed the 'general intellect' in the name of maximising profit (see Berardi 2009; Dean 2009).

Notes

1 Toneelgroep Amsterdam was founded by Van Hove's predecessor, the radical playwright-director Gerardjan Rijnders (b. 1949), who was an assistant to East German director Fritz

Marquardt while he worked in Amsterdam for several years after leaving the GDR. It was the first experimental theatre company associated with the 1960s Dutch theatre revolution to subsequently merge, in 1987, with a resident, municipal theatre, thereby taking the radical performance 'avant-garde' from the fringe right to the city's main stage. This merger formed what is now the largest resident repertory ensemble in the Netherlands, based at the historic Stadsschouwburg at the city's Leidseplein.

2   Van Hove, born in Antwerp and trained at the Brussels conservatoire, started off creating imagistic performance collages, staged in empty buildings in his home town, with his first company AKT, the 'Antwerps Kollektief voor Teaterprojekten'. Their work already featured the bare architectural spaces created by Versweyveld. Soon after, they began directing texts from the Western canonical repertoire, such as Euripides' *Bacchae* and Shakespeare's *Macbeth* in 1987, and Schiller's *Don Karlos* in 1988. They then moved to the Netherlands, where the inseparable duo have spent most of their career: Before his appointment as artistic director of Toneelgroep Amsterdam in 2001, van Hove lead Eindhoven-based touring company Zuidelijk Toneel as well as being artistic director of the annual Holland Festival from 1997. Already van Hove's earliest work became recognised within the New York performance scene; in the early 1980s, his pieces were prominently reviewed in the *Drama Review* (see Willinger 1981 and 1983). This led to the director's association with the New York Theatre Workshop, and over the years he formed his own local 'ensemble', working with a cast of regular actors on productions such as Eugene O'Neill's *More Stately Mansions* (1997), Tennessee Williams's *Streetcar Named Desire* (1998), Molière's *Misanthrope* (2007) and Lillian Hellman's *Little Foxes* (2010). Van Hove also created a number of productions in Germany, at Deutsches Schauspielhaus Hamburg, Schaubühne Berlin and Kammerspiele München, and he directed opera and musicals as well, for example Wagner's *Ring* cycle for the Flemish Opera Antwerp, and the Dutch version of the musical *Rent*.

3   Studying graphic design at the Antwerp Academy of the Arts, Cassiers mingled with the local experimental performance scene, which at the time also included van Hove; he even played the lead role in van Hove's 1981 experimental performance piece *Geruchten*. Later, Cassiers created ambitious youth theatre work. From the outset, most of his productions were based on novels by Ian McEwan, Martin Amis, Marguerite Duras, Tolstoy or Pushkin. In the mid-1990s, in *Rotjoch* (Cassiers's version of Patrick McCabe's *Butcher Boy*), he introduced projections of texts, and soon after, live cameras, creating his signature style. After running the Rotterdam-based Ro Theater as artistic co-director (with Alize Zandwijk) from 1998 until 2006, Cassiers took over Het Toneelhuis in his Belgian home town. Similar to the merger of Rijnders's Toneelgroep with the local Stadsschouwburg ensemble at Amsterdam in 1987, it had been formed as the Antwerp Koninklijke Nederlandse Schouwburg (KNS), merged in 1998 with the Blauwe Maandag Companie of director Luk Perceval, which was one of the key 'second-generation' Flemish experimental theatre companies to continue the 1960s revolution in Dutch-speaking theatre. In 2006, Perceval moved on to the Berlin Schaubühne and then, in 2009, to Hamburg's Thalia Theater.

4   I discussed this production in detail in Boenisch 2007. Cassiers created the cycle over the period of four years with dramaturg Erwin Jans, author Eric de Kuyper, set designer Marc Warning and the media collective Kantoor voor Bewegend Beeld ('Office for Moving Image') for Ro Theater Rotterdam.

5   Theatre here echoes a central tenet of Žižek's political critique, which hinges on a similar relational *Aufhebung* of the modern transcendental subject: 'What matters is not the location of the Self in objective reality, the impossible-real of "what I am objectively", but *how*

I am located in my own fantasy, how my own fantasy sustains my being as subject' (Žižek 2012, 707).

6 The audience was later, in a final scene change after 257 minutes, asked to retake their seats in the auditorium, and the doors of the venue were closed again for the final demise of Antony and Cleopatra.

7 'The personal and the grand, the micro and the macro, always go hand in hand. The beauty is precisely that private circumstances have influence on world politics, and vice versa. How that happens, is exactly what interests me in theatre' (van Hove, quoted in Coussens 2008, 4).

8 'The basic structure of perception mediated by media is such that there is no experience of a connection among the individual images received but above all no connection between the receiving and sending of signs; there is no experience of a relation between address and answer' (Lehmann 2006, 185).

9 'As soon as I have arrived at presentation from representation, the question "What is represented?" has an entirely different meaning. In representation, of course, it would be the object that is represented. But what is presented in the representation in the sense of *darstellen*? The answer is obvious: the self!' (Henrich 2003, 200; see also Žižek 2012, ch. 3, 'Fichte's Choice').

10 Both postdramatic theories in theatre studies and the post-foundational line of thinking in critical philosophy see the central aspects that define their postulated 'paradigm shifts' as always already at work within the (dramatic or political) structures they seem to overcome.

8

Theatre in the age of semiocapitalism: on *Regie*, realism and political critique

Paint bombs smashed against the walls and hit the face and body of the medic-turned-activist Thomas Stockmann, the protagonist of Ibsen's 1882 drama *An Enemy of the People*. He had just disclosed in a public meeting his discovery that the city's spa waters are contaminated with industrial waste from local factories, the discovery which his own brother, the city councillor, seeks to hush up. Yet, the audience in Thomas Ostermeier's 2012 production was no longer certain whether to side unequivocally with this activist who promises to sort out all problems. Already in Ibsen's original drama, Stockmann uses his speech to the public to discuss 'greater issues' than the poisoned wells. At this point, Ostermeier (b. 1968) and his dramaturg Florian Borchmeyer (b. 1974), who had translated the playtext into present-day colloquial German, inserted *The Coming Insurrection* into their production. This controversial anti-globalisation manifesto from 2007, published on the Internet by an anonymous French anarchist group calling itself The Invisible Committee, was hailed by some as a programmatic statement of the 'Occupy' protests. Others, especially in Germany, were very critical of its references to the thought of Martin Heidegger and Carl Schmitt, philosophers involved in Nazi ideology.[1] Ostermeier thereby highlighted a similar ambivalence in Ibsen's protagonist, who also attacks corrupt politicians and longs for a new society. Stockmann's call for the extermination of the political class was later copied verbatim in Adolf Hitler's *Mein Kampf*, as the programme booklet reminded us, presenting Ibsen's drama and Hitler's appropriation side by side. The production went on to replace the semi-comedic portrayal of the local assembly on stage with a debate with the actual audience in the auditorium. Actor David Ruland, in his role as newspaper editor Aslaksen, directly questioned the audience with the air of a contemporary TV talk show host, and microphones were passed to those wishing to make statements. This debate naturally differed each night, sometimes ending after a few casual comments, on other occasions developing into long, heated exchanges between factions in the audience.

Ein Volksfeind thus continued the way in which Ostermeier's previous Ibsen productions, such as *Nora* (2002) and the 2005 *Hedda Gabler*, echoed current affairs and the contemporary cosmopolitan lifestyle of his (and our) generation. Ostermeier sums up his transformative approach towards canonical playtexts:

> There is a literary core, and it is from there we develop our new material. This is more than a theatre of interpretation! It is a theatre of creation, and not at all of transmogrified originals – but of processes of research, concentration, and a collective intensification towards the production. (In Raddatz 2013, 15f.)

While his *Volksfeind* (and similarly, his celebrated *Hamlet* from 2008) was somewhat exceptional for the director's neo-realistic aesthetics in the suspension of the fourth wall, the productions' explicit political resonances were not. The fluid interference between the world of the plot, the theatral situation and the socio-cultural and material realities and political issues outside the theatre have become characteristic forces driving Ostermeier's *Regie* ever since he came to fame by introducing British 'In-Yer-Face' playwriting to German audiences at his Baracke theatre in the late 1990s.[2] Nowadays, a typical Schaubühne's season brochure, such as the spring 2014 edition, opens with an interview between Ostermeier and political philosopher Antonio Negri, where their main topic of conversation is the contemporary crisis of capitalism.

A similar politically motivated porosity between representation, presentation and present realities marks the work of Frank Castorf, the other pronounced political Berlin theatre *Intendant*. Yet, he takes his productions to an opposite aesthetic extreme. Whereas (West German) Ostermeier situates his productions in the recognisable present, (East German) Castorf (b. 1951) places his stage versions, for instance, of novels and novellas by Ibsen's Eastern contemporaries Dostoevsky, Bulgakov and Chekhov in a no less real, yet resolutely foreign, hostile and dirty other world. The director's stubborn refusal to integrate within the clean, homogenised world of Western capitalism has been most visibly expressed by the three letters 'OST' (East) that have been mounted on the top of the Volksbühne building ever since Castorf took over as the theatre's artistic director in 1992.[3] In contrast to the commodified authenticity and realism of global mass media, his work offers a realism underpinned by this resistant attitude. Castorf himself speaks of seeking to infuse his work with 'the simple concept of reality' (Castorf 2002, 75) – albeit a reality that often seems more akin to the abyss of the psychological Real as described by Lacanian psychoanalysis.

The *Regie* of both directors exploits a heightened (hyper-)realism, which fully acknowledges the material reality of the performance itself. Within the singular space of the stage, their productions present the spectators with configurations of different realities, thereby creating parallax perspectives that invite various layers of recognition. Ostermeier blends fictional realities with elements of the present so that distant times and spaces resonate with each other. As he shows us that the drama of Ibsen's bourgeois protagonists still takes place in living-rooms in today's Berlin, he confronts his twenty-first-century audience with the Other in our selves. Classic dramatic texts by Ibsen, Shakespeare and others function as an 'outside eye' whose perspective offer a distancing otherness to our everyday experience. This otherness is heightened by the sets created by Ostermeier's regular scenographer Jan Pappelbaum (b. 1966), an architect trained at the Weimar Bauhaus. In *Ein Volksfeind*, he created a black box that was far more abstract than previous sets. The space initially portrayed Stockmann's living-room, while doubling as newspaper office and assembly hall in later acts. During brief scene changes, where the actors themselves changed the scenery even while the final moments of the previous scene were still playing, they simply wrote the new location on the wall. Similarly, the artwork by visual artist Katharina Ziemke sketched out scenic elements such as a radio, a lamp and an espresso machine in chalk.

Castorf, meanwhile, forces us (often rather violently) to confront our selves in the extreme Other, as he explores the similarity of sensitivities and mental attitudes in the distinct time periods of late Tsarist Russia and today's late capitalism. His stage spaces at once evoke a hyper-real, yet almost mythological 'Russian' foreignness that is then permeated with anachronistic familiar clips and images from contemporary movies, daily soaps or other iconic pop-cultural citations. For the director's 2013 staging of Chekhov's *The Duel*, designer Aleksandar Denić (famous for his work with Serbian film director Emir Kusturica) created such a hyper-real set. It staged the essence of a desperate Caucasian village. In its centre was a huge wooden cabin, which was surrounded by the onion dome of the compulsory church and heaps of steaming, earthy-brown coal. A large billboard, reminiscent of the placards with socialist propaganda slogans one used to find across the communist countries, was mounted. Its inscription in red Cyrillic letters read, in translation, 'You, my brother, have been spoiled by the Germans. Yes, the Germans!' (see Figure 19). The fact that only a handful of audience members were able to decipher this Russian signage – formerly lingua franca in communist East Germany – perfectly expressed the strangeness, difference and resistance which have characterised Castorf's provocative work from the start of his career in the GDR. Illustrating what an American reviewer once described as the director's 'genus disorder' (Byrne 2009), *The Duel* presented an all-female cast, except for the Chekhovian stock doctor character. Instead of introducing direct references, Castorf's *Regie* then added numerous distant resonances into the staging of Chekhov's 1891 novella: a late 1960s Czech sci-fi movie (in which a single group of women survives a nuclear apocalypse, the director's prompt for his eccentric casting idea), graphic clips (visibly including men) from the black-and-white movie version of Henry Miller's notorious *Quiet Days in Clichy*, whose topic mirrors the amorous flight into the countryside that sets Chekhov's plot in motion.[4] These movie snippets were projected on a large screen that towered over the stage, reminiscent of a drive-in cinema. Across the four-hour performance, this screen also broadcast the live-feed shots created by a visible camera crew on stage. Their images were the only means by which the audience was able to follow the many scenes that took place within the closed four walls of the wooden cabin. Furthermore, the production included Castorf's characteristic references to American warfare. During several air raids that were obviously not from Chekhov, the characters gathered in a bunker underneath their hut, speaking ominously of 'the Americans' and their invasion; Chekhov's fictional village is situated in present-day Georgia, which was invaded by the Russian

Figure 19 Strangeness, difference and resistance: the audience for Frank Castorf's 2013 production *The Duel* after Anton Chekhov's 1891 novella was only able to follow the scenes that took place within the wooden cabin via the live-feed projection on a huge screen that towered over Aleksandar Denić's set. On screen Lilith Stangenberg as Nadeshda (right) and Kathrin Wehlisch as Ilja Kirilin. Photo: Thomas Aurin.

army in 2008. There were also visual allusions to global capitalism (some US-branded barrels of oil), alongside the typical citations from popular culture, such as film posters from Spielberg's *Duel* and from another Western movie of the same name, which were prominently mounted in the set, as well as popular music. In *The Duel*, alongside Castorf's preferred rock songs (including Neil Young and Jimi Hendrix), we heard some Austrian chansons and Eastern European classical music.

Both Ostermeier and Castorf are committed to the legacy of German political theatre in the Brechtian tradition. Ostermeier studied in the directing class of Manfred Karge, and Heiner Müller's work was formative for Castorf. Both consider a distinct theatral realism as a vital force to safeguard at least some political efficacy of theatre art against the all-absorbing machinery of today's global 'communicative capitalism' (Dean 2009). They put the theatral forces of *kinesis* and *aisthesis* in play in order to tackle a similar symbolic and imaginary totalitarianism to that which Herbert Marcuse once ascribed to the post-World War II 'advanced industrial society' (see Marcuse [1964] 2002). Since Marcuse's day, we have seen the development of what Italian activist Bifo Berardi described as 'semiocapitalism' (Berardi 2009), which (in the Western hemisphere) is largely dissociated from the material production of goods and the exploitation of manual labour and instead makes its profits from exploiting immaterial intellectual labour and financial capital. This configuration – Jodi Dean terms it with similar emphasis 'communicative capitalism' – has even further solidified such an all-pervasive discursive framework, characterised by the valorisation of any societal relation and any cultural manifestation, including art and theatre, in terms of economic value and functional efficiency alone. Mark Fisher calls this unchallenged narrative 'capitalist realism', evoking the doctrine of 'socialist realism' in the communist countries (see Fisher 2009).[5] Enmeshed in the global 'creative industry', even art and theatre are in danger of becoming tools of this uncritical ideology. As Fisher pointed out, capitalist realism no longer only attempts a retrospective incorporation of critical energy into the hegemonic ideology, but it serves the purpose of what he calls *precorporation* of critical, subversive positions in the first place: the staging of a playful 'gestural anti-capitalism [which] actually reinforces it' (9, 12). Similarly sceptical, Jodi Dean sees any artistic attempt to put forward alternative configurations of the sensible, through performances, films, novels or visual art, as merely a momentary illusion of activism to placate our conscience. According to her, such artistic pseudo-activism not only remains without consequence, but in fact redirects energies and engagement away from actual political intervention (Dean 2012, 11).

Ostermeier and Castorf reflect two generations and two artistic, as well as personal, biographies from the former German states. Their strategies of political *Regie* also point towards two alternative responses of theatre art to these fundamental challenges of communicative capitalism. Their outlines of a realism, which is perhaps best described as a 'negative realism', seek to counter the capitalist imperatives of functionality and efficiency by instilling an inefficient (hence 'negative') theatrical excess of play. It is often perceived in their work as a 'profanation' of classical plays, a reproach we should directly associate with Agamben's use of this term (Agamben 2007).[6] Rather than 'telling how it really is' and 'unmasking' ideology and hegemony, this realism, on the contrary, puts its theatral mask on. It seems to draw the conclusion from Slavoj Žižek's important assertion that critique of ideology does not work by *removing* some 'rose-tinted glasses' that prevent us from seeing the 'real' reality. Instead, it must make us *put on* 'anti-ideology glasses' to expose ideology; Žižek found the perfect illustration for this claim in John Carpenter's 1988 film *They Live* (see Žižek 2012, 999; the discussion also opens Žižek's *Pervert's Guide to Ideology* movie). Where Ostermeier's and Castorf's *Regie* brings the worlds of Ibsen and Chekhov into a collision with the ultimate present of the theatre situation, it creates a dis-functional theatral excess of senseable meanings. This playful surplus works as 'theatral anti-ideology glasses' that offer a critical 'X-ray' of ideology as these affective dimensions engage in a play with one of the most crucial forces behind ideology: the appeal and fascination of 'enjoyment', of what Lacan calls *jouissance*. It makes us do things while being fully aware that they are against our own interest, which the psychoanalytical perspective captures in the formula of festishistic disavowal, 'I know very well, but nevertheless …'. The two directors' insistence on realism taps, in different ways, into the force of *jouissance* through the theatrical play of meaning, corporeality and affect. It asserts the openness, the gaps, ambiguities and inconsistencies within the texts of Chekhov or Ibsen, without simply 'filling' or deciding them. The excess of this negative realism, which this chapter will explore further, then prepares the ground for a symbolic and imaginary remapping of the world. The frictions prompt a cognitive mapping, and thereby support a political strategy which Žižek gleaned from Hegel. In contrast to Jodi Dean he insists that the real political act always *precedes* any actual intervention in the world. It consists, above all, in the (re)structuring of our symbolic and imaginary order (a Rancièrian re-partitioning of the sensible) in a way that no longer precludes actual interventions, but that – against the lure of *jouissance* – makes them possible, if not necessary, in the first place. It is this work of restructuring our symbolic, imaginary and affective perception of reality and our investment in semiocapitalist *jouissance*, which the 'negative realism' of Castorf's and Ostermeier's *Regie* attempts, by negotiating, for instance, the political extremism of Ibsen's Stockmann, or the clear-sighted Count Myshkin, the eponymous 'idiot' of Dostoevsky's novel.

Composing the 'signifying stress': Frank Castorf

Since 1999 it has been impossible to speak about Frank Castorf's theatre work without mentioning the portacabin. In *Dämonen*, the director's first adaptation of a Dostoevsky novel ('Demons', the German title of *The Possessed*), his long-term design partner Bert Neumann (b. 1960) put a veritable bungalow on stage.[7] The audience was only able to peek through the windows and some large veranda doors. The scenes inside the construction, which critics frequently compared to the container building of the then new TV series *Big Brother*, were only relayed through cameras. Over the years, the experiments of Castorf, Neumann and video director Jan Speckenbach (b. 1970) became ever more radical. For *Der Idiot* (*The Idiot*, 2002), they transformed the entire interior of the Volksbühne, mounting a 400-square-metre set of the 'Neustadt' (New City). It covered over the entire space of the usual auditorium with a huge city piazza that was surrounded by bars, a travel agent's, a sex shop and other businesses, and where the audience was able to wander before the performance and during the interval. The spectators, meanwhile, were seated on multi-storey scaffolding mounted on the theatre's revolving stage (the 'Romantic World', as some neon signage revealed), enclosed by an entire street whose two-storey buildings were fully accessible to the actors (see Figures 20 and 21). The revolving stage was then turned so that the audience always faced the locus of the relevant scene. The gaze into the interior of these buildings was partly obscured; monitors and screens of various sizes were the only way of following most of the action in this production. Permutations of this basic concept have remained one of Castorf's trademarks, whether his sets are designed by Neumann or his other regular partner Aleksandar Denić.

Many discussions of these productions foreground aspects of visibility and mediatisation. The director's unconventional use of live-feed broadcasting, however, did not serve to contrast mediatised images with their material production, as in Katie Mitchell's work, for instance (see Boenisch 2010a, 164f.). As Erika Fischer-Lichte rightly emphasised, these sets call upon and challenge the audience's viewing habits, rehearsed through the daily use of TV and digital mass and social media. Already at the time when formats such as *Big Brother* and reality soaps were still new and

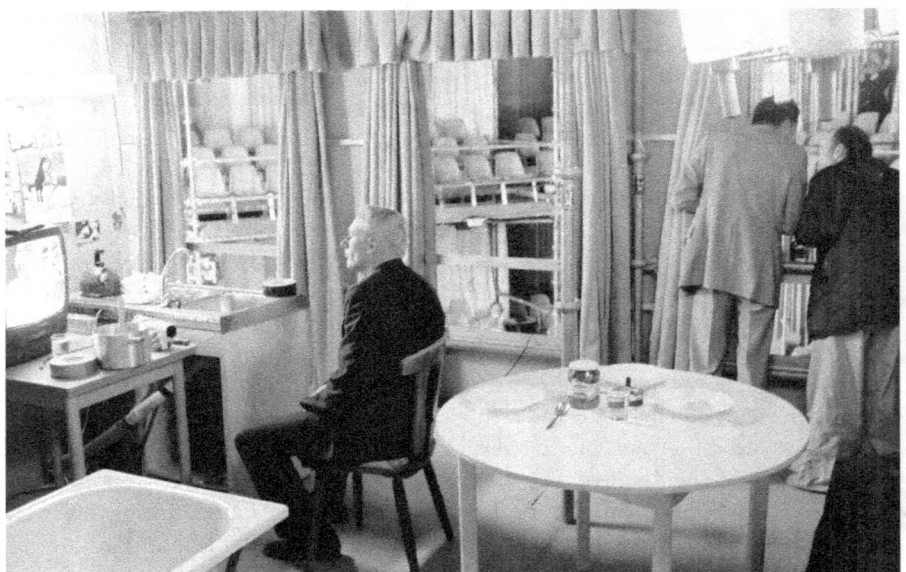

Figures 20 and 21 Playing with the spectators' desire for reality: for Frank Castorf's *Idiot* after Dostoevsky's novel (2002), designer Bert Neumann transformed the entire interior of the Volksbühne auditorium into a 400-square-metre city. The audience was seated on a multi-storey portacabin construction mounted on the revolving stage (Figure 20, above). Through the windows of the buildings, the spectators were only able to catch some glimpses of the play's action. Figure 21 (below) shows the performers' reverse perspective, from the set towards the audience's seating (from left, Herbert Fritsch on the chair, Kurt Naumann Skubowius and Martin Wuttke as Myshkin). Photos: Thomas Aurin.

causing (public and academic) excitement, Castorf refused outright the central privilege which the ideology of capitalist realism affords to immediacy, authenticity and intimacy. The extreme performances of his actors, which call on slapstick as much as on overexcited declamation, hysteric gesturation and at times even dangerous physical stunts, had been a long-established strategy in his work to counteract stage realism. The integration of live broadcast then added another, rather different 'reality effect', as Speckenbach pointed out:

> This idea [of reality] is correlated with the nature of the performer, not with the character they portray. Thus along with TV technology, reality enters the theatre – yet not the exterior, the outside (which is present in some documentary images, which remain, however, mere citations of reality), but the inner reality of the stage itself. The heavy make-up and the colourful light contribute their part to stimulate a mood that is different from 'realism'. (Speckenbach 2002, 82)

The 'fifth wall' of the screen, especially where it showed close-ups of the actors' faces and bodies, functioned as *cache*, to use Speckenbach's description, which he borrowed from film theorist André Bazin (83): it covers up, but thereby also makes us aware of what is being excluded from the image. As *cache*, their performance strategy at once heightens the 'inner reality of the stage' and its phenomenological materiality, but it does so by taking it away from the audience, as the live action withdraws into the interior of Neumann's buildings. Towards the end of Castorf's six-hour *Idiot*, for instance, there is an hour-long period when the audience do not see anybody on stage, in front of the Neustadt's many buildings. With all curtains drawn, and every action taking place out of direct sight, in one of the interior spaces, the spectators were only able to watch on screens. As Fischer-Lichte noted, 'every minute of the video increased the desire for the actors' "real" bodies; a desire that was repeatedly frustrated' (Fischer-Lichte 2008, 71).

Fischer-Lichte aligned this effect with earlier aspects of Castorf's *Regie*, such as his frequent cross-casting that had been an aspect of his work long before the recent *Duel*. Best known for cross-casting is his 1996 production of Carl Zuckmayer's World War II play *Des Teufels General*, a major work of Castorf's initial Volksbühne years, in which actress Corinna Harfouch played the protagonist, *Luftwaffe* general Harras (see Fischer-Lichte 2008, 87). According to Fischer-Lichte, both cross-dressing and the live video images blurred the line between the semiotic and the phenomenological layer of the performance and thereby emphasised 'unpredictable perceptual shifts between the order of representation and the order of presence' (157) She described such shifts as 'perceptual multistability', articulating an effect similar to the parallax perspective discussed in the previous chapter. Castorf's *Regie* certainly complements strategies we have encountered in van Hove's and Cassiers's work. Crucially, though, he insists that the truly important aspects are the effect and the thinking engendered by these formal strategies of his *Regie*:

> I often feel that the form has been understood. But actually, the form is the least relevant aspect. Much more important, however, is a certain way of thinking, and also a certain

ethics. What I often see is merely a copy of the form. But theatre has got to be a state of emergency. Not enough people realise this. (Castorf 2012b)

Castorf's *Regie* produces this chaotic 'state of emergency' by what I described as 'compositing' (see Boenisch 2010b). In place of any linear coherence of a dramatic narrative, this quintessentially postdramatic mode of theatral presentation relies on the discontinuous, asynchronic coexistence of various semiotic and kinetic layers with mutually exclusive aisthetic perspectives. It amasses wildly associative material so that even vaguely clear perspectives get lost.

This deliberately unwieldy *Regie* under GDR censorship served as camouflage for political critique. Later, Castorf's four- to six-hour-long productions expressed his deliberate stance against the absolutist regime of capitalist realism. In doing so (and Castorf's evocation of ethics certainly reminds us of this crucial intention), his work attempted to represent the 'heterocosm' that characterises our globalised world and which standard dramaturgic formulae and media clichés fail to address.[8] For Castorf (in a notable contrast to Ostermeier), this resulted in turning away from producing classic plays from the Western dramatic repertoire:

> I am getting more and more estranged by the calculated modelling and closure of drama, and by its suggestion that reality can be conquered – so that I can say: ah, that's the story, ah, it's as easy as that in the world. This doesn't correspond to my experience of reality. I am fascinated by antagonisms and by what I cannot explain, by vague intuitions. ... Novels offer more of the complexity I find in reality, and it's only logical that I can't even come close to masterworks like *The Possessed*. (Castorf 2001, 22)

Castorf's assertion seems reminiscent of the ominous reference to Dostoevsky that concluded György Lukács's *Theory of the Novel* (1916), where he boldly claimed that Dostoevsky had not written novels at all, but belonged to an altogether new era.[9] There was no straightforward orientation in his work, as it refused the illusion of 'total representability' characteristic for novelistic fiction, and even more so for dramatic fiction. Castorf's *Regie* repeated Dostoevsky's polyphony of the Real, which Mikhail Bakhtin famously described:

> *A plurality of independent and unmerged voices and consciousnesses, a genuine polyphony of fully valid voices is in fact the chief characteristic of Dostoevsky's novels.* What unfolds in his works is not a multitude of characters and fates in a single objective world, illuminated by a single authorial consciousness; *rather a plurality of consciousnesses, with equal rights and each with his own world*, combine but are not merged in the unity of the event. Dostoevsky's major heroes are, by the very nature of his creative design, *not only objects of authorial discourse but also subjects of their own directly signifying discourse.* In no way, then, can a character's discourse be exhausted by the usual functions of characterization and plot development. (Bakhtin [1929] 1984, 6; original emphases)

Castorf was initially drawn to Dostoevsky after he had directed Sartre's *Schmutzige Hände* (*Dirty Hands*) in 1998, which was his first production to explicitly engage with the warfare in former Yugoslavia. Initially, the director worked on Camus's dramatic adaptation of *The Possessed*, yet he found

> that something is lacking from his Dostoevsky. So it became a duty to rediscover Dostoevsky's contradictory flights of thought about evil and the apocalypse, and his almost Beckettian sense of humour. All of that is missing from Camus. In order to portray the pathos and the obsession of these people who are set on each other, I had to almost double in size his dramatic adaptation. (Castorf 1999b)

Castorf reintroduced the plurality of signifying discourses into his *Dämonen*. His six Dostoevsky plays, as well as his other 'Russian' productions, therefore became far more than rereadings of nineteenth-century narratives through the lens of the issues of twenty-first-century neoliberal 'communicative capitalism'. The (historical) foreignness of Dostoevsky's narratives and the (negative) realism of Castorf's *Regie* generated a decentring force, which challenged our spectatorial desire and thereby installed the typical 'engaged distance' which we have regularly encountered in our exploration of contemporary *Regie*. It emphasised our own distance from the past, and at the same time installed a distance that wrenched our immediate concerns and issues from easy appropriation and direct availability. The resulting theatral chronotope, to use another Bakhtinian term, displayed a complex pluri-dimensionality of space and time, which, as Günther Heeg suggested, points to a fundamental principle of *Regie*, far beyond Castorf's work:

> Neither the updating of the past nor its sheer persistence marks the transformation of *Regietheater*. Moreover, it creates a space in between the times, in which different times meet, get into conflict and disintegrate, compacting spatially and exposed as chronotopos. In the chronotope of Castorf's *Dämonen*, the ideas and narratives of the past make their appearance as failed and abandoned. ... The fragments and remains of ideas, which were to change or restore the world, make a ghostly return. (Heeg 2008, 32)

In Castorf's composite realism, this 'ghostly' diffusion of spaces 'in between the times' afforded the opening for 'the Real' to break through, in the sense of Hans-Thies Lehmann's notion of the 'irruption of the real' in postdramatic theatre (Lehmann 2006, 99). Here, the task of *Regie* was to set up the friction between contradictory forces on every level of theatrical presentation, and not to produce a singular, clear narrative and representation.

Castorf's insertion of Chekhov's short story *Peasants* into the well-known plot of *Three Sisters*, in his *Nach Moskau! Nach Moskau!* ('To Moscow! To Moscow!', 2010), was a further paradigmatic instance of this multiplication of perspectives. This composite montage of narratives again inserted the Bakhtinian plurality of consciousnesses and discourses; Castorf thus, one might say, 'dostoevskied' Chekhov. Where the play tells of the sisters' longing to return to Moscow, the novella introduces a peasant family who have just returned, having lived and worked in Moscow. In both narratives, a fire plays a climactic role, which Castorf fully exploited for his montage. Both groups of characters were played by the same actors, except for Kathrin Angerer's

Natasha, who functioned as the central dramaturgic link. The action took place in a single set by Neumann that juxtaposed a lush veranda-type space on one side with the dirty interior of the peasant's hut on the other. As Castorf's composite *Regie* extends the polyphony and plurality of numerous intertwining discourses even further, his productions present a theatral equivalent to the complexity of our present-day global reality, to which Castorf referred in his comment cited above. Where the symbolic regime of capitalist realism and its cultural Imaginary glance over it, he thus repeated the 'signifying stress' of our life under capitalist conditions. This is how Eric Santner described the constant demand to signify and interpret, and yet to constantly fail at signifying and interpreting (Santner 2006, 33). At the same time, the excess of signification and of layers of sense and meaning evokes the Lacanian notion of the Real.

Dostoevsky's novels present us, indeed, with hysteria, obsession, lust, perversion, depression and melancholy. From a Lacanian perspective, they grapple not merely with the psychological realm of desire, but with the abyss of the ultimately negative force of the drive.[10] The negative force of the drive underpins Dostoevsky's novels and engenders a transgressive dynamic, which Castorf sought to capture in his productions through theatral play. Žižek emphasises the 'acephalous character of the drive' as an a-subjective, impersonal force which is the complementing opposite, the negative mirror image of Nietzschean individual will (Žižek 2012, 549). For him, the drive is not simply a primordial human condition, but points towards the libidinal motor driving the ideology of capitalist realism:

> The drive inheres in capitalism at a more fundamental, *systemic*, level: the drive is that which propels forward the entire capitalist machinery, it is the impersonal compulsion to engage in the endless circular movement of expanded self-reproduction. (Žižek 2012, 497)

It is this compulsion that forms the ground of Castorf's 'negative realism'. His *Regie*, however, did not seek to access this dimension through *the representation* of drive by means of plots and characters, action and behaviour. Aesthetically, this engagement with the condition of drive allowed his *Regie* to go beyond psychological realism and its focus on the individual and his/her antagonistic entanglement within capitalist realities, which Ostermeier chose as his point of departure.

> The drive has nothing whatsoever to do with psychology ... Freud defined *Trieb* (drive) as a limit-concept situated between biology and psychology, or nature and culture – a natural force known only through its psychic representatives. But we should take a step further here and read Freud more radically: the drive is natural, but the natural thrown out of joint, distorted or deformed by culture; it is culture in its natural state. (Žižek 2012, 547)

Castorf's productions stage through the negative, unproductive, inefficient and unprofitable force of play such 'natural', 'out of joint' realities of the drive.

This shows in the seemingly chaotic progress of Castorf's rehearsal work, which critic Robin Detje described after observing the creation of *Erniedrigte und Beleidigte* (*The Humiliated and Insulted*) in 2001, Castorf's second Dostoevsky adaptation:

> Castorf holds a pocket edition of the novel and ploughs through it chapter by chapter. There is no road map. He chooses the most difficult path, straight into the jungle, a path many would find impossible.
>
> ...
>
> The only possible way to do the scenes has been found, and it will not be rehearsed again. It is dropped like a hot potato. Then everybody continues plowing through Dostoyevsky's book. The monstrous task of recording what has been decided lies with the assistant director, who will diligently create something like a shooting script for the opening night: 7 percent of Dostoyevsky, or maybe a little more, plus the blocking, the timing, and the actual lines. Synthesizing the scattered, forgotten work of long weeks of rehearsal is an effort of blood, sweat, and tears, of screaming and crying fits. Opening night performances often still contain unrehearsed material. Improvisation remains Castorf's fetish. It is needed to reach the 'authentic', 'the real'. The goal of rehearsals is to rechart the ocean of human behaviour, human drives, and human guilt. No maps are allowed. (Detje 2005, 12, 15)

This reality of an 'ocean of human behaviour, human drives, and human guilt', which demarcates the Lacanian Real, clearly cannot be adequately represented merely by 'acting it'. Castorf's *Regie* therefore pervades the dramatic fiction of the novel with the blood, sweat, tears and screaming fits of the performers and – not to forget – the disorientation and tiredness of the spectators in their 'signifying stress', shared by actors and performers in these exhausting productions. Castorf's compositing never added random layers that had not already been there in the original novel in all its plurality, which Bakhtin marvellously described. The composite of amassed material, association, people, images and spaces was an attempt to render by theatral means the polyphony of consciousnesses, and to make it sense-able for the spectators. The semiotic, kinetic and aisthetic excess of simultaneous, heterogeneous, incompatible events, sounds and images, of concealing and disclosing, of theatrical realism and material reality of the performance, provided what can be compared to the notion of *Anstoss* in Fichte's pre-Hegelian idealism: an obstacle that is also the incitement that sets the very process to which it reacts in motion.[11]

The polyphonic character of Castorf's *Regie* instils into the seamless logic of capitalist realism and its imperative of total representability a repetition that exposes the gap and non-identity of reality with our symbolic and imaginary orders. The tissue of reality (the fictional reality of the play/novel *and* the spectatorial reality in the theatre *and* thirdly, the 'public' reality outside the theatre) becomes fissured, and the disavowed real breaks through. At the same time, as Bakhtin stressed with regard to the effect of Dostoevsky's plurifocality, the consciousness of a character 'is not turned into an object, is not closed, does not become a simple object of the author's consciousness' (Bakhtin [1929] 1984, 7). This certainly applies to Castorf's *Regie*. He no longer makes a claim to singular authority over characters, the plot or even the performance. His productions refuse to reify the tensions and forces that underpin Dostoyevsky's narratives; they refuse to become easily available as a commodified representation offered for spectacular consumption. As spectators, we are consistently frustrated, as we feel we are missing out on the 'full picture', for instance, when events happen out of our direct sight. Yet, precisely for this reason, the ideology of the 'full picture', of 'authenticity' and 'immediacy', which is perpetuated by our semiocapitalist machinery of digital and social media – without much distinction between factual news and invented fiction – is challenged and disclosed as a mere illusion. In fact, 'missing out' is our ultimate reality, and not our personal failure. Pace Jodi Dean's provocation against the efficacy of subversive gestures in contemporary art, Castorf's theatre thus takes side with Philippe Pignarre and Isabelle Stengers, who argue that the one possible breakthrough against the dominating logic of capitalist realism is based on the suspension of reason, understood here not as the value of enlightenment, but as its perversion in the form of the capitalist demand for functionality, efficiency and consumability (Pignarre and Stengers 2011). We experience, instead, the painful *jouissance* of our existence once we refuse to indulge in the pleasure of non-stop consuming and thereby withstand the 'signifying stress' of capitalist realism. It is this dimension that makes Castorf's excessive theatral play anything but a 'project of idle self-fulfillment, but a genuinely political process' (Fischer-Lichte 2006, 12).

Recognising reality from the inside of theatre: Thomas Ostermeier

Whereas the interpolated *Coming Insurrection* manifesto was the dramaturgic key to unlock Thomas Ostermeier's *Enemy of the People*, a central clue for his 2008 *Hamlet* was – theatre. As metaphor, of course, 'theatre', and the confusion of reality and appearance, is a central preoccupation of the play itself. Yet, there was also 'Theater', Germany's 1980 contribution to the Eurovision Song Contest by pop singer Katja Ebstein, a song which Ostermeier's Hamlet (played by his principal lead actor Lars Eidinger) repeatedly intoned throughout the performance. The song talks about actors who 'act as their role demands', while 'one never sees how they really feel inside' – central aspects of this production's take on the Hamlet character.[12] *Hamlet* marked a pivotal moment in Ostermeier's production work. Compared with Jan Pappelbaum's filmic sets and their pronounced 'neo(n)-realism' (see Boenisch 2010c), exemplarily in *Woyzeck* (2003) and the lavish living-room realism of his *Hedda Gabler* and Norén's *Demons* (2010), the sets for Ostermeier's Shakespeare productions indicated a decisive step forward in his realist *Regie*. The designs appeared to visually confirm the intent to be more than a direct extension and mimetic replication of twenty-first-century realities on stage. For *Hamlet*, Pappelbaum scaled the stage space back to an empty, vast playing field, covered with earth, and a curtain, as well as a long table at the rear. The resonances with contemporary sensibilities were now focused on the character, and on the performers' play.[13] Across seven years and more than 250 performances, Eidinger's Hamlet noticeably morphed, from an initially altogether intolerable, spoiled upper-class royal living almost autistically in his own delusion, whom spectators of early performances encountered, into a victim who stands little chance against the political plotting of the parent generation. His only means of resistance is his refusal to perform as demanded.

In contrast to Castorf's play with an outright theatral 'signifying stress', the immediate recognisability of the characters and their situation remained central to Ostermeier's realism. He created theatral short-circuits between the fictional representation, the theatral reality and the public world outside by integrating recognisable current topics (such as the financial crisis in *Ein Volksfeind*), character types and behavioural patterns observed in contemporary life. As a result, in a way that is typical for Ostermeier's *Regie*,

> a shared 'structure of feeling' (rather than any psychological exploration) helped his performers to unlock their characters, just as a shared 'structure of feeling' (rather than a mere *Zeitgeist*) established the critical connection with the spectators. (Boenisch 2010c, 344)

In *Ein Volksfeind*, the (in contrast to Ibsen's original) consistently young group of friends, who would soon become enemies, was such a case.[14] Equal in age to the majority of the Schaubühne ensemble, as well as to its audiences, in *Volksfeind*'s first scene, they sat around the long kitchen table like in a typical Berlin *Wohngemeinschaft* community of flat sharers, and rehearsed songs for their band over a pot of spaghetti and some bottles of red wine (see Figure 22). The Stockmanns were portrayed as a young family, struggling with their new responsibility of parenting while still maintaining a 'studenty' lifestyle. Correspondingly, rather than the political frustration of a lifetime (as in Ibsen's original), Stockmann's activism was here shown as the youthful idealism of a group of university friends who set out to change the world and now found their ideals confronted with the demands of actual events and a city's *Realpolitik*.

Compared with Castorf, Ostermeier's scenarios often appear only too familiar. Importantly, though, his *Regie* does not stop here. What he had described in the Schaubühne's original mission statement from 2000 as a 'new realism', is anything but the mere continuation of mediatised soap-opera realism on stage, as some critics seemed to imply: 'Realism is not the simple depiction of the world as it looks. It is a view on the world with an attitude that demands change' (Schaubühne 2000, 15). Rather than an aesthetic mode of presentation, his realism thus understands itself as a form of critique of ideology. The realism of the nineteenth-century novel disclosed, as Louis Althusser stressed, 'in the form of *"seeing"*, *"perceiving"* and *"feeling"* (which is not the form of *knowing*) ... the *ideology* from which it is born, in which it bathes, from which it detaches itself as art, and to which it alludes' (Althusser 1971, 222; original emphasis). Rather than exploring and deconstructing past ideologies (of Ibsen, Shakespeare or even the contemporary playwrights he stages), Ostermeier's *Regie* uses the classical plays to 'detach itself as art' from the pervasive world of capitalist realism. It is for this reason that his *Regie* does not need the exaggerated excess and other strategies of defamiliarisation that characterise Castorf's approach; the very difference of ideological structures of feeling – in the full sense of Raymond Williams's concept – between Ibsen's time and our own, let alone the Elizabethan worldview and contemporary ideology, is enough to rupture the given economy of standardised 'sensibilities', precisely as they incorporate a 'foreign' perspective that is

Figure 22 'Realism is not the simple depiction of the world as it looks': in Thomas Ostermeier's production of Ibsen's *An Enemy of the People* (Schaubühne Berlin, 2012/2014), the Stockmanns' living-room resembled a contemporary Berlin flat share. Before falling out over the contamination of the spa baths, the youthful university friends, over a pot of spaghetti and some red wine, rehearsed for their band (from left: Moritz Gottwald as Billing, Christoph Gawenda as Thomas Stockmann, Eva Meckbach as Katharina Stockmann and Andreas Schröders as Hovstad; set design: Jan Pappelbaum, with a chalk artwork by Katharina Ziemke). Photo: Arno Declair.

inevitably 'out of joint' and no longer commensurate with contemporary partitions of the sensible. In Ostermeier's work, the recognisability of a fictional, foreign world – and equally, the strangeness of a recognisable world, in the Brechtian tradition of defamiliarisation – aims to break through the clichés and standardised behavioural patterns that (as accepted 'partition of the sensible') invite easy recognition and seamless identification with a represented world and its characters.

The most basic form of Ostermeier's realism is thus another parallax dissensus: an experiential, sensorial distance that emerges from the ultimate incompatibility of two equally truthful observations. Rather than reifying the 'foreign body' of the playtext as historicising stage production, Ostermeier refused to stage Ibsen's play as if it were set in 1882. He instead emphasised that it was an expressly contemporary play for Ibsen and his audience; for them, it was not about a remote society 150 years ago, so it should not be if you stage it today. Equally, a twenty-first-century actor who gives body to a Shakespearean protagonist produces the same contradictions that were obvious for a 1603 public. They observed a 'difference in sameness' between an ostensibly Danish prince and the current, Elizabethan and later Jacobean topics that underpinned the dramatic conflicts of Shakespeare's works. The characteristic dramaturgic short-circuiting at the heart of his plays creates a multiple, even parallax perception, which Ostermeier's realism seeks to maintain in performance. Similarly, his *Regie* attempts to create a congruence of the sensibilities of representation and reality that comes close to the congruence of Ibsen's world of his plays and the world of the public in his time, through which Ibsen's naturalism was once able to cause controversy and scandal.

It is worth noting that Althusser, in his cited reflection on the realist novel, highlighted seeing, perceiving and feeling, thus effectively the dynamic forces of the 'magic' triangle of theatrality. At the same time, he contrasted these forces with knowledge, evoking Hegel's doubts about rational 'understanding' alone. Here, the very dynamics of 'not knowing' allows realism to achieve some minimal detachment from its ideological ground. Althusser elaborated his point by arguing that in their 'political' novels, authors such as Tolstoy, Balzac and Solzhenitsyn

> give us a 'view' of the ideology to which their work alludes and with which it is constantly fed, a view which presupposes a *retreat*, an *internal distantiation* from the very ideology from which their novels emerged. They makes us 'perceive' (but not know) in some sense *from the inside*, by an *internal distance*, the very ideology in which they are held. (Althusser 1971, 222f.; original emphasis)

The topology implied in Althusser's statement expresses the shift that is crucial for realist *Regie*, too. The, in the full sense of the word, critical distance is not the spectator's safe retreat into the anonymity of the darkened auditorium, from which to watch a representation of reality as 'objective' observer. Rather, the 'internal distance' evoked here is introduced by being addressed and involved equally as spectator, and as public, so that the boundaries between these two positions within the theatral square become blurred. Ostermeier's changes to act IV in his *Volksfeind* marked precisely this redoubling of the spectatorial address. His *Regie* created such a perception 'from the inside', as the audience became the addressees of Stockmann's contemporary manifesto and then even had the right to respond and debate. Elsewhere, Ostermeier sought for the reflexive internal distance in his productions by explicitly asserting the fundamental principle of theatral play. In his earlier work, the director – who had been greatly influenced by Meyerholdian biomechanics, as well as Stanislavskian psycho-physicality – employed, above all, the kinetic energy of the performing body to insert momentary ruptures into the living-room realism. *Hamlet* again stands for the turning point, where the emphasis consistently shifted towards the reality of the theatral situation. Lars Eidinger, playing Hamlet, had extensive liberty (within a rather precisely conceived dramaturgic framework) to break through the fourth wall and engage directly with the audience, reacting for instance to audience members seeking the bathroom during the three-hour performance with no interval, engaging with someone who had fallen asleep or even seemingly stopping the performance to discuss the meaning of a specific line with his audience. Additionally, the spectators watched a small cast doubling roles, most notably Judith Rosmair, who made no attempt to hide her changes between Gertrude and Ophelia.[15]

In contrast to postmodern performance, the material reality of the theatral situation was never presented as superior to the fictional world of the play; the emphasis was, precisely, on achieving a theatral 'retreat' from both realities. According to the logic of parallax play, the fluid shifting between the worlds of representation, presentation and the present appeared more like different perspectives on the same subject, the ultimate reality of life. Ostermeier's 2007 production of Rainer Werner Fassbinder's 1979 movie *Die Ehe der Maria Braun* ('The Marriage of Maria Braun'), originally created away from his Schaubühne at Kammerspiele Munich the year before *Hamlet*, became the blueprint for the pronounced *Spiel* of theatricality within the director's framework of a critical, 'negative' realism.[16] *Maria Braun* outlined this strategy particularly plainly, as the production refrained from blending the fictional level with present-day sensibilities. The present was hinted at in the very beginning, when the actors, who were on stage from the moment the audience entered the theatre, watch a slide-show of images from the Third Reich, read out love letters to the Führer and then start reading out the script of Fassbinder's movie and begin to embody the script. The attitude portrayed was that of finding a box of personal items in one's grandparents' attic, and with this same attitude of, again, internal distanciation, rather than knowing, Ostermeier approached Fassbinder's narrative.

Fassbinder's movies are notorious for their heightened, at times crass naturalism, portraying a world full of dirt, drugs, alcohol and sex, as an ultimate foil to the image of the clean, organised and industrious post-war (West) German society. His harsh critique of the latent fascism and of the other disavowed undersides of the economic success of Germany's *Wirtschaftswunder* capitalism often used comparisons with erotic attraction (to goods and money), sexual exploitation and prostitution – a basic conceit of his *Maria Braun*, too. At the same time, Fassbinder's films are extremely stylised and never deny that what we see is staged and performed; a characteristic trait of his work since his beginnings in theatre. Aesthetically, Fassbinder's excessive realism seems more akin to Castorf's stage aesthetics discussed above. In its difference, Ostermeier's stage version therefore outlines his own distinct approach to a critical realism even more clearly. His production was originally part of a series of productions of socio-critical drama by Bavarian authors (Fleisser, Achternbusch) which Ostermeier staged for the Munich Kammerspiele, confronting topics of his adolescence in a small Bavarian town. Ostermeier chose to work from the script, rather than adapting the movie and its distinct visual aesthetics. Designer Nina Wetzel created a 1950s-style interior, with several groups of distinct period chairs, sofas and coffee-tables spread across the room, surrounded by curtains on all sides. In this rather concrete performance space, Brigitte Hobmeier as Maria Braun remained the only constant character, and thus the production's singular focal point. Four male actors (Jean-Pierre Cornu, Steven Scharf, Hans Kremer and Bernd Moss in the original production) meanwhile shared amongst them the more than twenty other roles from the movie, including female characters such as Maria's mother, and Maria's black US-Army lover, whom she murders after her husband, who was believed dead, eventually returns from wartime captivity. The actors cross-dressed, used masks, costumes and hairpieces. They never renounced the attitude of a playful 'borrowing' of their characters; they performed, for instance, the female characters, not as 'drag' travesty, but in their own, male voices. A simple sign – a periwig, a pair of glasses or a jumper – indicated each of their different characters, allowing quick switches between the roles they played.

At the same time, the actors swiftly reconfigured the space for the fast sequence of scenes. The chairs and tables served as sole props to turn the scene into a car, a restaurant, a prison and a train carriage. In addition to the elegant choreography of scenes, video designer Sebastien Dupouey (b. 1969) assembled a montage of historic footage – Hitler speeches, newsreels of air raids during the war, scenes from post-war news and 1950s German cities – which were projected onto props, such as a suitcase during the train journey, onto the rear curtain and also onto the costumes and the actors' bodies (see Figure 23). In the final scene – where Maria commits suicide after finding out that she had been a pawn all along in a secret financial agreement between her jailed husband Hermann and her lover, the much older entrepreneur Karl Oswald – a projection of flames seemed to consume Maria's body against the acoustic background of a radio broadcast of Germany winning the 1954 football World Cup.

Sublating Fassbinder's filmic extremism through heightened theatral playfulness had an interesting effect. The same harsh analysis of West German ideology and its support by lies and disavowal, which despite the movie's success had remained unpalatable to the German establishment, turned into a mainstream success in Ostermeier's production. It was invited to the Berlin Theatertreffen, toured internationally and was eventually revived and restaged in 2014. The production thoroughly relied on what Alain Badiou termed 'theater ideas', which are unique to the theatre and thus distinct from both the realms of everyday life and of politics: they 'cannot be produced in any other place or by any other means' (Badiou [1988] 2005a, 72). Rancière similarly stresses that the domains of art and politics should not be conflated. Rather, their link should be understood as a homology, not as identity. For him, art constitutes a field of 'metapolitics' (Rancière 2009a, 33). It is on the basis of this separation that Ostermeier's *Regie* creates within the acts of performing and spectating internal distance and an at least minimal retreat from the hegemonic partitions of the sensible. The emphasis of the reality of theatral play as a central cornerstone of Ostermeier's realism opens different perspectives. *Ein Volksfeind* with its chalk-board set and open scene changes eventually united the theatrality of *Maria Braun* and of the director's Shakespearean works with the neo(n)-realism of his productions of European and US naturalist classics, from Ibsen and O'Neill to Lilian Hellman. The reality of theatral play – based on a rigorous performing technique – cracked open the represented fictional reality, much like the, in Lehmann's term, 'irruption' of another reality (of disavowed warfare) in *Blasted* by Sarah Kane, the playwright whose work most resonated with Ostermeier during his formative Baracke years of the late 1990s.

Ostermeier is often considered, not least by German theatre academics, to be a conventional director lacking the avant-garde edge seemingly expected from *Regietheater*. His explicit recourse to clear recognisability, if not critical identification with the characters and situations in his productions, indeed relies on a mix of solid post-Stanislavskian *Regie* technique and a post-Brechtian political criticality. It thus embodies the ideal of the theatre training at Berlin's Ernst Busch theatre academy,

Figure 23 Reinvested realism, full of a pronounced play of 'theatre ideas': in Ostermeier's stage adaptation of Fassbinder's movie *Die Ehe der Maria Braun* (*The Marriage of Maria Braun*), Brigitte Hobmeier as Maria Braun was the sole consistent focal point. Four male performers, in an elegant choreography and with simple theatral means, shared all other roles (Kammerspiele München, 2007; set design: Nina Wetzel; video: Sebastien Dupouey; at the back: Steven Scharf, left, and Bernd Moss). Photo: Arno Declair.

from which Ostermeier graduated and where he now himself teaches as a professor on the *Regie* class. The political act of his *Regie* is, indeed, not to be found on a purely aesthetic level. It is a strictly relational act facilitated by his reinvested realism, which culminates in the creation of a theatral community that brings together human beings not least on an affective level. His *Regie* thus counteracts the socio-cultural effect of the encompassing narcissistic individualisation of our society, which Mark Kingwell described as 'empathy deficit' (Kingwell 2012, 22). Ostermeier's theatre explores conventional theatral means and established patterns of spectatorial engagement with characters, situations and stories, precisely in order to break through the reproduction of the ever-same prefabricated models of interpersonal relations, clichés of emotion and identification, on the part of both performers and spectators. Together with his frequent reminders about the original values of bourgeois culture, embodied by Schiller's call for liberty, his *Regie* work refuses to surrender realism as a critical tool to the cultural industries and to the almost hermetically sealed narratives of global mass media.

In many ways, Ostermeier's seeming conservatism can be understood as in fact a radical political strategy, which echoes the 'minimal condition' for a true act and true change outlined by Žižek:

> In some political constellations, such as the late capitalist dynamic in which only constant self-revolutionizing can maintain the system, those who refuse to change anything are effectively the agents of true change: the change of the very principle of change. ... This persistence of the Old, its 'stuckness', is the only possible site of the rise of the New: in short, *the minimal definition of the New is as an Old which gets stuck and thereby refuses to pass away.* (Žižek 2012, 482–3; original emphasis)

Articulating itself as ultimate Badiouian 'theater ideas', while being 'stuck' in the old forms of naturalism and realist aesthetics, Ostermeier's theatre asserts its difference and distance, and precisely thereby attempts never to lose sight of its grounding in contemporary social reality. It is a critical realism that no longer copies reality, but in a Hegelian sense sublates it, using the means of theatral play.

Two versions of *Regie* as dialectic mediation

Rather than designating an aesthetic doctrine, the variants of realism in Castorf's and Ostermeier's political *Regie* reveal the directors' concrete aesthetico-political attempts to articulate a politics of theatre performance that seeks to come to terms with the appeal and the very perfidy of communicative capitalism. Against the production of identical copies, which is the ideal of digital repetition and reproduction, and against the hegemonic strategy of 'precorporating' critical resistance, their work posits the force of 'impure repetition', where the negative excess of theatral play sublates both the playtext *and* reality. The symbolic and imaginary universe offered by a playtext, novel or film is exploited to open up a distanced perspective from which the productions tackle the hegemonic partition of the sensible installed by capitalist realism as well as the predicaments of our everyday reality. The 'internal distantiation' allows for a materialist analysis of these aesthetico-political realities. This is why we must defend the autonomous realm of theatre art which, as a space for critical reflections, does not surrender to demands of capitalist efficiency, functionality and easy consumability. At the same time, we need to comprehend the dialectic twist that, to paraphrase Hegel, behind the curtain of *Regie*, there is still, despite the insistence on theatrical autonomy, only ever what reality and its ultimate negative force has put there.

In their respective outlines of a realist *Regie*, Castorf and Ostermeier suggest two distinct approaches to a Hegelian dialectic mediation of both the playtext and of the material and ideological conditions of our reality. Castorf starts with a negation by first inducing into the text the symbolic and imaginary realities of popular culture, films, music and not least theatre itself. At the next step of performance, then, the excess of theatricality in his hour-long productions, along with the sheer force of his performers, serves as 'negation of the negation'. Here, the forces of theatrical play are used at once to permeate the representation with an entire range of human psychoses and hysteria, while at the same time rechannelling the negative power of the Real (which we have aligned with Žižek's extended understanding of the Freudian death drive, see Žižek 2012, 546f.) against the attraction and enjoyment of capitalist realism. Castorf's *Regie*, in many ways 'irrational', seems reminiscent of the power of wit and humour in Hegelian-era Romantic art, which he described as the force which

> makes everything which attempts to objectify itself and to gain a fixed form in reality, or to even have this form in the reality beyond art, collapse and disappear by the sheer power of subjective ideas, flashes of thought, and striking ways of perceiving it. (Hegel 1955, 564)

Castorf's *Regie* thus turns capitalism's appeal of excessive enjoyment against itself. Ostermeier, meanwhile, takes a different path of dialectic mediation. He starts from a negation through theatrical play and technique, heightening the dynamic interplay of *semiosis*, *kinesis* and *aisthesis* by means of a thorough analysis of the dramatic circumstances, situations and actions, and by employing all available theatral means (bodies, spaces, images, music and rhythms) to convey and add to the poignancy of these circumstances and situations.

Next, reality enters as negation of the negation: the performers' and directors' own experiences and observations are used to complete the 'theatrical appearing' of these dramatic situations. That way, the represented reality of the text is not straightforwardly redoubled, but is connected with contingent elements of the actors', the director's and spectators' own lives. We return to reality, yet our perspective on it has changed: rather than affirming the given order of the sensible, this dialectic sublation breaks through one-dimensional copies of the reality; it likewise challenges the suggestion of a fictional reality that were utterly remote from any of our everyday concerns. Instead of battling capitalism directly with its own dynamic forces, Ostermeier's *Regie* overtly questions, counters, and thereby seeks to undermine its appeal. The ambiguous position of Thomas Stockmann in *Ein Volksfeind* is a pertinent example, and the audience is equally left negotiating its relation to Hamlet and Maria Braun. The strategy of his dialectic move can therefore be linked to another Žižekian rereading of a well-known concept: the logic of the symptom (see Žižek 2012, 520–9). It is connected to the Hegelian understanding of totality as encompassing the whole plus its self-contradictions, inconsistencies and structural antagonisms that appear to undermine the 'truth' of the notion (in the sense of its transparent self-identity). Žižek goes beyond Hegel by suggesting that these 'symptoms' are far more than the 'inbuilt', dormant contradictions that just wait to be exposed. For him, Hegel's famous statement that 'the Whole is the Truth', by evoking an excessive, 'negative' totality that can never be complete, points towards the future, similar to the notion of *voir venir* in Malabou's sense:

> [T]he symptom is not a secondary expression of some substantial content already dwelling deep in the subject – on the contrary, the symptom is 'open', coming from the future, pointing towards a content that will only come to be through the symptom. (Žižek 2012, 527)

We can draw on this logic of symptom to analyse Ostermeier's short-circuiting between Ibsen's drama and the later verbatim citation by Hitler, the insertion of the contemporary political manifesto *The Coming Insurrection* or the approach towards *Maria Braun* from the without of the present performance situation.

More than thematic extensions of motifs already articulated in the plays, these interventions of his *Regie* foster a 'symptomatic actualisation' of the (virtual) 'whole' of the play – they come into the play, as it were, from its future of our present. Conversely, this logic of the symptom also inserts the spectatorial position, desires and acts into the orbit of the play and its 'whole'. Both realist strategies of *Regie* discussed here make such a crucial attempt to come to terms (whether successfully or not is of course a matter of debate) with 'our insertion *at the level of desire* in the remorseless meat-grinder of Capital [and] our own complicity in planetary networks of oppression' (Fisher 2009, 15; original emphasis). Ostermeier's work with alternative symbolic and imaginary frameworks of identification, and equally Castorf's engagement with the Real and its dynamics of the drive, in their effect, are avenues of a Hegelian reflexive mediation that correspond to Žižek's manifesto of achieving true comprehension and true grasp precisely by 'looking awry', by adopting a partial, even distorting perspective:

> As a rule, it is not a reading of a thick book by Hegel himself, but some striking, detailed observation – often wrong or at least one-sided – made by an interpreter that allows us to grasp Hegel's thought in its living moment. (Žižek 2012, 280)

Ostermeier and Castorf similarly enable us to grasp Ibsen or Shakespeare, Chekhov or Dostoevsky 'in their living moment', on the basis of the contingent, ultimately playful, striking and necessarily 'wrong' interpretations of their *Regie* – 'wrong' because they tap into the negative truth of the playtext, where it breaks through the established norms of our hegemonic order of the sensible. For this reason, the past texts make us perceive and sense (and not necessarily 'know' or 'understand') our own 'living moment' from the distance of their inside, and thereby bring us a step closer to truth – as long as we do not understand 'truth' as senseless, stupid identical replication of the illusion of an objective, neutral state of how 'things really are'. It is the truth of the Lacanian Real: an impossible truth of symptomal tensions, self-limitations and contradictions that clash with its own surface order of aesthetico-political sensibility. These are the political stakes of *Regie* today. Without an engaged, subjective perspective, there is nothing but a consumable, reproducible, reified commodity – the 'ideal' flat world of semiocapitalism. What *Regie* thus truly messes up is not the authorial privilege of the playwright, but the very order of the sensible, precisely in its refusal to 'orderly' represent, illustrate and to thus play by the rules of the established hegemonic aesthetico-political order of things, affirming its easy, comfortable and alluring clichés of thinking.

Notes

1 A German left-wing weekly magazine summarised the controversy in its headline, 'This is all but left!' (Thumfart 2010).
2 Ostermeier was appointed to lead the Baracke ('Shed'), a temporary space for new work established by the Deutsches Theater in a disused theatre workshop earmarked for demolition, in 1996, while still finishing his studies at the Ernst Busch conservatoire. Three seasons later, he was appointed artistic director of the Berlin Schaubühne, the prime German theatre associated with *Regietheater*, which was brought to fame by Peter Stein in the 1970s and 1980s (see also Boenisch 2010c).
3 Castorf was renowned for controversial deconstructionist takes on classical plays, which had regularly caused him trouble with East German authorities, and later for his outspoken resistance to German unification (see Carlson 2009, ch. 5). By the late 1990s, however, he changed his approach (see Castorf 1998). In a recent interview, he confirmed:

> Until 1998, I created radical, anarchic theatre. Then I discovered Dostoevsky and realised his greatness. In this moment I came to know humility and realised what it means for an artist to unconditionally put one's own talent into the service of another artist. (Castorf 2012a)

> His successful Dostoevsky adaptations, *Demons* (1999), *The Humiliated and Insulted* (2001), *The Idiot* (2002) and *Crime and Punishment* (2005), were, however, followed by a gradual demise in which many regular performers and dramaturgs left the Volksbühne, to the degree that Marvin Carlson considered Castorf's star as 'distinctly faded' (in Delgado and Rebellato 2010, 119). Yet, his more recent turn to Chekhov – with *The Duel* and his previous *Three Sisters* adaptation – saw many former protagonists (not least Martin Wuttke, Sophie Rois and Kathrin Angerer) reuniting with the director, and continued Castorf's success. He was chosen to direct Wagner's *Ring* cycle at Bayreuth in 2013, and after several years of absence, his work was once again selected for the Theatertreffen in 2014, albeit with a production of Celine's *Journey to the End of the Night* which he directed at Residenztheater, Munich, the theatre where he had produced his first show in West Germany in 1988. Castorf has announced his retirement from the Volksbühne, once launched by Max Reinhardt and later home to Erwin Piscator and Benno Besson, with the theatre's centenary in 2016.

4 In *The Duel*, Petersburg civil servant Laevsky escapes to a remote Caucasian village with someone else's wife, only to get bored and find himself involved in a duel with the Darwinist zoologist Von Koren, the ominous German alluded to in the line quoted on Denić's billboard. Von Koren's desire to exterminate worthless humans like the Petersburg escapee (not unlike Stockmann's utterances in Ibsen's play) uncannily prefigures fascist

ideology. It echoes a similar speech from Dostoevsky's *Demons*, which Castorf inserted into his *Three Sisters* adaptation *Nach Moskau! Nach Moskau!*, assigning the text to the sisters' upstart sister-in-law Natasha.

5   Interestingly, Ostermeier already used the term 'capitalist realism' during his time at the Baracke. For him, it stood for seemingly radical directorial gestures, which were void of any socio-political force and relevance, and which implicitly even promoted neoliberal ideology; a self-proclaimed 'critical' aesthetics which in fact, in Ostermeier's perspective, 'suits those in power very well' (Ostermeier 1999, 76).

6   Their theatral realism further resonates with Fredric Jameson's analysis of a central affective impulse in realism, which he sees mediating what he describes as tension between the linear temporality of the narrative and the eternal present of the body (Jameson 2013a). This tension accurately describes the cultural dynamism we have tried to capture here in the model of the theatral triangle of *semiosis*, *kinesis* and *aisthesis*, which these forms of political *Regie* exploit.

7   Neumann has been head designer at the Volksbühne since Castorf's appointment in 1992. Since their early collaborations, most notably Schiller's *Robbers* in 1990, Neumann's designs have brought remnants of desolate realities into the theatre spaces. Before installing his almost filmic set for the first time on the theatre's main stage for *Dämonen*, Neumann had experimented with actual interior designs in his work with Rene Pollesch at the Volksbühne's then second space, the Prater theatre.

8   The term is borrowed from Linda Hutcheon's adaptation theory, albeit not from her discussion of stage adaptations but of the 'interactive' mode of digital adaptations. Hutcheon describes the latter as engaging experientially with a virtual 'heterocosm' (Hutcheon 2006, 50f.). I previously suggested that Castorf employs a similar logic in order to tackle the realities of communicative capitalism (see Boenisch 2010b).

9   It is no accident that Castorf's ongoing exploration of Dostoevsky, and over time other Russian authors, began in 1999, a crucial transitional year, when Germany's post-unification excitement as well as melancholia over the loss of East Germany waned. At the same time, the Balkan wars, the first European warfare since 1945, were a first indication of our present historic moment of cultural clashes and global warfare.

10 On the Lacanian distinction between drive and desire, and its association with capitalist realism, see Žižek 2012, 496–504.

11 For Fichte, *Anstoss* designates something that is ultimately subjective, yet still not produced by the I. It thus marks 'a realm of irreducible otherness, of absolute contingency and incomprehensibility' at the very core of the subject, and not purely an external push (Žižek 2012, 150). Žižek describes this basic core of subjectivity elsewhere with Hegel's term the 'night of the world'. It is precisely this uncanny contingency that characterises Castorf's *Regie*. Like Fichte, the standard reproach to his work is that of purely subjectivist eccentricity and of overblown egomania. Žižek's rereading of Fichte thus provides important prompts that, in our context, help us to reconceive the discourse of subjective authority and authorship in *Regietheater* (see Žižek 2012, ch. 3, 'Fichte's Choice').

12 My own approximate translation. In German, the lyrics read: 'Sie setzen jeden Abend eine Maske auf, und sie spielen wie die Rolle es verlangt. ... Sie sind König, Bettler, Clown im Rampenlicht, doch wie's tief in ihnen aussieht sieht man nicht.'

13 After *Hamlet*, Ostermeier directed *Othello*, 2010, and then *Measure for Measure*, 2011, which was set within a vast, undefined metallic space.

14 The adaptation cut Captain Horster, and merged the characters of Stockmann's (in Ibsen's original rather dull) wife and his politically engaged adult daughter, who works

as a teacher at a local night school, into a single character of a young mum who had just returned to her job as a teacher after the couple had their first baby.
15 Rosmair, who created the role, now alternates performances with Lucy Wirth and Jenny König.
16 The production, which the director considers a pivotal work in the development of his *Regie*, transferred to the Schaubühne with the original cast in 2009. In 2014, Ostermeier revived and restaged the production with an entirely new cast.

Conclusion. The future of *Regie*?

Across its two parts, this book has speculated about the theatral practice named *Regie*. Prompted by a somewhat contingent selection of theatre events in German and Flemish theatre seen by me over the past decade or so, I have posited a concrete notion of *Regie* as theatral play, as dialectic act of mediation and as speculative style of thinking. Both sets of four chapters have repeatedly and somewhat obstinately moved past the same issues, problems, ideas and suggestions, and with each encounter looked at them from a different perspective and from another point of view. The book hence has made no attempt at hiding my own *Regie*. It certainly does not seek to offer a 'truthful representation and interpretation of the work' of contemporary theatre directors and the history they draw on, and neither do I consider this the prime task of theatre direction. Instead, this study presents itself as an *Inszenierung* of *Regie* that attempts to activate the same movement of speculative mediation, the very energies of dialectic sublation that characterise and drive *Regie*.

Regie is, then, more than another, pompous Germanic term to mystify existing ideas of direction and *mise en scène*. All these concepts, of course, revolve around the same core. They are parallax perspectives on the same object (and subject), each offering something which escapes the other approaches. Together, these notions form another triangular constellation at the heart of contemporary European theatre:

- **Direction** captures the *practical* aspect of putting a playtext on stage and mounting a production. It describes the craft and labour of making theatre, which is addressed in writings by artists such as Anne Bogart (2001, etc.), Mike Alfreds (2007), Declan Donnellan (2005) and Katie Mitchell (2008), to name but a few contemporary directors and their books which I use in my own teaching of direction.

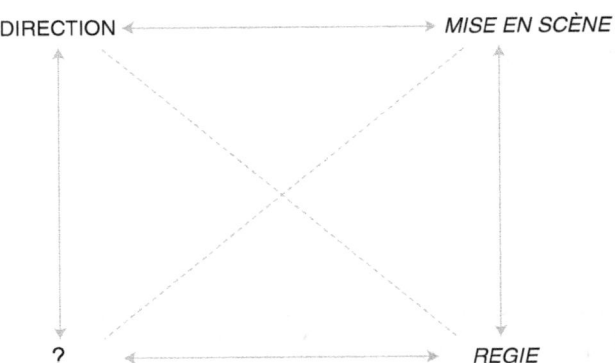

Figure 24 The 'theatral square', applied to the relations of direction, *mise en scène* and *Regie*.

Direction is, thus, situated on the *theatrical* level, understood here without any of the term's negative connotations.

- **Mise en scène** is an *analytic* concept which expresses the dynamic process of emitting and releasing the playtext on stage, as comprehensively described by Patrice Pavis (2013, etc.). It transforms literary writing into a multi-dimensional, sensory experience in the theatre, triggering the 'autopoietic feedback loop' between stage and audience which Erika Fischer-Lichte uses as a heuristic notion to describe the performative effect generated by *mise en scène*. It does refer to the 'directorial concept' or 'intention' of the director. Related to the analytic use of its German translation as **Inszenierung**, which – in contrast to the *Aufführung*, the individual performance on the night – designates their common core (frequently expressed in English as staging or production), *mise en scène* sets in motion (and is set in motion) through this framework of direction. It is thus an analytic tool situated at the level of mediation between the theatrical and the theatral.

- **Regie** is an *aesthetic* concept, in the full sense of Rancière's use of this term. It is both historically associated with the aesthetic regime of arts and it engages with the aesthetic level of the sensible. *Regie* expresses a cultural process of 'making sense' (of *mise en sens*, as I described it in Part I of this study), which traverses the symbolic order of discourse as well as the imaginary order of channelling desire, which a critical analysis of theatre performance from the perspectives of Foucauldian discourse analysis and Lacanian psychoanalysis foregrounds. Engaging with and intervening in the semiotic, kinetic and aisthetic dimensions of the socio-political sensible, *Regie* is always political, even though it operates as an artistic process in its own autonomous field which is not politics (see Rancière 2009a). It is a critical concept that marks the fabric of *theatral* thinking, a playful (re-) partitioning of the common sensible which is prompted by the cultural force of *thea*, that common process of public showing and gazing that links theatre and theory.

We can then further extend this triangle of direction, *mise en scène* and *Regie*, as it maps onto the theatral square (of character/performer and spectator/public) introduced in

Chapter 7 (see Figures 17 and 24). Theatre research has only very recently started its foray into the fourth corner, mapping out a new subdiscipline of 'rehearsal studies', most notably with Gay McAuley's proposition of rehearsal ethnography (McAuley 2012) and by Lavender and Harvie's edited collection on rehearsal practices (2010) – a suggestion to be debated further. In the visualisation above, I therefore leave this fourth corner of the theatral square open for future debate.

My own concern throughout this book was with the perspective of *Regie* as 'public play of *thea*', as I described it in Chapter 2. In a necessarily 'wrong' act of (negative) repeating and 'playing' with the direction and *mises en scène* of the directors I discussed, my aim has been to foster the 'appearing' of some truths of (rather than about) *Regie* and its thinking, in order to further assist us with a

> critical re-examination of the philosophical foundations of theatre and performance, of the forms of knowledge about ourselves and the world we live in which these cultural practices enhance and develop, of their ethical consequences and the epistemological assumptions they are based on. (Rokem 2009, 228)

Since its emergence in the nineteenth century, *Regie* has opened spaces for such critical examination and for such thinking, within the 'aesthetic' realm of theatre that insists on its autonomy from the demands and imperatives of everyday life and its underlying hegemonic ideologies and discourses. From this autonomous examination through play, *Regie* propels theatre, the art of cultural traditions and memories of the past, back into a present and forward into the future. Around Hegel's time, it was a present dominated by the empirical regime of natural sciences and the formal reasoning of logic; our present is governed by the pervasive 'business ontology in which it is *simply obvious* that everything in society … should be run as a business' (Fisher 2009, 17; original emphasis). This includes theatre, as it is increasingly absorbed by the so-called cultural industry. Against this global neoliberal conformity of the twenty-first century, which defines the 'good citizen' as a well-behaved consumer of goods, bite-sized, chewable chunks of information and spectacle, *Regie* supplies us, as actors and spectators, with an attitude of playfulness that fosters thinking and imagining, by activating and exploiting the theatral dynamics of meaning, motion and affective perception. The negotiations of *Regie* – against the imperative of 'doing the play(text)' and 'producing a show' – create a secure, autonomous theatral space *vis-à-vis* the text and the demands of everyday life. Militating against what Peter Brook once, and still validly, described as 'deadly theatre', *Regie* opens up a living space of thinking, and of thinking differently, a vital room for possibilities, a vibrant place for dissensus. *Regie* is a public intervention through theatre and theatral thinking, even a utopia, similar to Schiller's intervention through his chorus and his utopia of human play and liberty.

Instead of clarifying, illustrating and ascertaining unambiguous clear meaning and rather than suggesting the immediate availability of everything as commodity, the play of *Regie* problematises any such uniform clarity. It throws doubt on comfortable truths and accepted givens, and thereby confronts performers, theatre-makers and the spectating public alike with difficulties, with risk and with responsibilities – with the very 'carnival of thinking' that unsettles the rigour of fixed partitions of the sensible and opens up alternatives in the face of the ever-same, insisting that there must be and will be different perspectives and different 'senses'. *Regie* creates and celebrates the shared communities of 'active interpreters, who develop their own translations in order to appropriate the "story" and make it their own', whom Rancière put at the centre of any true emancipation of the spectator (Rancière 2009b, 22). The playfulness of this inefficient, unprofitable 'magic' of thinking and interpreting takes away the fear of 'thinking for ourselves', of 'interfering' and of 'thinking differently'. It gives access to and offers a perspective – its perspective and our own perspective against the fixed logic of representation. For this reason, *Regie*, in its very play with classic texts, from Greek tragedy to Shakespeare and great novels, from Ibsen to contemporary plays and new writing, is able to take seriously all our own subjective fears, passions, concerns, anger and irrational gut feelings as artists and spectators, turning them into the very ground for the 'concrete universality' of these classics.

For a while it had been fashionable to discard the cultural legacy of dramatic theatre and of the 'classical canon'. The traditions of playwriting and of putting on plays were regarded as epitomes of the cultural capital of a white, Western bourgeoisie in the field of theatre, remote from struggles and concerns in the socio-political conditions of the twenty-first century. Yet, these conditions are defined by the logic of capital positing itself as the one and only, single universal narrative and signifier, and as the sole link to transcend any division of nation, gender, race or class. Should we not at least attempt to reclaim the legacy of our Western European cultural capital in order to confront this homogenising logic with a different narrative and a different proposition of what is 'sensible'? The speculative theatral mediation of these canonical texts, which *Regie* unlocks, may counter with its own claim for universality. The text becomes the lens through which we can focus on the social, 'public' realities of today's globalised economy of semiocapitalism in our acts of interpreting the world around us. The mediation of these texts through the acts of directing and spectating, their sublation through *thea* and theatral thinking, may then allow us to collectively take ownership and to share (rather than possess and consume) the scenes and senses of this cultural capital, so it becomes a starting point for our 'recognition or reappropriation of the hitherto alienated social order' (Jameson 2010, 107). *Regie*, as this very agent of mediation and sublation as well as of a cultural partitioning and part-taking of the common sensible, is predicated on the irresolvable distance and difference, on the antagonistic tension, on the excess engendered by each text. *Regie* zooms into the molecular fabric of the texts and their symptomal self-limitations and celebrates them, in its 'negative' Hegelian stance, as their actual 'truth' that playfully remaps standardised patterns.

Assuming ownership of these traditions and extending them into the future through the dialectic force of *Regie* and its speculative dynamics of theatral thinking does therefore not at all mean ignoring all the antagonisms and contradictions inherent in this unapologetically white, male, European and bourgeois legacy of 'the canon' of classics. On the contrary. It invites us to confront them and to 'play' with the very impossibility of resolving these tensions, using them as the force to drive forward our thinking and to 'see what is coming' as a result of this playful confrontation. Against the boredom, the apathy and the empathy deficit spread by the homogenised media imaginary of semiocapitalism and the dictate of its symbolic order, such dialectic critical activity of recognising the object of play in its full contradictory ambiguities as our own construction, as inevitably connected to our subjective activity (and responsibility) of spectating, relating and engaging invites us to try out, in the act of play, a different relation to the world and to its dominant institutions and ideologies: hence, to play with a different 'partition of the sensible'. This play begins with assuming a (critical) distance as first prerequisite for liberty. In the spirit of the Rancièrian goal of emancipation, *Regie* is our ally in theatre in order to make a claim in the face of the global hegemony of capital by insisting on the 'universal particular' of culture: of a human community, bound not by the circle of production and consumption, but by common playing and thinking and the shared force of *thea*. For the future of theatre, we might do worse than remind ourselves of Schiller's imperative: we are fully human beings only when we have (and claim) the liberty to play, and thereby to think – freely, autonomously, differently.

> Genosse du bist nicht umsonst gestorben
> Gefallen an der Front der Dialektik
> Wie löst man einen Widerspruch Indem
> Man sich hinein begibt geradeaus
> Heiner Müller

Figure 25 Christoph Gawenda as Thomas Stockmann in the final scene of Thomas Ostermeier's *An Enemy of the People* (set design: Jan Pappelbaum; Schaubühne Berlin, 2012/2014). Photo: Arno Declair.

BIBLIOGRAPHY

Adorno, Theodor W. ([1970] 2002), *Aesthetic Theory*. Trans. Robert Hullot-Kentor. London and New York: Continuum.
—— (2004), *Philosophy of Modern Music*. Trans. Anne G. Mitchell and Wensley V. Blomster. London and New York: Continuum.
Aerts, Ruben (2014), 'De zaak uit handen geven doen we per definitie niet: Over 25 jaar op bühne met Toneelspelersgezelschap STAN', *Gazet van Antwerpen/Metropool Noord*, 20 March, copy in tg STAN Press Archive 'JDX 2014', n.p.
Agamben, Giorgio (2007), *Profanations*. Trans. Jeff Fort. New York: Zone Books.
Akáts, Franz von ('Grüner') (1841), *Kunst der Scenik in ästhetischer und ökonomischer Hinsicht*. Vienna: Mausberger, http://books.google.de/books?id=9g0tAAAAYAAJ, accessed 31 November 2014.
Alfreds, Mike (2007), *Different Every Night: Freeing the Actor*. London: Nick Hern.
Alston, Adam (2013), 'Audience Participation and Neoliberal Value: Risk, Agency and Responsibility in Immersive Theatre', *Performance Research* 18(2), 128–38.
Althusser, Louis (1971), *Lenin and Philosophy, and Other Essays*. Trans. Ben Brewster. London: New Left Books.
Antoine, André (1903), 'Causerie sur la mise en scène', *La Revue de Paris*, March–April, 596–612.
Artaud, Antonin (1958), *The Theatre and its Double*. Trans. Mary Caroline Richards. New York: Grove Press.
Auslander, Philip (1997), *From Acting to Performance: Essays in Modernism and Postmodernism*. London and New York: Routledge.
Bab, Julius (1928), *Das Theater der Gegenwart: Geschichte der dramatischen Bühne seit 1870*. Leipzig: J.J. Weber.
Badiou, Alain ([1988] 2005a), *Being and Event*. Trans. Oliver Feltham. London and New York: Continuum.
—— (2005b), *Handbook of Inaesthetics*. Trans. Alberto Toscano. Stanford: Stanford University Press.
—— (2006), 'Drawing', *Lacanian Ink* 28, 45, 42–9.
—— (2007), *The Century*. Cambridge: Polity.
—— (2008), 'Rhapsody for the Theatre: A Short Philosophical Treatise'. Trans. Bruno Bosteels. *Theatre Survey* 49(2), 187–238.
Bakhtin, Mikhail ([1929] 1984), *Problems of Dostoevsky's Poetics*. Ed. and trans. Caryl Emerson. Minneapolis and London: University of Minnesota Press.
Bal, Mieke (1996), *Double Exposures: The Subject of Cultural Analysis*. London and New York: Routledge.

Balme, Christopher B. (2007), *Pacific Performances: Theatricality and Cross-Cultural Encounter in the South Seas*. Basingstoke and New York: Palgrave Macmillan.
——(2008), 'Werktreue: Aufstieg und Niedergang eines fundamentalistischen Begriffs', in Ortrud Gutjahr, ed., *Regietheater: Wie sich über Inszenierungen streiten lässt*. Würzburg: Königshausen & Neumann, 43–50.
Barish, Jonas (1981), *The Antitheatrical Prejudice*. Berkeley: University of California Press.
Barthes, Roland ([1954] 1972), 'Baudelaire's Theater', in *Critical Essays*. Trans. Richard Howard. Evanston: Northwestern University Press, 25–31.
——(1980), *Camera Lucida: Essays on Photography*. Trans. Richard Howard. New York: Hill & Wang.
Baugh, Christopher (2005), *Theatre, Performance, and Technology*. Basingstoke and New York: Palgrave Macmillan.
Behrendt, Eva, Barbara Burckhardt and Franz Wille (2008), 'Warten auf die Wahrheit: Ein Gespräch mit Constanze Becker, Jens Harzer und Ulrich Matthes über ihre Arbeit mit Jürgen Gosch', *Theater Heute* 13, 92–102.
Beiser, Frederick (2005), *Schiller as Philosopher: A Re-examination*. Oxford: Oxford University Press.
Benjamin, Walter (2003), *Understanding Brecht*. Trans. Anna Bostock. London and New York: Verso.
Berardi, Franco 'Bifo' (2009), *The Soul at Work: From Alienation to Autonomy*. Trans. Francesca Cadel and Giuseppina Mecchia. Los Angeles: Semiotext(e).
Bergman, Gösta M. (1966), 'Der Eintritt des Berufsregiseurs in die deutschsprachige Bühne', *Maske und Kothurn* 12(1), 63–91.
Bersani, Leo (2010), *Is the Rectum a Grave? And Other Essays*. Chicago and London: University of Chicago Press.
Blanchart, Paul (1948), *Histoire de la mise en scène*. Paris: Presses Universitaires de France.
Bluth, Karl Theodor (1928), *Leopold Jessner: Zum fünfzigsten Geburtstag*. Berlin: Oesterheld & Co.
Boenisch, Peter M. (2006), 'Aesthetic Art to Aisthetic Act. Theatre, Media, Intermedial Performance', in Chiel Kattenbelt and Freda Chapple, eds, *Intermediality in Theatre and Performance*. Amsterdam and New York: Rodopi, 103–16.
——(2007), 'Multisensuality and Postdramatic *Mise-en-Scène*: The Ro Theater's *Proust*-Project', in Malgorzata Sugiera and Mateusz Borowski, eds, *Fictional Realities/Real Fictions: Contemporary Theatre in Search of a New Mimetic Paradigm*. Newcastle: Cambridge Scholars Publishing, 121–34.
——(2008), 'Exposing the Classics: Michael Thalheimer's *Regie* beyond the Text', *Contemporary Theatre Review* 18(1), 30–43.
——(2010a), 'Towards a Theatre of Encounter and Experience: Reflexive Dramaturgies and Classic Texts', *Contemporary Theatre Review* 20(2), 162–72.
——(2010b), 'Frank Castorf and the Berlin Volksbühne: The Humiliated and Insulted (2001)', in Sarah Bay-Cheng, Chiel Kattenbelt, Andy Lavender and Robin Nelson, eds, *Mapping Intermediality in Performance*. Amsterdam: Amsterdam University Press, 196–202.
——(2010c), 'Thomas Ostermeier: Mission Neo(n)realism and a Theatre of Actors and Authors', in Maria M. Delgado and Dan Rebellato, eds, *Contemporary European Theatre Directors*. Abingdon and New York: Routledge, 339–59.
——(2012) 'Acts of Spectating: The Dramaturgy of the Audience's Experience in Contemporary Theatre', in *Critical Stages* 7, Special Topic 'The Spectator', ed. Patrice Pavis, www.criticalstages.org/criticalstages7. Revised version in Katalin Trencsényi and Bernadette Cochrane, eds, *New Dramaturgy: International Perspectives on Theory and Practice*. London: Methuen, 2014, 225–41.
——(2014a), 'What Happened to our Nation of Culture? Staging the Theatre of the Other Germany', in Nadine Holdsworth, ed., *Theatre and National Re-imaginings*. Abingdon and New York: Routledge.
——(2014b), 'Who's Watching? Me! – Theatrality, the Žižekian Subject and Spectatorship', in Broderick Chow and Alex Mangold, eds, *Žižek and Performance*, Basingstoke and New York: Palgrave Macmillan.
——(2014c), 'Creating X-rays of the Text to Dissect the Present: An Interview with Ivo van Hove', in Margherita Laera, ed., *Theatre and Adaptation: Return, Rewrite, Repeat*. London and New York: Methuen.
Bogart, Anne (2001), *A Director Prepares: Seven Essays on Art and Theatre*. London and New York: Routledge.
Böhler, Michael J. (1972), 'Die Bedeutung Schillers für Hegels Ästhetik', *PMLA* 87(2), 182–91.
Boltanski, Luc, and Eve Chiapello (2005), *The New Spirit of Capitalism*. Trans. Gregory Elliott. London and New York: Verso.
Bowie, Andrew (2003), *Aesthetics and Subjectivity: From Kant to Nietzsche*, 2nd edn. Manchester: Manchester University Press.
Bradby, David, and David Williams (1988), *Directors' Theatre*. Basingstoke: Macmillan.

Braun, Edward (1982), *The Director and the Stage: From Naturalism to Grotowski*. London: Methuen.
Brauneck, Manfred (1988), *Klassiker der Schauspielregie*. Reinbek: Rowohlt.
Bruford, W.H. (1950), *Theatre, Drama and Audience in Goethe's Germany*. London: Routledge & Kegan Paul.
Burckhardt, Barabara (2009), 'Herr K. und Herr K.: Zwei Seelen wohnen in Andreas Kriegenburg's Brust. Ein Gesprächsporträt', *Theater Heute* 13, 92–100.
Burns, Elizabeth (1972), *Theatricality: A Study of Convention in the Theatre and in Social Life*. New York and London: Longman.
Butler, Judith, Ernesto Laclau and Slavoj Žižek (2000), *Contingency, Hegemony, Universality: Contemporary Dialogues on the Left*. London and New York: Verso.
Byrne, Kevin (2009), 'Genus Disorder: Frank Castorf's "Kean/Hamletmachine" at the Volksbühne Berlin', *Western European Stages* 21(2), 13–14.
Carlson, Marvin (2009), *Theatre is More Beautiful than War: German Stage Directing in the Late Twentieth Century*. Iowa City: University of Iowa Press.
Carroll, Noël (1996), *Theorizing the Moving Image*. Cambridge: Cambridge University Press.
Carter, Huntley (1914), *The Theatre of Max Reinhardt*. London and New York: B. Blom.
Castorf, Frank (1998), 'Auf der Suche nach dem trojanischen Pferd. Ein Theater Heute Gespräch', *Theater Heute* 13, 24–39.
——(1999a), 'Tschi-Tschi-Tschingiskhaan!', interview with Peter Laudenbach, *tip* 12, 99, n.p.
——(1999b), '"Ich bin kein Feind": Frank Castorf über die Schönheit des Terrorismus', interview with Frank Dietschreit, *Märkische Allgemeine Zeitung*, 18 May, n.p.
——(2001), '"Ich bin ein Querulant": Interview – Der Regisseur Frank Castorf über Größenwahn, langweiliges Theater, "Big Brother" und seine neue Arbeit für die Wiener Festwochen', *Profil* 22, 28 May, 130–1.
——(2002), 'Nicht Realismus, sondern Realität: Frank Castorf spricht über seine Arbeit', in Carl Hegemann, ed., *Politik und Verbrechen: Einbruch der Realität*. Berlin: Alexander Verlag, 71–9.
——(2012a), 'Da kriege ich das Kotzen', interview, *Cicero* 4, www.cicero.de/salon/da-kriege-ich-das-kotzen/49000, accessed 24 February 2014.
——(2012b), '"Theater muss Partisanentum sein": Interview mit Frank Castorf und Kathrin Angerer', *Zitty*, 22 November, www.zitty.de/interview-mit-casdorf-und-kathrin-angerer.html, accessed 27 February 2014.
Cole, Toby, and Helen Krich Chinoy (1963), *Directors on Directing: A Source Book of the Modern Theatre*, rev. edn. Indianapolis and New York: Bobbs-Merrill.
Colson, Sara (2005), 'De perceptie van Guy Cassiers' multimedial Proustcyclus', in Het Ro Theater, eds, *Proust 4: De kant van Marcel – Script & Werkboek*, Amsterdam: UIT&FB, 132–50.
Conrad, Joseph (2009), *Heart of Darkness*. Ed. Judith Boss and David Widger, www.gutenberg.org/files/219/219-h/219-h.htm, accessed 31 November 2014.
Coussens, Evelyne (2008), 'Anton & Cleo's tergend sterven', *Etcetera* 26(112), June, 3–7.
Craig, Edward Gordon ([1911] 2009), *On the Art of the Theatre*. Ed. Franc Chamberlain. Abingdon and New York: Routledge.
Crary, Jonathan (2001), *Suspensions of Perception: Attention, Spectacle, and Modern Culture*. Cambridge, MA: MIT Press.
——(2014), *24/7: Late Capitalism and the Ends of Sleep*. London and New York: Verso.
Cull, Laura (2012), 'Performance as Philosophy: Responding to the Problem of "Application"', *Theatre Research International* 37(1), 20–7.
——(2013), 'Philosophy as Drama: Deleuze and Dramatization in the Context of Performance Philosophy', *Modern Drama*, Special Issue 'Drama and Philosophy', 56(4), 498–520.
Cusset, François (2008), *French Theory: How Foucault, Derrida, Deleuze, & Co. Transformed the Intellectual Life of the United States*. Trans. Jeff Fort with Josephine Berganza and Marlon Jones. Minneapolis and London: University of Minnesota Press.
Davis, Tracy C., and Thomas Postlewait, eds (2003), *Theatricality*. Cambridge: Cambridge University Press.
Dean, Jodi (2009), *Democracy and other Neoliberal Fantasies: Communicative Capitalism and Left Politics*. Durham, NC: Duke University Press.
——(2012), *The Communist Horizon*. London and New York: Verso.
de Cock, Michael (2007), 'Ibsen on Speed: Interview with the Four tg STAN Actors', *Knack*, 5 September, www.stan.be/content.asp?path=qws9y29n, accessed 16 August 2013.
de Hart, Steven (1981), *The Meininger Theatre 1776–1926*. Ann Arbor, MI: UMI Research Press.
Deleuze, Gilles ([1964] 2000), *Proust and Signs*. Trans. Richard Howard. London: Athlone.
Delgado, Maria M., and Paul Heritage, eds (1996), *In Contact with the Gods: Directors Talk Theatre*. Manchester: Manchester University Press.

Delgado, Maria M., and Dan Rebellato, eds (2010), *Contemporary European Theatre Directors*. Abingdon and New York: Routledge.
Demaitre, Ann (1972), 'The Theater of Cruelty and Alchemy: Artaud and *Le Grand Oeuvre*', *Journal of the History of Ideas* 33(2), 237–50.
Demets, Paul (2004), 'The Lawyer in the Actor: Interview with STAN's Four Actors', *Knack*, 4 February, www.stan.be/content.asp?path=ot8gccd8, accessed 17 August 2013.
Derrida, Jacques (2001), *Writing and Difference*. Trans. Alan Bass. London and New York: Routledge.
Detje, Robin (2005), 'Remembering Never-Ever Land: How Frank Castorf Reconjured Berlin's Volksbühne', *Theater* 35(2), 5–17.
Dollimore, Jonathan ([1984] 2004), *Radical Tragedy: Religion, Ideology and Power in the Drama of Shakespeare and his Contemporaries*, 3rd edn. Basingstoke and New York: Palgrave Macmillan.
Dollimore, Jonathan, and Alan Sinfield (1985), eds, *Political Shakespeare: Essays in Cultural Materialism*. Manchester: Manchester University Press.
Donnellan, Declan (2005), *The Actor and the Target*. London: Nick Hern.
Dort, Bernard (1971), 'Condition sociologique de la mise en scène théâtrale', in *Théâtre réel: Essais de critique 1967–1970*. Paris: Seuil, 51–66.
Düffel, John von (2011), 'Michael Thalheimer: Das Bauchsystem', in Melanie Hinz and Jens Roselt, eds *Chaos und Konzept: Proben und Probieren im Theater*. Berlin: Alexander, 51–70.
Eagleton, Terry (1988), 'The Ideology of the Aesthetic', *Poetics Today* 9(2), 327–38.
——(1990), 'Schiller and Hegemony', in *The Ideology of the Aesthetic*. Oxford: Blackwell, 102–19.
Feinberg, Anat (2010), 'The Unknown Leopold Jessner: German Theatre and Jewish Identity', in Freddie, Rokem and Jeanette R. Malkin, eds, *Jews and the Making of Modern German Theatre*. Iowa City: University of Iowa Press, 232–60.
Feingold, Michael (2004) 'Nora Gets her Gun: Did Ibsen's *A Doll's House* Need Updating? Berlin's Thomas Ostermeier Gave it a Shot', *Village Voice*, 17 November, 71.
Féral, Josette (1982), 'Performance and Theatricality: The Subject Demystified', *Modern Drama* 25(1), 170–81.
Fiebach, Joachim (2002), 'Theatricality: From Oral Traditions to Televised "Realities"', *SubStance*, Special Issue 'Theatricality', 31(2/3), issue 98/99, 17–41.
Finburgh, Clare, and Carl Lavery, eds (2011), *Contemporary French Theatre and Performance*. Basingstoke: Palgrave Macmillan.
Firmin-Didot, Catherine (2005), 'Antagonistic in Antwerp: An Interview with the Four Actors from tg STAN', *Télérama*, 9 November, www.stan.be/content.asp?path=su9q6zxw, accessed 17 August 2013.
Fischer, E. Kurt (1932), *Königsberger Hartungsche Dramaturgie: 150 Jahre Theaterkultur im Spiegel der Kritik*. Königsberg: Hartung.
Fischer-Lichte, Erika (1993), *Kurze Geschichte des deutschen Theaters*. Tübingen and Basle: Francke.
——(1995), 'From Theatre to Theatricality: How to Construct Reality', *Theatre Research International* 20(2), 97–105.
——(2002), *History of European Drama and Theatre*. Trans. Jo Riley. London and New York: Routledge.
——(2004), *Ästhetik des Performativen*. Frankfurt am Main: Suhrkamp.
——(2006), 'Frank Castorfs Spiele mit dem Theater: Wie das Neue in die Welt kommt', *Forum Modernes Theater* 21(1), 5–23.
——(2008), *The Transformative Power of Performance: A New Aesthetics*. Trans. Saskya Iris Jain. Abingdon and New York: Routledge.
Fischer-Lichte, Erika, Christian Horn, Sandra Umathum and Matthias Warstat, eds (2005), *Diskurse des Theatralen*. Tübingen and Basle: Francke.
Fisher, Mark (2009), *Capitalist Realism: Is There No Alternative?* Winchester and Washington, DC: Zero Books.
Förster, Eckart (2012), *The Twenty-Five Years of Philosophy: A Systematic Reconstruction*. Trans. Brady Bowman. Cambridge, MA: Harvard University Press.
Fouquières, Louis Becq de (1884), *L'art de la mise en scène: essai d'esthétique théâtrale*. Paris: G. Charpentier, www.gutenberg.org/ebooks/12489/, accessed 31 November 2014.
Frenzel, Herbert A., ed. (1984), *Geschichte des Theaters: Daten und Dokumente, 1470–1890*, 2nd edn. Munich: dtv.
Fried, Michael (1980), *Absorption and Theatricality: Painting and Beholder in the Age of Diderot*. Berkeley: University of California Press.
Fuchs, Georg ([1909] 1959), *Revolution in the Theatre: Conclusions Concerning the Munich Artists' Theatre*. Abridged and adapted by Constance Connor Kuhn. Ithaca, NY: Cornell University Press.
Gardner, Lyn (2009), 'The Roman Tragedies', review, *Guardian*, 21 November, www.guardian.co.uk/stage/2009/nov/21/roman-tragedies-lyn-gardner-review, accessed 30 November 2013.

Giannachi, Gabriella, and Mary Luckhurst, eds (1998), *On Directing: Interviews with Directors*. London: Faber and Faber.
Goethe, Johann Wolfgang von ([1813] 1900), 'Shakespeare and No End', in *Criticisms, Reflections, and Maxims of Goethe*. Ed. and trans. W.B. Rönnfeldt. London and New York: Scott, 3–20, http://openlibrary.org/books/OL24606422M/Criticisms_reflections_and_maxims, accessed 31 November 2014.
Golub, Spencer (1984), *Evreinov: The Theater of Paradox and Transformation*. Ann Arbor: University of Michigan Press.
Gosch, Jürgen (2004), 'Der Campinghocker: Erfahrungen mit Thomas Dannemann', *Theater Heute* 13, 90–2.
Greenberg, Clement ([1961] 1992), *Art and Culture: Critical Essays*. Boston: Beacon Press.
Gronemeyer, Nicole, and Bernd Stegemann, eds (2009), *Regie*. Berlin: Theater der Zeit.
Groys, Boris (2010), *Going Public*. Berlin: Sternberg.
——(2011), 'Subjectivity as Medium of the Media', *Radical Philosophy* 169, 7–9.
Günther, Matthias (2010), 'Erkundungen für den Goldrahmen: Ein Streifzug durch das Probengeflecht der Münchner Kammerspiele', *Theater Heute* 1, 6–15.
Gutjahr, Ortrud, ed. (2008), *Regietheater: Wie sich über Inszenierungen streiten lässt*. Würzburg: Königshausen & Neumann.
Hagemann, Carl (1904), *Regie: Die Kunst der szenischen Darstellung*, 2nd edn. Berlin and Leipzig: Schuster & Loeffler.
Hammermeister, Kai (2002), *The German Aesthetic Tradition*. Cambridge: Cambridge University Press.
Heddon, Deirdre, and Jane Milling (2006), *Devising Performance: A Critical History*. Basingstoke and New York: Palgrave Macmillan.
Heeg, Günther (2008), 'Die Zeitgenossenschaft des Theaters', in Ortrud Gutjahr, ed., *Regietheater: Wie sich über Inszenierungen streiten lässt*. Würzburg: Königshausen & Neumann, 29–42.
Hegel, Georg Wilhelm Friedrich (1955), *Ästhetik*. Ed. Friedrich Bassenge. Berlin: Aufbau.
——(1986a), *Phänomenologie des Geistes*, *Werke*, vol. I. Ed. Eva Moldenhauer and Karl Markus Michel. Frankfurt am Main: Suhrkamp.
——(1986b), *Wissenschaft der Logik I*, *Werke*, vol. V. Ed. Eva Moldenhauer and Karl Markus Michel. Frankfurt am Main: Suhrkamp.
——(1986c), *Wissenschaft der Logik II*, *Werke*, vol. VI. Ed. Eva Moldenhauer and Karl Markus Michel. Frankfurt am Main: Suhrkamp.
Hegemann, Carl (2011), 'Gleichzeitigkeit von Kunst und Nicht-Kunst im Theater', in Marion Tiedtke and Philipp Schulte, eds, *Die Kunst der Bühne: Positionen des zeitgenössischen Theaters*. Berlin: Theater der Zeit, 76–84.
Heilmann, Matthias (2005), *Leopold Jessner, Intendant der Republik: Der Weg eines deutsch-jüdischen Regisseurs aus Ostpreußen*. Tübingen: Niemeyer.
Hein, Dieter, and Andreas Schulz, eds (1996), *Bürgerkultur im 19. Jahrhundert: Bildung, Kunst und Lebenswelt*. Munich: C.H. Beck.
Henrich, Dieter (2003), *Between Kant and Hegel: Lectures on German Idealism*. Ed. David S. Pacini. Cambridge, MA: Harvard University Press.
——(2010), *Hegel im Kontext*. Berlin: Suhrkamp.
Hinz, Melanie, and Jens Roselt, eds (2011), *Chaos und Konzept: Proben und Probieren im Theater*. Berlin: Alexander.
Hiss, Guido (2009): *Synthetische Visionen. Theater als Gesamtkunstwerk von 1800 bis 2000*. Munich: E-Podium.
Höbel, Wolfgang (2006), 'Ausweitung der Schamzone: Ein Plädoyer für die zeitgenössische Bühnenkunst', *Der Spiegel* 11, 168–70.
Höfele, Andreas (1992), 'Leopold Jessner's Shakespeare Productions 1920-1930', *Theatre History Studies* 12, 139–56.
Hove, Ivo van (2008), 'De kunst is een onteembar wild dier: Over de betekenis van kunst voor onze samenleving'. Machiavellilezing, 29 January, www.stichtingmachiavelli.nl/upload/Machiavellilezing%20Ivo%20van%20Hove.pdf accessed 30 November 2013.
Hutcheon, Linda (2006), *A Theory of Adaptation*. Abingdon and New York: Routledge.
Innes, Christopher, and Maria Shevtsova (2013), *Theatre Directing*. Cambridge: Cambridge University Press.
Jameson, Fredric (2009), *Valences of the Dialectic*. London and New York: Verso.
——(2010), *The Hegel Variations*. London and New York: Verso.
——(2013a), *The Antinomies of Realism*. London and New York: Verso.
——([2002] 2013b), *A Singular Modernity*. London and New York: Verso.
Jessner, Leopold (1979), *Schriften: Theater der zwanziger Jahre*. Ed. Hugo Fetting. Berlin: Henschelverlag.

Jestrovic, Silvija (2002), 'Theatricality as Estrangement of Art and Life in the Russian Avant-Garde', *SubStance*, Special Issue 'Theatricality', 31(2/3), issue 98/99, 42–56.
Kalb, Jonathan (2009), 'Nothing to do with Patience: Michael Thalheimer', *Theater* 39(1), 28–39.
Karatani, Kojin (2003), *Transcritique: On Kant and Marx*. Trans. Sabu Kohso. Cambridge, MA: MIT Press.
Kehlmann, Daniel (2009), 'Die Lichtprobe', www.fr-online.de/kultur/spezials/die-lichtprobe/-/1473358/2725516/-/index.html, accessed 10 August 2013.
Kelleher, Joe, and Nicholas Ridout, eds (2006), *Contemporary Theatres in Europe*. Abingdon and New York: Routledge.
Kennedy, Dennis (2009), *The Spectator and the Spectacle: Audiences in Modernity and Postmodernity*. Cambridge: Cambridge University Press.
Kerr, Alfred (1981), *Mit Schleuder und Harfe: Theaterkritiken aus drei Jahrzehnten*. Ed. Hugo Fetting. Berlin: Henschelverlag.
Kingwell, Mark (2012), *Unruly Voices: Essays on Democracy, Civility and the Human Imagination*. Windsor, ON: Biblioasis.
Koller, Ann Marie (1984), *The Theatre Duke: Georg II of Saxe-Meiningen and the German Stage*. Stanford: Stanford University Press.
Kortner, Fritz ([1959] 1979), *Aller Tage Abend*. Munich: Kindler.
Koselleck, Reinhart ([1959] 1988), *Critique and Crisis: Enlightenment and the Pathogenesis of Modern Society*. Cambridge, MA: MIT Press.
Kotte, Andreas (1998), 'Theatralität: Ein Begriff sucht seinen Gegenstand', *Forum Modernes Theater* 13(2), 117–33.
Krauss, Rosalind (1987), 'Theories of Art after Minimalism and Pop', in Hal Foster, ed., *Discussions in Contemporary Culture 1*. Seattle: Bay Press, 56–87.
Kriegenburg, Andreas (2008), 'Figuren, die es nicht schaffen, ihre Phantasie und Lebenszeit zu verkaufen', in Ortrud Gutjahr, ed., *Regietheater: Wie sich über Inszenierungen streiten lässt*. Würzburg: Königshausen & Neumann, 137–51.
——(2011), 'Die meisten Regisseure, die ich kenne, sind asozial', *DT Magazin* 4, 4–7.
Kuhn, Helmut ([1931] 1966), 'Die Vollendung der klassischen deutschen Ästhetik durch Hegel', in *Schriften zur Ästhetik*. Munich: Kosel, 15–144.
Kümmel, Peter (2009), 'Vom Zittern der Zeit: Ein Gespräch mit dem Theaterregisseur Jürgen Gosch und dem Schauspieler Ulrich Matthes', *Die Zeit*, 7 May, www.zeit.de/2009/20/Interview-Gosch-Matthes, accessed 10 August 2013.
Lavender, Andrew, and Jen Harvie, eds (2010), *Making Contemporary Theatre: International Rehearsal Processes*. Manchester: Manchester University Press.
Lazarowicz, Klaus, and Christopher Balme, eds (1991), *Texte zur Theorie des Theaters*. Stuttgart: Reclam.
Lehmann, Hans-Thies (2006), *Postdramatic Theatre*. Trans. Karen Jürs-Munby. Abingdon and New York: Routledge. Adapted from *Postdramatisches Theater*. Frankfurt am Main: Verlag der Autoren, 1999.
——(2011), 'Michael Thalheimer, Gestenchoreograph', in Marion Tiedtke and Philipp Schulte, eds, *Die Kunst der Bühne: Positionen des zeitgenössischen Theaters*. Berlin: Theater der Zeit, 85–95.
——(2013), *Tragödie und dramatisches Theater*. Berlin: Alexander.
Levine, David (2007), 'Michael Thalheimer', http://bombsite.com/issues/999/articles/3036, accessed 10 August 2013.
Lewald, August (1837), 'In die Szene setzen', *Allgemeine Theater-Revue* 3, 249–308 [Stuttgart and Tübingen: Cotta], http://books.google.de/books?id=gOhMAAAAcAAJ, accessed 31 November 2014.
Lindau, Paul (1901), 'Laube und Dingelstedt, zwei Regisseure', *Nord und Süd* 98(292), 60–82.
Lottmann, Joachim (2006), 'Hau ab, du Arsch!', *Der Spiegel* 10, 164–7.
Lowe, Donald M. (1982), *History of Bourgeois Perception*. Chicago: University of Chicago Press.
Lukács, George ([1914] 1965), 'The Sociology of Modern Drama'. Trans. Lee Baxandall. *Tulane Drama Review* 9(4), 146–70.
Lukanitschewa, Svetlana (2013), *Das Theatralitätskonzept von Nikolai Evreinov: Die Entdeckung der Kultur als Performance*. Tübingen: Francke.
McAuley, Gay (2012), *Not Magic but Work: An Ethnographic Account of a Rehearsal Process*. Manchester: Manchester University Press.
McCarter, Jeremy (2004), 'Super-Ego Size Me', *New York Sun*, 16 December, 19, www.nysun.com/arts/superego-size-me/6364/, accessed 11 July 2012.
Malabou, Catherine (2005), *The Future of Hegel: Plasticity, Temporality, and Dialectic*. Trans. Lisabeth During. Abingdon and New York: Routledge.
Marchart, Oliver (2007), *Post-foundational Political Thought: Political Difference in Nancy, Lefort, Badiou and Laclau*. Edinburgh: Edinburgh University Press.

Marcuse, Herbert (1955), *Reason and Revolution: Hegel and the Rise of Social Theory*, 2nd edn with supplementary chapter. London: Routledge & Kegan Paul.
——([1955] 1987), *Eros and Civilization: A Philosophical Enquiry into Freud*. London: Routledge & Kegan Paul.
——([1964] 2002) *One-Dimensional Man: Studies in the Ideology of Advanced Industrial Society*. Abingdon and New York: Routledge.
Martin, Roxane (2007), *La féerie romantique sur les scènes parisiennes 1791–1864*. Paris: Honoré Champion.
——(2014), *L'émergence de la notion de mise en scène dans le paysage théâtral français 1789–1914*. Paris: Classiques Garnier.
Marx, Karl (1857), *Grundrisse der Politischen Ökonomie/Outline of the Critique of Political Economy*, www.marxists.org/archive/marx/works/1857/grundrisse, accessed 31 November 2014.
Marx, Karl, and Friedrich Engels (1976), *Collected Works*, vol. V. New York: International Publishers.
——([1848] 1985), *The Communist Manifesto*. London: Penguin.
Marx, Peter W. (2005), 'Challenging the Ghosts: Leopold Jessner's *Hamlet*', *Theatre Research International* 30(1), 72–87.
——(2006a), *Max Reinhardt: Vom bürgerlichen Theater zur metropolitanen Kultur*. Tübingen: Francke.
——(2006b), 'Consuming the Canon: Theatre, Commodification, and Social Mobility in Late Nineteenth-Century German Theatre', *Theatre Research International* 31(2), 129–44.
Menke, Bettine (2007), 'Wozu Schiller den Chor gebraucht', in Bettine Menke and Christoph Menke, eds, *Tragödie Trauerspiel Spektakel*. Berlin: Theater der Zeit, 72–100.
Mercier, Louis-Sébastien (1773), *Du théâtre, ou Nouvel essai sur l'art dramatique*. Amsterdam: Harrevelt, http://archive.org/details/duthtreounou00merc, accessed 31 November 2014.
Miller, Jacques-Alain (2007), 'A Reading of the Seminar *From an Other to the other*'. Trans. Barbara P. Fulks. *Lacanian Ink* 29, 6–61.
——(2009), 'The Prisons of Jouissance'. Trans. Barbara P. Fulks. *Lacanian Ink* 33, 36–55.
Mitchell, Katie (2008), *The Director's Craft: A Handbook for the Theatre*. Abingdon and New York: Routledge.
Mitter, Shomit, and Maria Shevtsova, eds (2005), *Fifty Key Theatre Directors*. Abingdon and New York: Routledge.
Mouffe, Chantal (2005), *The Return of the Political*. London and New York: Verso.
Müllenmeister, Horst (1956), 'Leopold Jessner: Geschichte eines Regiestils'. Unpublished doctoral dissertation, University of Cologne.
Münz, Rudolf (1979), *Das andere Theater: Studien über ein deutschsprachiges teatro dell'arte der Lessingzeit*. Berlin: Henschel.
——(1998), *Theatralität und Theater: Zur Historiographie von Theatralitätsgefügen*. Ed. Gisbert Amm. Berlin: Schwarzkopf & Schwarzkopf.
Osborne, John (1988), *The Meiningen Court Theatre 1866–1890*. Cambridge: Cambridge University Press.
Ostermeier, Thomas (1999), 'Ob es so oder so oder anders geht! Ein Gespräch', *Theater Heute* 13, 66–76.
——(2003), 'Formal das Alltägliche betonen: Thomas Ostermeier gegen Theater als Angstveranstaltung, *Freitag* 45, 31 October, www.freitag.de/autoren/der-freitag/formal-das-alltagliche-betonen, accessed 10 March 2014.
——(2009), 'Erkenntnisse über die Wirklichkeit des menschlichen Miteinanders: Plädoyer für ein realistisches Theater', in Kai-Michael Hartig, ed., *Kräfte messen: Das Körber Studio Junge Regie*, vol. VI. Hamburg: Ed. Körber Stiftung, 48–51.
Pavis, Patrice (1982), 'Towards a Semiology of the *Mise en Scène*?', in *Languages of the Stage: Essays in the Semiology of the Theatre*. New York: Performing Arts Journal Publications, 131–63.
——(1990), *Le théâtre au croisement des cultures*. Paris: José Corti.
——(1992), 'From Page to Stage: A Difficult Birth', in *Theatre at the Crossroads of Culture*. Trans. Loren Kruger. London and New York: Routledge, 24–47.
——(1998), *Dictionary of the Theatre: Terms, Concepts, and Analysis*. Trans. Christine Shantz. Toronto: University of Toronto Press.
——(2003), *Analyzing Performance: Theater, Dance, and Film*. Trans. David Williams. Ann Arbor: University of Michigan Press.
——[1982] (2007) *Vers une théorie de la pratique théâtrale: voix et images de la scène*, 4th rev. edn. Villeneuve: Presses Universitaires de Septentrion.
——(2008), 'On Faithfulness: The Difficulties Experienced by the Text/Performance Couple', *Theatre Research International* 33(2), 117–26.
——(2010), 'The Director's New Tasks', in Maria M. Delgado and Dan Rebellato, eds, *Contemporary European Theatre Directors*. Abingdon and New York: Routledge, 395–411.

——(2013), *Contemporary Mise en Scène: Staging Theatre Today*. Trans. Joel Anderson. Abingdon and New York: Routledge. Adapted from *La mise en scène contemporaine: origines, tendances, perspectives*. Paris: Armand Collin, 2007.
Pignarre, Philippe, and Isabelle Stengers (2011), *Capitalist Sorcery: Breaking the Spell*. Trans. and ed. Andrew Goffey. Basingstoke and New York: Palgrave Macmillan.
Pippin, Robert B. (2005), 'What Was Abstract Art? (From the Point of View of Hegel)', in *The Persistence of Subjectivity: On the Kantian Aftermath*. Cambridge: Cambridge University Press, 279–306.
——(2008), *Hegel's Practical Philosophy: Rational Agency as Ethical Life*. Cambridge: Cambridge University Press.
——(2014), *After the Beautiful: Hegel and the Philosophy of Pictorial Modernism*. Chicago: University of Chicago Press.
Pirchan, Emil (1949), *Zweitausend Jahre Bühnenbild*. Vienna: Bellaria.
Poschmann, Gerda (1997), *Der nicht mehr dramatische Theatertext: Aktuelle Bühnenstücke und ihre dramaturgische Analyse*. Tübingen: Niemeyer.
Prütting, Lenz (2006), '"Werktreue": Historische und systematische Aspekte einer theaterpolitischen Debatte über die Grenzen der Theaterarbeit', *Forum Modernes Theater* 21(2), 107–89.
Puchner, Martin (2009), 'The Theatre of Alain Badiou', *Theatre Research International* 34(3), 256–66.
Raddatz, Frank (2013), 'Die Systemfrage. Der Beliner Schaubühnen-Chef Thomas Ostermeier und Thomas Oberender, Intendant der Beliner Festspiele, im Gespräch', *Theater der Zeit* 12, 12–19.
Rancière, Jacques (1999), *Disagreement: Politics and Philosophy*. Trans. Julie Rose. Minneapolis and London: University of Minnesota Press.
——(2004), *The Politics of Aesthetics*. Trans. Gabriel Rockhill. London and New York: Continuum.
——(2007), *The Future of the Image*. Trans. Gregory Elliott. London and New York: Verso.
——(2009a), *Aesthetics and its Discontents*. Trans. Steven Corcoran. Cambridge: Polity.
——(2009b), *The Emancipated Spectator*. Trans. Gregory Elliott. London and New York: Verso.
——(2009c), *The Aesthetic Unconscious*. Trans. Debra Keates and James Swenson. Cambridge: Polity.
——(2010), *Dissensus: On Politics and Aesthetics*. Ed. and trans. Steven Corcoran. London and New York: Continuum.
——(2013), *Aisthesis: Scenes from the Aesthetic Regime of Art*. Trans. Zakir Paul. London and New York: Verso.
Reinelt, Janelle (2004), 'Theatre and Politics: Encountering Badiou', *Performance Research*, Special Issue 'Civility', 9(4), 87–94.
——(2011), 'Rethinking the Public Sphere for a Global Age', *Performance Research* 16(2), 16–27.
Ricklefs, Sven (1994), 'Andreas Kriegenburg', in Anke Roeder and Sven Ricklefs, eds, *Junge Regisseure*. Frankfurt am Main: Fischer, 97–108.
Roenneke, Rudolf (1912), 'Franz Dingelstedts Wirksamkeit am Weimarer Hoftheater: Ein Beitrag zur Theatergeschichte des 19. Jahrhunderts'. Unpublished dissertation, Greifswald University, http://archive.org/details/3865762, accessed 31 November 2014.
Rokem, Freddie (2009), 'Editorial', *Theatre Research International* 34(3), 227–9.
Rokem, Freddie, and Jeanette R. Malkin, eds (2010), *Jews and the Making of Modern German Theatre*. Iowa City: University of Iowa Press.
Rose, Gillian ([1981] 2009), *Hegel contra Sociology*. London and New York: Verso.
Roselt, Jens (2009), 'Vom Diener zum Despoten: Zur Vorgeschichte der modernen Theaterregie im 19. Jahrhundert', in Nicole Gronemeyer and Bernd Stegemann, eds, *Regie*. Berlin: Theater der Zeit, 23–37.
Roubine, Jean-Jacques (1980), *Théâtre et mise en scène 1880–1980*. Paris: Presses Universitaires France.
Rühle, Günther (1976), 'Leopold Jeßner: Die Revolution im Staatstheater', in *Theater in unserer Zeit*. Frankfurt am Main: Suhrkamp, 47–81.
Santner, Eric L. (2006), *On Creaturely Life: Rilke, Benjamin, Sebald*. Chicago: University of Chicago Press.
Sarrazac, Jean-Pierre (2005), 'Genèse de la mise en scène moderne: une hypothèse', *Genesis* 26, 35–50.
Schaubühne am Lehniner Platz (2000), 'Der Auftrag', originally published in the season brochure, spring 2000, reprinted as 'Wir müssen von vorn anfangen', *Die Tageszeitung*, 20 January, 15.
Schiller, Friedrich ([1782] 1818), 'Über das gegenwärtige teutsche Theater', in *Sämtliche Werke*, vol. II. Stuttgart: Cotta, 365–76.
——(1970), *Vom Pathetischen und Erhabenen: Schriften zur Dramentheorie*. Ed. Klaus L. Berghahn. Stuttgart: Reclam.
——([1793] 2003), 'Kallias or Concerning Beauty: Letters to Gottfried Körner', in *Classic and Romantic German Aesthetics*, ed. J.M. Bernstein, Cambridge: Cambridge University Press, 145–84.
——([1795] 2009), *Über die ästhetische Erziehung des Menschen*. Ed. Stefan Matuschek. Frankfurt: Suhrkamp.

Schlegel, August Wilhelm (1817), *Über Dramatische Kunst und Literatur: Vorlesungen, Erster Theil*, 2nd edn. Heidelberg: Mohr und Winter, http://books.google.de/books?id=f0I4AQAAIAAJ, accessed 31 November 2014.
Schneider, Rebecca, and Gabrielle Cody, eds (2002), *Re:direction: A Theoretical and Practical Guide*. London and New York: Routledge.
Schrader, Bärbel, and Jürgen Schebera (1977), 'Politischer Skandal und ästhetisches Ereignis: Leopold Jessners *Wilhelm Tell*', in *Die 'goldenen' zwanziger Jahre: Kunst und Kultur der Weimarer Republik*. Vienna, Cologne and Graz: Böhlau, 49–67.
Schramm, Helmar (1990), 'Theatralität und Öffentlichkeit. Vorstudien zur Begriffsgeschichte von "Theater"', in Karlheinz Barck, Martin Fontius and Wolfgang Thierse, eds, *Ästhetische Grundbegriffe: Studien zu einem historischen Wörterbuch*. Berlin: Akademie Verlag, 202–42.
——(1995a), 'The Surveying of Hell. On Theatricality and Styles of Thinking', *Theatre Research International* 20(2), 114–18.
——(1995b), 'The Open Book of Alchemy in/on the Mute Language of Theatre: "Theatricality" as a Key for Current Theatre/Research', *Theatre Research International* 20(2), 156–64.
——(1996), *Karneval des Denkens: Theatralität im Spiegel philosophischer Texte des 16. und 17. Jahrhunderts*. Berlin: Akademie Verlag.
Schütt, Hans-Dieter (2004), 'Unter Eis? Unter der Haut: Michael Thalheimer – einer der radikalsten Regisseure des deutschen Theaters', *Neues Deutschland*, 29/30 May, 19.
Seel, Martin (2003), *Ästhetik des Erscheinens*. Frankfurt am Main: Suhrkamp.
Seyhan, Azade (1992), *Representation and its Discontents: The Critical Legacy of German Romanticism*. Berkeley: University of California Press.
Sharpe, Lesley (1995), *Schiller's Aesthetic Essays: Two Centuries of Criticism*. Columbia, SC: Camden House.
——(2005), 'Schiller and the Mannheim National Theatre', *Modern Language Review* 100(1), 121–37.
Sharpe, Matthew, and Geoff Boucher (2010), *Žižek and Politics: A Critical Introduction*. Edinburgh: Edinburgh University Press.
Shepherd, Simon (2012), *Direction: Readings in Theatre Practice*. Basingstoke and New York: Palgrave Macmillan.
Shevtsova, Maria, and Christopher Innes (2009), *Directors/Directing: Conversations on Theatre*. Cambridge: Cambridge University Press.
Sloterdijk, Peter (2013), *In the World Interior of Capital: Towards a Philosophical Theory of Globalization*. Trans. Wieland Hoban. Cambridge: Polity.
Speckenbach, Jan (2002), 'Der Einbruch der Fernsehtechnologie', in Carl Hegemann, ed., *Politik und Verbrechen: Einbruch der Realität*. Berlin: Alexander, 80–4.
Stegemann, Bernd (2013), *Kritik des Theaters*. Berlin: Theater der Zeit.
Stemann, Nicolas (2009), 'Wo gibt's hier Spaghetti?', *Süddeutsche Zeitung*, 30 July, www.sueddeutsche.de/kultur/daniel-kehlmann-und-das-regietheater-wo-gibts-hier-spaghetti-1.172450, accessed 10 August 2013.
Styan, J.L. (1982), *Max Reinhardt: Directors in Perspective*. Cambridge: Cambridge University Press.
Szondi, Peter (1974a), 'Antike und Moderne in der Ästhetik der Goethezeit', in *Poetik und Geschichtsphilosophie I*. Ed. Senta Metz and Hans-Hagen Hildebrandt. Frankfurt am Main: Suhrkamp, 11–265.
——(1974b), 'Hegels Lehre von der Dichtung', in *Poetik und Geschichtsphilosophie I*. Ed. Senta Metz and Hans-Hagen Hildebrandt. Frankfurt am Main: Suhrkamp, 267–512.
——([1956] 1987), *Theory of the Modern Drama*. Trans. Michael Hays. Minneapolis: University of Minneapolis Press.
Thalheimer, Michael (2008), 'Diese Arbeit am pulsierenden Zentrum der Stücke', in Ortrud Gutjahr, ed., *Regietheater: Wie sich über Inszenierungen streiten lässt*. Würzburg: Königshausen & Neumann, 189–200.
Thiele, Rita (2008), 'Zuschauen wie die Zeit vergeht: Die Bühnenräume von Johannes Schütz', in Stefan Tigges, ed., *Dramatische Transformationen: Zu gegenwärtigen Schreib- und Aufführungsstrategien im deutschsprachigen Theater*. Bielefeld: Transcript, 263–72.
Thumfart, Johannes (2010), 'Links ist das nicht!', *Jungle World* 47, http://jungle-world.com/artikel/2010/47/42175.html, accessed 24 February 2014.
Tiedtke, Marion (2011), 'Das Spiel im Spiel: Der Regisseur Andreas Kriegenburg', in Marion Tiedtke and Philipp Schulte, eds, *Die Kunst der Bühne: Positionen des zeitgenössischen Theaters*. Berlin: Theater der Zeit, 110–21.
Turner, Victor (1986), *The Anthropology of Performance*. New York: PAJ.
van den Berg, Klaus (2007), 'Michael Thalheimer: Seducing the Audience with Suggestive Images', *Theatre Forum* 30, 65–72.

van den Dries, Luc (2001), 'Theatre Group STAN', *Performance Research* 6(3), 46–51.
van den Dries, Luc, and Thomas Crombez (2010), 'Jan Fabre and STAN: Two Models of Postdramatic Theatre in the Avant-Garde Tradition', *Contemporary Theatre Review* 20(4), 421–31.
Veinstein, André (1955), *La mise en scène théâtrale et sa condition esthétique*. Paris: Flammarion.
Waldenfels, Bernhard (2010), *Sinne und Künste im Wechselspiel: Modi ästhetischer Erfahrung*. Berlin: Suhrkamp.
Weber, Samuel (2004), *Theatricality as Medium*. New York: Fordham University Press.
Weinzierl, Ulrich (2011), 'Gewalt ist die einz'ge Sicherheit', *Die Welt*, 14 March, www.welt.de/print/die_welt/kultur/article12810012/Gewalt-ist-die-einzge-Sicherheit.html, accessed 10 August 2013.
Whitmore, Jon (1994), *Directing Postmodern Theater: Shaping Signification in Performance*. Ann Arbor: University of Michigan Press.
Williams, Simon (1990), *Shakespeare on the German Stage*, vol. I, *1586–1914*. Cambridge: Cambridge University Press.
Willinger, David (1981), 'Van Hove's *Geruchten*', *Drama Review* 25(2), 116–18.
——(1983), 'Van Hove's *Disease Germs*', *Drama Review* 27(1), 93–7.
Wilms, Bernd (2008), 'Der Ensemble-Solist. Ulrich Matthes, ein Schauspieler des Jahres', *Theater Heute* 13, 112–14.
Wilson Nightingale, Andrea (2004), *Spectacles of Truth in Classical Greek Philosophy: Theoria in its Cultural Contexts*. Cambridge: Cambridge University Press.
Winds, Adolf (1925), *Geschichte der Regie*. Stuttgart and Berlin: Deutsche Verlags-Anstalt.
Winnacker, Susanne, and Christine Peters (1999), 'tg STAN: Stop Thinking about Names! Interview with Jolente De Keersmaeker, Damiaan De Schrijver and Frank Vercruyssen', originally published in *Mousonturm Portrait* 9, 1999, www.stan.be/content.asp?path=qws94dm3, accessed 16 August 2013.
Worthen, W.B. (1998), 'Drama, Performativity and Performance', *PMLA* 113(5), 1093–107.
Žižek, Slavoj (1989), *The Sublime Object of Ideology*. London and New York: Verso.
——(1992), *Looking Awry: An Introduction to Jacques Lacan through Popular Culture*. Cambridge, MA: MIT Press.
——(1999), *The Ticklish Subject: The Absent Centre of Political Ontology*. London and New York: Verso.
——(2004), *Organs without Bodies: Deleuze and Consequences*. London and New York: Routledge.
——(2006a), *How to Read Lacan*, London: Granta.
——(2006b), *The Parallax View*. Cambridge, MA: MIT Press.
——(2007), *The Indivisible Remainder: On Schelling and Related Matters*. London and New York: Verso.
——(2010), *Living in the End Times*. London and New York: Verso.
——(2012), *Less Than Nothing: Hegel and the Shadow of Dialectical Materialism*. London and New York: Verso.
Zupančič, Alenka (2006), 'Real-Spiel', in Felix Ensslin, ed., *Spieltrieb: Schillers Ästhetik heute*. Berlin: Theater der Zeit, 200–11.

INDEX

actualisation 75–8, 80–2, 87, 89, 113, 119–20, 139
   concrete 46, 78, 107, 115
adaptation 19–21, 71, 128, 135, 155, 173, 188
Adorno, Theodor 49–50, 72
   non-identity of identity 50
Aeschylos
   Oresteia 109–10
aesthetic regime of art 9, 17, 21, 24–6, 28, 30–2, 34, 38, 40, 42, 45, 54–5, 66, 90, 98
aesthetico-political order 63, 186
aesthetics 25, 48, 60, 64, 191
   aesthetic experience 24, 27, 30, 45
   of appearing 119, 139
   politics of 31
Agamben, Giorgio 168
agency 51, 152
   subjective 159, 161
aisthesis 10, 39, 41, 54, 69, 78, 86, 91, 99, 137, 187
   aisthetic dynamics 82, 87
   aisthetic experience 122, 153–4
   aisthetic perception 156
Akáts, Franz von 20–1, 26–7
alchemy 40–1, 43, 50–2, 65
Althusser, Louis 17, 177, 179
Altmann, Olaf 109–12

Anschauung 34, 65
Antoine, André 16, 19, 25, 31, 76
apparition 113
appearance 25, 48, 56, 60–1, 113, 137, 173, 176
appearing 25, 113, 119–20, 122–4, 127, 130, 138–9, 158, 184, 190
Appia, Adolphe 76, 81
Artaud, Antonin 35, 52, 70, 109, 114
äussere Regie 31
auteur 7–8, 46, 129
authority 7–8, 11, 48, 67, 70, 89, 114, 119–20, 127–9, 134, 160, 175, 187
authorship 7–8, 52, 89, 187
autonomy 31, 56, 60, 62–3, 66–7, 89, 191

Badiou, Alain 9, 22, 27, 60, 103, 113, 115, 147, 160, 181
Bakhtin, Mikhail 39, 172, 175
   chronotope 173
   polyphony 172–5
Barthes, Roland 25, 34
   punctum 25
Bassermann, Albert 74, 86–7
beauty 25–6, 50, 56, 59–60, 63, 67, 70, 90, 129, 163

Index

becoming 44, 82–3, 107–8, 138–9, 157–8
Benjamin, Walter 38, 51, 55, 69
Berardi, Franco 'Bifo' 5, 46, 50, 161, 167
Bergman, Ingmar
  Scenes from a Marriage 142, 144, 150
Bernlef, J.
  Hersenschimmen (Out of Mind) 154–9
Bersani, Leo 45, 152
Bildung 3, 57, 74
Bradby, David 2, 4, 8
Brahm, Otto 16, 25, 32, 76, 81, 83
Brecht, Bertolt 10, 38, 69–70, 86–8
Brook, Peter 8, 81, 191
Büchner, Georg
  Woyzeck 109, 176
Burns, Elizabeth 37, 51

cache 171
Camus, Albert 173
canonical texts 21, 75–7, 80, 160–1, 192
Cassiers, Guy 144–6, 151–9, 162
Castorf, Frank 98, 131, 151, 165–9, 171–7, 180, 184–7
Chekhov, Anton
  The Duel 166–7, 187
  The Seagull 101–5
  Three Sisters 173, 187
  Uncle Vanya 101–3, 105–6
chorus 10, 30, 55–6, 61, 63–70, 109, 120, 124, 191
communicative capitalism 5, 17, 41, 46, 99, 160–1, 167–8, 173, 183, 187
compositing 172
concept, directorial 20, 88–9, 114, 136, 190
concrete actualisation 46, 78, 107, 115
concrete universality 46, 80, 88–9, 103, 113, 192
concretisation 81, 89, 114, 139
conflict, dramatic 81–2, 179
Conrad, Joseph
  Heart of Darkness 131, 133
consciousnesses 46–7, 113, 152, 172–3, 175
context 28–9, 48, 151
contingency 25, 30, 60, 80–1, 99, 120, 139, 161, 184–7
contradiction, dialectic 10, 26, 34, 47–8, 59, 70, 79, 81, 89, 99, 127, 178, 186, 192
Corneille, Pierre 24
counterpoint 16, 67, 99, 124, 131, 135–6, 153

Craig, Edward Gordon 70, 76, 81
critique, political 82, 126, 129, 168, 172, 177
cultural capital 8, 74, 80, 108, 192
cultural institution 7, 41, 68
cultural relation 34

Dalberg, Heribert von 19, 56, 71
Dean, Jodi 5, 17, 41, 46, 160–1, 167–9, 176
deconstruction 64, 114, 129, 161
defamiliarisation 85, 88, 177–8
Deleuze, Gilles
  apprenticeship to signs 153–4
  desubstantialisation of affects 157–8
  sterile surface 157–8
Denić, Aleksandar 166–9
Derrida, Jacques
  closure of representation 109, 138, 150
Deutsches Theater Berlin 101, 133
Devrient, Eduard 20, 27
dialectic thinking 4, 9, 48, 67, 75, 79, 103
Dialogregie 87
Diderot, Denis 15, 35, 37, 51, 57
Dingelstedt, Franz von 9, 20, 27–8
directors' theatre 1–7, 67, 97
  see also Regietheater
discourse 17, 26, 173, 190–1
dissensus 1, 5, 23, 26, 30, 39, 41, 47, 62, 89, 178, 191
distance 28–30, 79, 83, 89, 91, 122, 134, 144, 147, 183–5, 193
  critical 159, 179
  engaged 173
  historic 77, 137
  internal 179, 181
  minimal 66
  negative 119
  reflexive 82, 114, 119, 124, 127
Dostoevsky, Fjodor
  Dämonen (The Possessed) 169, 172–3, 187
  Der Idiot (The Idiot) 169, 171, 186

Ekhof, Conrad 18–19
emancipation 70, 159, 193
emergence 31, 138–9, 157
ensemble 1–2, 27, 136, 162
essence 18, 43, 45, 113, 139, 161
Evreinov, Nicolai 35
ex-position 115, 119, 154

Fassbinder, Rainer Werner
  Die Ehe der Maria Braun (*The Marriage of Maria Braun*) 180–4
fiction, dramatic 64, 68, 78, 82, 119, 122–4, 134–8, 144–7, 153, 172, 175–80
Fischer-Lichte, Erika 74, 119, 122, 171, 176
focalisation 20, 103, 111
foreign body 6, 55, 64, 178
form 7, 59–60, 67, 90–1, 103, 113–14, 138, 155, 158, 171, 177, 184
formal reasoning 42, 44, 191
Foucault, Michel 17, 29, 45
frame 23, 37, 127, 150, 152
freedom 56, 60, 68, 81
  see also liberty

gaze 26, 49, 115, 153, 158
Goethe, Johann Wolfgang von 18–19, 57, 59, 107–8, 134–5, 139
  Stella 122, 130–1, 134–6
Gorky, Maxim
  Zomergasten (*Summerfolk*) 122–5
Gosch, Jürgen 11, 97–111, 113–15, 119, 123, 127–8, 134
Greek theatre 15, 30, 38, 68, 71, 109
Groys, Boris 160

Hannetaire, Jean-Nicolas 19
Hauptmann, Gerhart 101, 108–11
  Die Ratten (*The Rats*) 109–10
Hegel, Georg Wilhelm Friedrich
  Absolute 43, 50–1, 56, 59, 129–31, 139
  Absolute Knowledge 50, 129–30, 139
  Absolute Spirit 51, 59
  abstract universality 80
  actuality 43–4, 113, 124, 138, 152
  Aesthetics 25, 31, 45, 48, 127
  dialectic 30, 42–50, 90, 99
  Phenomenology of Spirit 17, 41, 152
  restlessness 46, 50
  Science of Logic 45, 91
  sensuous appearing (of the Idea) 18, 25, 43, 49–50, 69, 80
  Spirit (*Geist*) 17, 41, 45–51, 59, 68, 81, 90, 152
  sublation (*Aufhebung*) 10, 75, 79, 82, 85–6, 101, 139, 152, 162, 192
  substance 34, 42, 45, 47, 85, 139, 154
  'thousand-eyed Argus' 48

Hegemann, Carl 151
historical realism 28, 30
historicism (in *Regie*) 28–30, 44, 65, 78, 98, 178
historicity 30, 43–4
Hove, Ivo van 142, 144, 146–9, 151, 159–63

Ibsen, Henrik 109–10, 120–2, 125, 139, 164, 166, 168, 177–8, 181, 185, 187–8, 192
  Ein Volksfeind (*An Enemy of the People*) 120–1, 164–6, 177, 179, 184
  JDX – A Public Enemy (*An Enemy of the People*) 120–5
  Nora (*A Doll's House*) 1, 122–7, 139, 165
idealism 7, 9, 33, 44, 56–66, 69, 75, 161, 175
ideology 2, 5, 17, 37, 152, 161, 168, 176–7, 179, 184
  critique of 168, 177
Iffland, August Wilhelm 19
illusion 64, 84–5, 123–4, 127, 152
imaginary 65, 157, 169, 184
imitation 28, 31, 89, 113
Inszenierung 9, 20, 22, 30, 44, 67, 69, 89, 91, 190
intermediality 146, 157
interpretation 3, 5, 8, 11, 18–19, 22, 47, 80–3, 119, 122, 147, 151, 185, 189
interpreter 80, 160, 185

Jameson, Fredric 34, 41, 43, 45–7, 50, 81, 187, 192
Jessner, Leopold 10, 20, 70, 73, 75–9, 81–9, 91, 103, 122, 149
  Grundmotiv 76, 78, 81–3, 87, 89
  step-stage (*Stufenbühne*) 83–4, 88

Kafka, Franz,
  Der Prozess (The Trial) 118–19, 123, 131, 136
Kammerspiele Munich 118, 162, 180, 182
Kant, Immanuel 26, 42, 54, 56, 59–60, 65, 72
  transcendental apperception 60
  transcendental approach 152
Karatani, Kojin 72
  transcritical perspective 63, 67–8, 70
Keersmaeker, Jolente De 119–20, 125–6, 128
kinesis 10, 39, 41–2, 54, 69, 78, 86, 91, 99, 137, 187
Koselleck, Reinhard 26, 62

Index

Kotte, Andreas 35, 42
Kriegenburg, Andreas 119–23, 130–8

Lacan, Jacques 47, 49, 65–6, 113, 147, 150, 168, 174
   anamorphosis 147
   jouissance 168–9
   Master Signifier 47
   'non-all' 55, 139
   objet petit a 49
   Real 49–51, 65–6, 160, 165, 172–5, 184–6
   split subject 153
Laube, Heinrich 9, 19–20, 27
Lehmann, Hans-Thies 10–11, 65, 69, 100, 107, 114–15, 147, 160, 163, 173, 181
   dramatic cosmos 86, 147
   irruption of the Real 65–6, 173, 181
   'response-ability' 159, 161
   withdrawal of representation 100
Lessing, Gotthold Ephraim 15, 57–8, 108, 110
   Emilia Galotti 108, 110
   Hamburg Dramaturgy 15, 57
Lewald, August 20, 27
liberty 56, 61, 63–4, 68, 70–1, 77, 82, 90, 129, 139, 159, 183, 191, 193
Lukács, György 46, 69, 172

Malabou, Catherine 34, 75, 80, 90, 138
Marcuse, Herbert 34, 40, 42–3, 45–6, 57, 62, 167
meaning 9–10, 18, 22, 31, 39, 45, 50, 66, 89, 109, 122, 128, 132, 137, 160
media 10, 21, 146, 150, 153, 160
mediation 9–11, 21–3, 25–6, 28–31, 45–6, 55–6, 63, 77–9, 81–3, 89, 98–9, 158–61, 183–5, 189–90, 192
   aesthetic mediation 25–6, 29–31, 34
mediatisation 146, 153, 158, 169
medium 5, 21–2, 25, 41, 44, 50, 57, 150
Meininger 16, 18–20, 24, 27–8, 76, 85
Mercier, Louis-Sébastien 18
milieu 76–7, 81, 88, 100–1, 109
mimesis 23–4, 26, 31
Mitchell, Katie 136, 169, 189
modernism 16, 31, 51, 76, 160
Molnár, Ferenc
   Liliom 98–100
multisensuality 146–7, 153–6, 158

Münz, Rudolf 10, 35–9, 42–3
   see also theatrality
Musil, Robert
   Der Mann ohne Eigenschaften (*The Man Without Qualities*) 154

narrator 132, 153–5
naturalism 16, 24, 26, 32, 63–4, 77, 179–80, 183
negation 10, 47, 68, 101, 103, 153, 184
negativity 43, 46–8, 65, 101, 103, 114

object 10, 24–6, 45, 48, 60, 124, 131, 151, 153, 158–60, 186, 189
objectivity, new (*Neue Sachlichkeit*) 76, 79, 81–2, 87, 98
Ostermeier, Thomas 1, 164–9, 172–88
ownership 68, 70, 75, 78, 135, 192

Pappelbaum, Jan 166, 176
parallax, theatral/spectatorial 65, 70, 72, 79, 82, 147, 150, 152–5, 157–61, 165, 178–80, 189
partition of the sensible 5, 8–9, 17, 22–3, 26, 30–1, 37–40, 42, 59, 62–3, 66, 69, 178, 181, 183
Pavis, Patrice 3–4, 10, 16, 18, 24, 75, 78–9, 81, 110, 130, 161
   émis en scène 130
   metteur en contradiction 79
   text-performance couple 10
perception 10, 17, 23, 33–42, 69, 146, 150, 156, 179
   affective 24, 169, 191
   modes of 37, 45
performativity 4, 31, 36, 48, 51, 119, 190
perspective 50, 64, 79, 89, 99, 114, 138, 150, 157, 173, 180–1, 184, 189, 192
   distanced 153, 155, 183
   foreign 177
   one-sided 122, 160, 186
   partial 80, 185
   subjective 115, 186
   unmediated 79
Pippin, Robert 34, 48, 127
Pirchan, Emil 83–4, 86–7
Piscator, Erwin 10, 75, 78, 187
plasticity 75, 80, 89–91, 103, 111
political act 23, 62, 169, 182

politicity *see* Rancière
position
  ambiguous (of spectating) 134, 184
  relational (of Regie) 56, 70
postdramatic theatre 87, 100, 144, 147, 161, 172–3
postmodernism 36, 98, 127, 152, 161, 180
potentiality 42, 44, 119, 138, 151, 158
presentation
  mode of 82, 90, 105, 177
  theatral level of 20, 30, 48, 50, 124, 144, 146, 150, 161
Proust, Michel
  Recherche du temps perdu 144–6, 153–7
psychological realism 36, 101, 133–4, 144, 174
public character of theatre 10, 22, 34, 39, 48, 58, 62, 68, 76, 150–2, 159, 175, 177, 179, 190–1

Rancière, Jacques
  emancipated spectator 65, 134, 159
  metapolitics 181
  politicity 5, 70, 161
  silent speech of things 9, 24–5, 34, 65, 73, 106
  see also aesthetic regime of art; dissensus; partition of the sensible; representative regime of art
realism 25, 28, 44, 51, 61–4, 82, 88–9, 144, 165, 168, 171–9
  capitalist 168, 171–7, 183–4, 187
  critical 180, 183
  negative 30, 168–9, 174, 180
reality 26, 41–6, 49–51, 60–2, 64–5, 113, 122, 142–6, 149–53, 175, 184
reality effect 171
reason (*Vernunft*) 29, 44, 59–60, 176
  speculative 41, 59
reflexivity 21–2, 43–6, 122–4, 135–9, 142–7, 150–60
Regietheater 1, 7, 17, 73, 76, 91, 97, 104, 173, 181
  see also directors' theatre
regisseur 3, 19–20, 32, 55
rehearsal 19, 27, 104–6, 127–8, 135–8, 175
Reinhardt, Max 9–10, 25, 27, 74, 76, 83, 85, 187
relational fabric 38
relational process 29, 45

representation 17, 21, 24–5, 27, 42–3, 45, 48, 98, 100–1, 119–20, 122, 137–8, 150, 158, 161
  mode of 85, 120
  negative 101
  withdrawal of *see* Lehmann
representative (representational) regime of art 17, 23–4, 26–7, 29–31, 62, 65–7, 80, 98, 144, 153, 157
resistance 166–7, 177
responsibility (of subject/spectator) 115, 119, 134, 147, 159–61, 191–3
rhythm 54, 87, 103, 111, 184
Ro Theater Rotterdam 154

scenography 26–7, 83
Schaubühne (Schiller) 57, 62, 71
Schaubühne Berlin 108, 110, 162, 177, 186–8
Schauspiel Frankfurt 108, 122, 134, 136
Schechner, Richard 35, 37, 86
Schiller, Friedrich
  Bride of Messina 10, 55, 63, 69
  Don Karlos 57, 59, 64
  form drive 60, 67
  freedom of play 59
  Kabale und Liebe 57, 59, 61
  Letters on the Aesthetic Education of Man 56, 60–2
  Maria Stuart 27, 55, 109–10
  play instinct 60
  (poetic) point of indifference 67
  sense drive 60, 67
  theatre as moral institution 10, 57, 60, 63, 65, 68, 71, 75, 77
  Wallenstein 28, 59
  Wilhelm Tell 55, 64, 73–7, 81–8, 91, 132, 135
  see also liberty
Schlegel, August Wilhelm 19, 28, 69
Schramm, Helmar 8, 10, 31, 35, 39–44, 52, 147, 151
  see also style of thinking; theatrality
Schrijver, Damiaan De 120–5
Schröder, Friedrich Ludwig 19
Schütz, Johannes 101–2, 105–6, 109–11
Seel, Martin 119, 138
self 46, 147, 152–3, 161, 163
self-consciousness 43, 50–1, 152, 154
self-identity 153, 185

semiocapitalism 5, 11, 50, 64, 167, 169, 171, 173, 175, 177, 179, 181, 183, 185–7, 192
semiosis 10, 39–42, 55, 78, 86, 91, 99, 137, 184, 187
sensory experience 22–6, 59–60, 76, 82, 115, 122, 190
set (stage) 24, 99, 101–6, 110–11, 118, 123–4, 130–1, 142–3, 155–7, 166–9, 176, 181
Shakespeare, William
   Coriolanus 147, 149–50
   Hamlet 75, 78, 154, 176, 179–80, 184, 188
   Julius Caesar 27–8, 147, 149
   Macbeth 19, 97, 99, 101, 104–5
   Richard III 75, 85
   Roman Tragedies 147–50, 152
sign (semiotics) 6, 25, 34, 111–3, 119, 154, 158–9
silent speech of things see Rancière
signifying stress 174–7
Sophocles
   Antigone 80, 109, 111
   Oedipus Rex 24, 109, 111
Speckenbach, Jan 169, 171
spectating
   act of 22, 49, 122, 137, 144, 147, 152
spectatorial engagement 137, 150, 183
spectatorial position 114, 150, 159, 185
speculative thinking 5, 30, 34, 41–8, 59, 90–1, 99
split spectator 153, 158
Staatstheater am Gendarmenmarkt Berlin 73, 75
Stanislavsky, Konstantin 16, 25
Stein, Peter 8, 70, 74, 91, 98, 101, 104, 133, 144, 186
style of thinking 8–9, 16, 34, 39–40, 42, 46, 54, 70, 90, 127, 137
subjectivity 90, 152, 160–1, 187
   negative 154, 157–8
Symbolic Order 17, 65, 158, 190, 192
Szondi, Peter 44, 66, 69, 144
   absoluteness of drama 24

text
   delivery of the 27, 87, 103, 109
   fidelity to the 80, 134
   true to the (*Texttreue*) 2, 11, 97, 107, 134
Textträger 87
tg STAN 11, 119–29, 132–8

Thalheimer, Michael 98–101, 107–14, 128, 134
Thalia Theater Hamburg 76, 162
thea 11, 33–4, 36–9, 41–3, 71, 78, 90, 107, 114, 122–3, 147, 158, 190, 193
   public play of 34, 39, 190
   pure 114
theatrality 10, 31, 34–43, 50, 55, 60, 69–70, 78, 81–2, 86–7, 90, 132, 138, 179–81, 184
   (cultural) fabric of (*Theatralitätsgefüge*) 10, 43, 70
   magic triangle 2, 10, 31, 39, 65, 179
   theatral mediation 11, 78, 82–3, 99, 126, 146, 192
   theatral presentation 132, 144, 146, 157, 172–3
   theatral square 152, 159, 179, 190–1
   theatral thinking 11, 34, 42–3, 50–1, 56, 70, 115, 127, 138, 190–2
   theatral triangle 78, 114, 187
   theatral truth 98, 111, 115
theatricality 34–7, 124, 132, 150
Toneelgroep Amsterdam 142, 148, 161–2
tragedy 54–5, 61, 63, 67, 100, 104, 107, 111, 123
true to the work 97, 99
truth 25, 28, 34, 36, 62–5, 98–9, 101, 106–7, 113–15, 128–9, 132, 160, 185–6, 190, 192
   aesthetic 25, 99
   speculative 99, 107, 115
truth-event 103, 112, 115
truthfulness 7, 16, 80, 98, 106, 113
truth of the text 98, 115

universality 43–4, 46, 80–2, 161, 192

Vercruyssen, Frank 119–28
Versweyveld, Jan 142, 148
virtuality 49, 119, 137, 151, 157–8, 185, 187
Volksbühne Berlin 75, 101, 169, 186–7
Vorstellung 43, 45

Wagner, Richard 16, 19–20, 70, 162, 186
Waldenfels, Bernhard 137
Wedekind, Frank 78, 107
Weimar court theatre 19–20, 57
Werktreue 97

Wilson, Robert 88, 109
Winds, Adolf 15, 19, 31
Wrede, Bert 109–10

Zadek, Peter 91, 98, 104, 133
Žižek, Slavoj
   anti-ideology glasses 168
   awry perspective 65
   (death) drive 60, 174, 185, 187, 192
   (decentred) subject 63
   (dialectic) materialism 44
   (Hegelian) Absolute/absolution 56, 129–30
   (Hegelian) dialectic process 129, 138–9
   organs without bodies 157
   parallax perspective 65, 72, 79, 147, 150, 153, 158, 160–1, 180
   symptom 184–5
Zupančič, Alenka 64–5, 93

EU authorised representative for GPSR:
Easy Access System Europe, Mustamäe tee 50,
10621 Tallinn, Estonia
gpsr.requests@easproject.com